Lecture Notes in Computer Scienc

Commenced Publication in 1973
Founding and Former Series Editors:
Gerhard Goos, Juris Hartmanis, and Jan van Leeuwen

David H. Akehurst   Régis Vogel
Richard F. Paige (Eds.)

Model Driven Architecture - Foundations and Applications

Third European Conference, ECMDA-FA 2007
Haifa, Israel, June 11-15, 2007
Proccedings

 Springer

Volume Editors

David H. Akehurst
University of Kent, U.K.
E-mail: D.H.Akehurst@kent.ac.uk

Régis Vogel
IHG, Madrid, Spain
E-mail: Regis.vogel@ihg.net

Richard F. Paige
The University of York, U.K.
E-mail: paige@cs.york.ac.uk

Library of Congress Control Number: 2007927648

CR Subject Classification (1998): C.2, D.2, D.3, F.3, C.3, H.4

LNCS Sublibrary: SL 2 – Programming and Software Engineering

ISSN   0302-9743
ISBN-10   3-540-72900-3 Springer Berlin Heidelberg New York
ISBN-13   978-3-540-72900-6 Springer Berlin Heidelberg New York

Springer is a part of Springer Science+Business Media

springer.com

© Springer-Verlag Berlin Heidelberg 2007
Printed in Germany

Typesetting: Camera-ready by author, data conversion by Scientific Publishing Services, Chennai, India
Printed on acid-free paper   SPIN: 12072637   06/3180   5 4 3 2 1 0

Preface

Model-driven architecture, and model-driven approaches in general, holds the promise of moving software development towards a higher level of abstraction. Given the challenges in the software industry of delivering more complex functionality with less effort, it is not really a question *whether* model-driven development will succeed, but rather a question of *when* it will break through. However, before this can happen, there are many challenging problems to conquer, both theoretical and pragmatic. This requires close collaboration between academic research and industrial application.

The goal of the European Conference on Model-Driven Architecture — Foundations and Applications (ECMDA-FA) is to bring together industry and academia to tackle the problems in model-driven development. This volume includes nine foundation papers and seven application papers. ECMDA-FA 2007 also hosted six workshops on both theoretical and practical aspects of MDA. Furthermore, the keynote speakers, Stuart Kent from Microsoft and Andy Schürr from TU Darmstadt, proved that both industry and academia are interested in MDA and its applications.

This third ECMDA-FA conference is the result of the work of the authors who submitted a total of 60 papers, the Program Committee members who produced careful and thoughtful reviews under significant time pressures, the people organizing the workshops, and of course the Steering Committee. Several hundreds of people worked hard to make this conference a success. We have the honor of speaking for all these people in this preface and we would like to thank each of them for their valuable contribution.

The ECMDA-FA 2007 conference was supported by the European Commission's Information Society Technologies (IST) initiative and by IBM.

June 2007   Dave Akehurst
                                                                    Regis Vogel

Organization

Organizing Committee

Conference Chair	Alan Hartman (IBM)
Program Co-chairs	David Akehurst (University of Kent)
	Regis Vogel (IHG)
Local Arrangements Chair	Ettie Gilead (IBM)
Workshops Chair	Arend Rensink (University of Twente)
Tools and Consultancy Chair	Regis Vogel (IHG)
Webmaster	Yair Harry (IBM)
Public Relations Chair	Jos Warmer (Ordina)
Publications Chair	Richard Paige (University of York)

Steering Committee

Alan Hartman (IBM, Chair)
David Akehurst (University of Kent)
Richard Paige (University of York)
Philippe Desfray (Softeam)

Regis Vogel (IHG)
Arend Rensink (University of Twente)
Jos Warmer (Ordina)

Program Committee

Jan Aagedal
David Akehurst
Uwe Assmann
Terry Bailey
Jean Bézivin
Xavier Blanc
Behzad Bordbar
Manfred Broy
Krysztof Czarnecki
Miguel de Miguel
Jean-Luc Dekeyser
Serge Demeyer
Philippe Desfray
Jürgen Dingel
Gregor Engels
Jeff Gray
Alan Hartman
Gabor Karsai

Roger Kilian-Kehr
Anneke Kleppe
Jason Mansell
Tom Mens
Veronique Normand
Richard Paige
Chris Raistrick
Arend Rensink
Bernhard Rumpe
Branislav Selic
Maarten Steen
Juha-Pekka Tolvanen
Andreas Ulrich
Marten van Sinderen
Regis Vogel
Gerd Wagner
Jos Warmer
Clay Williams

Additional Reviewers

Khalid Allem
Christian Basarke
Reda Bendraou
Javier F. Briones
Sebastian Cech
Anis Charfi
Norbert Diernhofer
Dolev Dotan
Cedric Dumoulin
Anne Etien
Alexander Förster
Joris van Geet
Steffen Goebel
Pieter van Gorp
Hans Grönniger
Florian Heidenreich
Antoine Honoré
Andrew Jackson
Eric Jouenne
Alexander Kofman
Dimitrios Kolovos
Holger Krahn

Katja Lehmann
Jérôme Le Noir
Stéphane Menoret
Parastoo Mohagheghi
Olaf Mulliawan
Ellen van Paesschen
Dirk Reiss
Andreas Roth
Andreas Rummler
Tim Schattkowsky
Stefan Scheidl
Martin Schindler
Hans Schippers
Marvin Schulze-Quester
Yahalomit Simionovici
Christian Soltenborn
Alin Stefanescu
Gernot Stenz
Todor Stoitsev
Hendrik Voigt
Yi Zhang
Steffen Zschaler

Table of Contents

An Open Source Domain-Specific Tools Framework to Support Model Driven Development of OSS

Achilleas Achilleos[1], Nektarios Georgalas[2], and Kun Yang[1]

[1] University of Essex, Dept. of Electronic Systems Engineering, UK
{aachila,kunyang}@essex.ac.uk
[2] British Telecom Group, UK
nektarios.georgalas@bt.com

Abstract. Telecommunications companies undergo massive transformations which reflect onto exacting requirements for controlling the costs of new Operation Support Systems (OSS) development and integration. This calls for the adoption of new approaches, which improve agility and reusability. Model Drive Development (MDD), as specified by OMG, can drastically tackle these issues and has, therefore, attracted the interest of the telecommunications industry. Equally important is the Open Source paradigm. For MDD to gain wide industrial adoption, tools should be available to facilitate the OSS development process. In this paper, we specify requirements MDD tools should meet for effective application of the approach. An extensive survey is then carried out to evaluate existing meta-modelling frameworks over the identified tools requirements. Eventually, we present the Integrated Eclipse Model driven Environment (IEME), which comprises a unified environment of bundled Eclipse-based MDD facilities that also supports the automatic generation of domain-specific tools.

Keywords: Meta-modelling, MDA, model-driven development, domain specific languages, modelling editor tools.

1 Introduction

Telecommunications companies undergo massive transformations to become agile organizations shifting from their traditional profile as telephony operators into providers of networked-based ICT services. Some of their main challenges are to reduce the costs of their IT operational support systems (OSS), increase agility, and design the OSS infrastructure to support fast delivery of new services and products. A major contributing factor in the cost of running OSS is the integration tax incurred when legacy is integrated with new OSS Components Off-The-Shelf (COTS). This is mainly due to the multiplicity of platforms and middleware used by the OSS. Although advances are being made by the OSS industry towards standardising OSS capabilities and information models, through the OSS/J initiative [1] and the Tele-Management Forum (TMF) [2], systems are still designed around specific middleware technologies such as CORBA, J2EE, and .NET. This preserves the problem of heavy costs and lengthy process cycles of OSS to new versions of such platforms.

D.H. Akehurst, R. Vogel, and R.F. Paige (Eds.): ECMDA-FA 2007, LNCS 4530, pp. 1–16, 2007.
© Springer-Verlag Berlin Heidelberg 2007

MDD of software, as specified by OMG [3], provides an approach that can drastically tackle the aforementioned issues. MDA provides clear distinction between models independent of technical details, namely, *Platform Independent Models (PIMs)* and models that include detail of the implementation technology, namely, *Platform Specific Models (PSMs)*. MDA comprises a set of standards that enable the definition of Domain Specific Languages (DSLs) used to specify a system's structure and behaviour. DSLs are represented as meta-models based on the Meta-Object Facility (MOF) and can be precisely defined using the Object Constraint Language (OCL) [4] for defining constraints over meta-models as well as actual models. With sequential transformations among various DSLs, using the Query/View/Transform (QVT) standard, system implementations can be produced for particular platforms. MOF expressed model data can be exchanged between compliant tools using XML Metadata Interchange (XMI) technology.

We have practically applied MDA in several case-studies that demonstrated the advantages it offers in the process of designing, developing and integrating OSS in terms of improved quality and lower costs [5], [6], [7], [8]. In order to capitalize on these advantages it is instrumental that the MDA standards are implemented in the tools used for OSS development. In the context of the NGOSS/MDA TMF Catalyst project [9], a practical evaluation of mainstream commercial tools showed limited, if any, implementation of the MDA standards with a strong proprietary flavour. That is, service providers are currently bound to limited exploitation of the MDA potential. Furthermore, service providers expend considerably on costly licenses and training in order to put such tools to enterprise-wide use, driving overall costs even higher. This is the reason why open source paradigms, such as Eclipse [10], have recently received significant attention and strong industrial support. In the TMF OpenOSS Catalyst [11] the general benefits of open source were investigated in the direction of driving down OSS development costs. However, OpenOSS did not cover the area of tooling.

This paper specifies high-level principles, which should be complied with by tools for sufficient facilitation of meta-modelling and MDA. These principles get refined into more concrete requirements through a state-of-the-art survey of meta-modelling tools. Based on these requirements, the paper presents IEME, an Eclipse-based open source environment providing key MDA facilities for the development of software systems. IEME brings together Eclipse initiatives that individually implement a certain MDA aspect. Specifically, IEME uses: (i) the Eclipse Modelling Framework (EMF) [12], the Eclipse implementation of MOF, for specifying the abstract syntax of meta-models; (iii) the Graphical Modelling Framework (GMF) [13] for specifying the concrete syntax of meta-models and generating dedicated graphical tools that support both the abstract and concrete semantics of a meta-model; (iv) the Atlas Transformation Language (ATL) [14] for specifying transformation rules among meta-models; and (v) the openArchitectureWare (oAW) [15] for building code generators and specifying constraints on meta-models and models .

The rest of the paper is organised as follows. Section 2 investigates the relationship between meta-modelling and DSL specification and lays out a rigorous set of requirements that an effective MDD tools framework should satisfy. Section 3 conducts a survey of tools with MDD capabilities and evaluates them using the identified requirements. Next, section 4 presents IEME and how it fulfils the identified requirements. Finally, section 5 discusses conclusions and future work.

2   Meta-models as Domain Specific Languages: MDD Tools Framework Requirements

According to Nytun, Prinz and Tveit [16]: *A metamodel is a model that defines a language completely including the concrete syntax, abstract syntax and semantics.*

Another definition describes meta-modelling [17] as: *The construction of an object oriented-model, which represents the abstract syntax of a language.*

Our view on meta-modelling aligns with the former statement. That is, meta-modelling is the process of complete and precise specification of a *domain-specific* modelling language, which in turn can be used to define models of that domain. This treatment places a meta-model one abstraction layer higher than domain models. This way, an indefinite hierarchy of abstraction layers can be built, where models at layer *n* are specified using the precise semantics of the language defined as a meta-model at layer *n+1*. In this setting, models situated at layer n are instances of meta-models at layer n+1.

MDA provides such a layered architecture limiting the number of abstraction layers to four. At the top level, M3, the meta-meta-model of MOF is situated, which provides a generic language for the definition of domain-specific languages. Layer M2 is populated by meta-models that represent MOF-defined domain-specific languages. Layer M1 hosts domain models written in M2-defined DSLs. Finally M0 hosts run-time domain objects that instantiate M1 domain entities.

Due to their focus on a certain domain, as opposed to generic modelling languages such as UML [18], it is necessary to produce a precise definition for the domain specific semantics of a DSL. This requires a DSL specification paradigm that can adequately facilitate the rigorous definition of the DSL abstract syntax, comprising a meta-model of the domain-specific concepts and constraints for precisely defining the domain concepts semantics. MDA is such a paradigm, as it provides MOF for meta-model specification and OCL for the specification of meta-model constraints. Furthermore, MDA can facilitate the definition of mappings between DSLs using QVT and the exchange of meta-model data using XMI.

In order to render practical the use of a DSL, a high-level notation should be available, allowing designers to produce models in this DSL. Therefore, alongside its abstract syntax, a DSL should encompass a concrete syntax definition specifying the way DSL abstract concepts can be represented within a design in a consistent manner. For easier use of the language, such DSL concrete syntax may be specified through a graphical notation, which can drive the development of DSL-specific graphical modelling tools. Developing such DSL tools can be a laborious and costly process, especially when considering the need of these tools to constantly evolve alongside modifications and extensions the DSL may incur in time. Therefore, looking at automating the process of generating DSL tools can be very beneficial. Automatic tool generation will require meta-tools, ie. more abstract DSL tool specification environments, providing a framework of meta-modelling and graphical facilities to precisely specify DSL abstract and concrete syntax.

All aforementioned features, also grounded on our previous work and MDA case-studies [5], [6], [7], [8], [9], describe general principles for the way we view MDD process applying in practice and the facilitation we believe is required by way of a MDD supporting tools framework. These principles are shaped into a specific set of requirements necessary to render a MDD framework practically efficient. The requirements are outlined below:

[R1] *Abstract syntax:* Any DSL shall be specified as a M2 meta-model using a semantic meta-meta language, such as MOF. An effective MDD framework must ensure completeness of the new modelling language through its meta-meta language.

[R2] *Concrete syntax:* A DSL shall additionally specify a notation, preferably graphical, to allow the concrete representation of its abstract concepts. This will enable better understanding of the language and will make its use easier in developing domain models.

[R3] *Meta-model level constraints:* Precision in the DSL semantics shall be provided by the specification of constraints onto the M2 meta-model (DSL abstract syntax) to ensure correctness of the language.

[R4] *Domain-specific modelling tools generation:* One to one mapping must be enabled between the DSL abstract concepts and their corresponding concrete representation, which shall lead to the generation of a DSL modelling tool environment. The tool will be used for the specification in DSL and management of M1 domain PIMs.

[R5] *Model level constraints:* It shall be possible to specify constraints onto the actual M1 domain PIMs. Therefore, domain-specific tools must provide a constraints specification facility.

[R6] *Model Transformations:* It shall be possible to transform a PIM to another PIM or PSM. This must be driven by mapping rules defined at M2 between the meta-models which represent the abstract syntax of the DSLs used to specify the original and resulting M1 domain models. The mapping rules should be embedded in the generated DSL modelling tool. In its M1 model manipulation capacity, the domain modelling tool should be able to execute the transformation but should provide no facility to change the mapping rules.

[R7] *Text-based generation:* A MDD framework shall generate text-based output from M1 domain models. This can lead to code generation in a programming, such as Java, or a markup language, such as XML.

[R8] *Standards Conformance:* Any MDD and supporting tools framework should be conformant to OMG's MDA standards, namely, MOF, XMI, QVT and OCL.

[R9] *Accelerated adoption:* Generated tools should be easy to use by the designers. In the context of this paper, we will restrain to assessing accelerated adoption by the extent the environment of the generated tool is compatible to a widely adopted and used development environment, such as Eclipse.

From a conceptual perspective, the aforementioned requirements drive a certain flow of steps, a way of working in other words, that characterise a structured and practically effective MDD process. Figure 1, illustrates thoroughly the proposed MDD process flow over OMG's 4-level architecture and the way each requirement matches the consecutive flow steps.

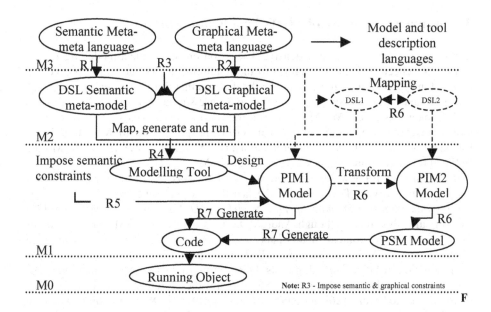

Fig. 1. Meta-modelling and frameworks

From a practical perspective, the requirements introduce a two-layered MDD tools framework, as illustrated in Figure 2. The top layer refers to meta-tool environments with capacity to specify abstract and concrete syntax of a DSL, meta-model level constraints and DSL transformations. The meta-tools generate graphical modelling tools, which occupy the lower layer and conform to the DSL specifications. The offspring tools can be used to develop domain models using the DSL, to specify domain model constraints and to automatically generate out of the domain models either code or other PIMs, as dictated by the embedded meta-model transformations.

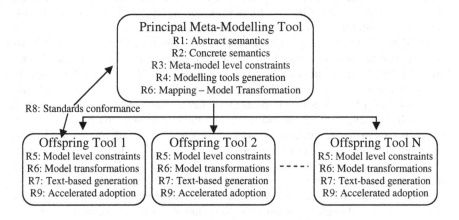

Fig. 2. Generation of offspring modelling editor tools

3   Comparative Study of MDD Tool Frameworks

In this section we provide an extensive discussion on major meta-modelling frame-works. We check how these conform to the requirements set and to the procedures outlined in Figure 1 and Figure 2. It must be denoted that those requirements were ex-tracted based on our experience from previous case studies [8], [9] performed using such frameworks (see XMF-Mosaic). The frameworks under study are two research tools; (i) Generic Modelling Environment (GME) [19], (ii) DOmain Modelling Envi-ronment (DOME) [20], two commercial tools; (iii) MetaEdit+ [21], (iv) XMF-Mosaic [22] and the open source framework project AndroMDA [23].

The first four frameworks selected are considered as the most suitable ones for contacting the survey. This is due to the fact that these are the most dominant ones and provide extensive *Domain Specific Modelling (DSM)* support; DSM Forum [24] supports also this idea. Although AndroMDA falls out of the DSM Forum group of tools is used in the context of this paper to demonstrate the high value of an open source project. DSM Forum focuses on DSL development and expresses the necessity for production of DSL supporting tools. DSM Forum industrial experiences and case studies [25] revealed that the use of DSM supplies the aforementioned benefits. Fur-thermore, related work [26] yet again acknowledged that DSM in conjunction with the MDA paradigm increase productivity significantly. The major problem though with such an approach was the inability of frameworks to generate the appropriate modelling tools. Nowadays meta-modelling frameworks have significantly improved and provide many of the required capabilities to the developers.

Primarily a framework needs to supply a precise meta-meta modelling language for the production of DSLs. This should cover both the definition of abstract properties and their concrete graphical representation. GME supports a proprietary meta-modelling language called MetaGME [19] that is based on UML class diagram nota-tion for the creation of new DSLs. Meta-models and models are represented and can be imported/exported using an XML format. MetaGME allows additionally definition of meta-model level constraints compliant with OCL 1.4. MetaGME's OCL imple-mentation allows the developer to generate a consistent DSL and its corresponding modelling editor. Additionally the framework allows the definition of OCL con-straints at the model level for checking low-level model attributes.

GME does not provide any explicit support for defining and executing model-to-model transformations. The code generation functionality is restricted since it only allows the developer to integrate its on generator as an API add-on. GME has been recently incorporated into a new Eclipse project called Generic Eclipse Modelling System (GEMS) [27]. Its goal is to bridge qualified meta-modelling projects, such as GME, with the Eclipse platform and its related modelling projects; EMF and GMF. The aim is similar to the integration we have performed by bridging several Eclipse based modelling projects together to form an effective meta-modelling environment.

DOME has its own proprietary tool specification language [28], which relies on concepts similar to UML. It covers abstract semantics definition but provides only ba-sic support for concrete semantics since the graphical appearance cannot be edited in a visual manner. Although the graphical representation is not very powerful it still en-ables tools generation for the defined DSLs. DOME does not support explicitly the OCL language but provides built-in support for certain types of frequently used meta-model level constraints; with the Alter language. Additionally Alter allows the developer to build code generators on the basis of the domain models defined. Concerning model transformations the tool does not provide any support. Models and meta-models are also expressed using XML syntax.

MetaEdit+ includes several tools that compose its MetaEngine and provides in overall a framework that minimizes the developer's workload. It implements a meta-meta language called GOPRR [29]. Each letter corresponds to an element of the language. The framework allows defining both the conceptual and graphical properties. From the DSL definition the modelling tool can be automatically generated including facilities such as diagramming editors, browsers and generators. Constraints can be also defined as data incorporated onto the meta-model definition. GOPRR meta-modelling definition enables MetaEdit+ to identify several rules from which a user can select the most appropriate ones. The user can even alter those rules to conform better to its requirements. Framework's support for model level constraints definition is limited. It provides also a Generator editor that facilitates both basic model-to-model transformations and code generation. The framework grants to the developer the ability to integrate its own model transformation engine or code generator package as an API add-on. In general it facilitates many of the requirements and it seems that its future direction aims towards the integration of the entire set of those features.

Table 1. Meta-modelling frameworks requirements conformance

RS	Tool features	GME	DOME	MetaEdit+	XMF-Mosaic	AndroMDA
R1	Abstract semantics	UML MetaGME	√	GOOPPR	XCore	UML 1.4 or MOF XMI
R2	Concrete semantics	UML MetaGME	Partially	√	√	×
R3	Meta-model level constraints	OCL 1.4 in MetaGME	Alter language	As data in meta-model	XOCL	OCL translated to Java, EJB-QL and HQL
R4	Modelling tools generation	√	√	√	√	×
R5	Model level constraints	OCL 1.4	×	Limited support	XOCL	×
R6	Transformations	×	×	Generator Editor or add-ons	XMap language	Defined in Java
R7	Code generation	As GME add-ons	Alter language	Generator Editor or add-ons	XMap language	Template-based
R8	MOF Compliant	Proprietary language	Proprietary language	Proprietary language	√	Limited support
	XMI-Compliant	XML format	XML format	XML format	XML format	√
	QVT Compliant	×	×	×	√	×
	OCL Compliant	√	×	×	Executable OCL	Limited support
R9	Accelerated adoption	×	×	×	Eclipse build	×

XMF-Mosaic is the last framework of the DSM Forum group studied in this survey, which is build onto the Eclipse platform. It incorporates all requirements identified and illustrated onto Figures 1 and 2. Table 1 also reveals that fact and displays the features each tool provides. XMF-Mosaic uses XCORE [30] as its meta-modelling language, which is based on the Meta Object Facility (MOF) [31] specification. XCORE is used for the specification of the meta-model properties. It also supplies tools like XBNF and XTools that facilitate the representation of the meta-model concepts into a so-called user interface model. XBNF is a grammar language and XTools is used to map domain concepts graphically. Additionally XTools specifies the tooling for the user interfaces of the generated modelling editor. With the use of two powerful languages XMap and executable OCL (XOCL) it fulfils the aspects of constraint checking, model transformations and text-based generation. XMap is used to define the mappings between DSLs to perform the model transformation and additionally can be used to define code generators. XOCL enables constraint definition on both meta-models and models. XMF Mosaic is a very powerful meta-modelling framework, which conforms to OMG specifications more than any other framework. Despite that fact XMF-Mosaic is a commercial product, which is not freely available and cannot be extended or modified unless the company releases a new version.

This is where the open source software community comes into action, since it covers the additional aspect of extensibility and subtracts software licence costs. AndroMDA [31] is a very good example of an open source extensible generator framework that adheres to the MDA paradigm. Its core features endeavour most of the requirements. It provides UML 1.4 meta-modelling language support and alternatively it allows using your own MOF XMI meta-model. Comes with pre-configured OCL constraints and allows the addition of own specific project constraints, which are translated into Java, Hibernate Query Language (HQL) and Enterprise JavaBeans Query Language (EJBQL) validation code. Constraints are enforced onto the meta-models. Additionally it provisions to define model-to-model transformations using Java and it is planned as part of the next major release of AndroMDA to provide support for the powerful QVT based ATL language. It provides also generation of text-based output using well known template engines.

Another valuable aspect of AndroMDA, along with the fact that it is open source, is its modular design that supplies a plug-in based architecture. This allows the developer to compose its own environment from various project blocks to suit specific requirements and needs. AndroMDA covers most of the requirements but it lacks support of the essential facet of modelling tools generation, which is an imperative feature of an MDA framework with DSM support. Furthermore, current support for constraint validation is deficient and model-to-model transformation using Java is not as powerful as with the use of a QVT based language. Finally setup of the development environment for AndroMDA and configuration of its building blocks can be quite tedious and troublesome. Due to that fact, an Eclipse-based integration is one of the primary objectives set by the AndroMDA project and is currently under the development process.

Eclipse open source platform provides solutions to the issues identified from the evaluation of the aforementioned frameworks and guides the effort in the formulation of a coherent MDA environment. Recognising its tremendous impact on the industrial world (e.g. XMF-Mosaic is build on the Eclipse platform) and the high-value of its related modelling projects we proceeded in formulating an open source environment, which integrates the necessary meta-modelling features. The environment is composed by several Eclipse projects in an intuitive manner that allows efficient application of model driven development. Further reference to the environment in this article is done in terms of its devised name that is Integrated Eclipse Modelling Environment (IEME).

4 Integrated Eclipse Modelling Environment

The development of IEME was mainly driven by the need to produce a meta-modelling framework satisfying the requirements identified in section 2. Due to the interest in keeping IEME an open source environment, relevant MDA project initiatives of the Eclipse platform were considered. These initiatives were carefully evaluated in practice as per their ability to best meet the aforementioned requirements and were suitably tailored and integrated in a coherent environment.

There are many reasons for choosing Eclipse as the platform for creating the framework. Primarily is its wide acceptance amongst developers and the fact that it is an extensible open source development platform (*R9*). This provides the ability to the developer to modify any of its features or tools and extend or add new tools to serve its company specialised needs. Additionally it offers the possibility to integrate IDEs such as Java and C/C++ that facilitate in increasing software systems productivity.

Figure 3 shows how the MDD process requirements are mapped accordingly to the capabilities of the integrated environment. Initially with the use of the Graphical Modelling Framework (GMF) diagram editor the domain meta-model can be defined

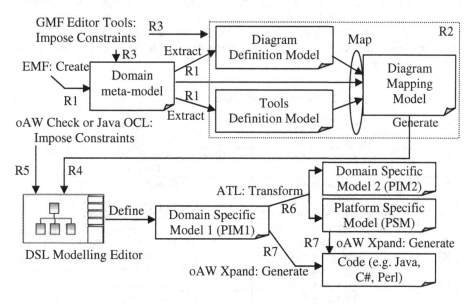

Fig. 3. Model driven development using the IEME

using the *ECore meta-meta modelling language (R1)*. Subsequently, the diagram and tools definition models can be extracted automatically from the domain meta-model. GMF translates the abstract syntax of the domain meta-model and generates the concrete syntax models. These are the *Diagram Definition Model (R2)*, which presents the diagrammatic figures and the *Tools Definition Model (R2)*, which presents the palette element tools. Both models represent the graphical elements of the generated modelling editor tool. The models can be further enhanced through the use of the GMF modelling editor tools provided.

Binding of the abstract and concrete syntax produces the *Diagram Mapping Model (R2)*, which includes the distinct concepts found in the three models. The generation model is extracted from this mapping model and the Eclipse Modelling Framework (EMF) Java Emitter Templates (JET) generation engine is used to generate the *DSL Modelling Editor (R4)* of the domain language. The modelling editor can be used to define graphically application domain specific models with their semantics set accordingly through the use of the properties view of the editor. Models can be further improved by the imposition of constraints using the *openArchitectureWare (oAW) Check language* or by *applying OCL statements through Java (R5)*. It must be denoted that *GMF modelling editor tools (R3)* provide capabilities for assigning both graphical and semantics constraints at the meta-model level during the editor's development process.

Atlas Transformation Language (ATL) is another component that can be used to define model-to-model transformations *(R6)*. The transformations are written in an ATL textual editor and are purely based onto the meta-model. Transformations can be from a platform independent model (PIM) to another platform independent model or even a platform specific model (PSM). Thus the only remaining aspect is the generation of the implementation from the model. The framework grants that capability with the use of the *oAW Xpand language (R7)*. Actually the generator is build out of templates written in the XPand language something that enables code generation in any possible language.

Table 2. IEME framework characteristics conformance

Reqs	Tool features	IEME
R1	Abstract semantics	ECore (EMF) – ECore Diagram (GMF)
R2	Concrete semantics	GMF (GMFGraph, GMFTool, GMFMap, GMFGen)
R3	Meta-model level constraints	GMF modelling editor tools
R4	Modelling tools generation	EMF JET Engine
R5	Model level constraints	oAW Check language or Java
R6	Transformations	Atlas Transformation Language (ATL)
R7	Code generation	oAW Xpand language
R8	MOF Compliant	EMF – implementation of MOF
	XMI Compliant	XMI meta-models and models
	QVT Compliant	ATL – implementation of QVT
	OCL Compliant	GMF, oAW Check, Java OCL
R9	Accelerated adoption	Build on the Eclipse Platform

The procedure described before and illustrated in Figure 3 shows that IEME is in fact a complete and coherent MDA/MDD framework. Additionally Table 2 presents how the framework reflects each of the requirements set and attests to the claim that it provides a pure meta-modelling environment. Following we give a more detailed overview of the core components of the environment to enable better understanding of its features and capabilities. It must be stated that the framework provides Java and C/C++ IDEs that are also built-in the environment using the extensible Eclipse plug-in architecture. IEME is composed by the following modelling core components delivering a versatile environment.

Eclipse Modelling Framework (EMF) [12] is the core of the environment. It's an extended implementation of MOF and lies at the meta-meta level. It is a modelling framework and code generation facility that serves as the meta-meta language for defining domain meta-models (ecore). EMF supplies its own tree-based editor for meta-model definition. The domain meta-model includes the semantics of the defined DSL. Furthermore it provides the facilities that are essential for the automatic generation of the corresponding tree-based editor tool. This tool enables the creation of models of the defined domain specific language.

Graphical Modelling Framework (GMF) [13] provides a generative component and runtime infrastructure for developing graphical editors. GMF provides graphical editor tools that allow the definition of the visual domain meta-model (ecorediagram), the diagram definition model (gmfgraph), the tooling definition model (gmftool) and the mapping model (gmfmap). The visual domain meta-model is the diagrammatic view of the domain meta-model, which provides better understanding of the defined DSL. Therefore definition of the visual domain meta-model using the GMF editor is preferred than the definition of the domain meta-model using the EMF tree-based

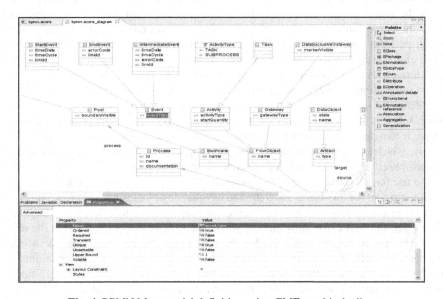

Fig. 4. BPMN Meta-model definition using GMF graphical editor

editor. Figure 4 shows an example of a visual domain meta-model definition using the GMF editor. It represents the domain meta-model semantics of the Business Process Modelling Notation (BPMN).

EMF and GMF combined and used in parallel provide the essential meta-meta languages and the supporting tools that drive the entire language development process. Most importantly they facilitate the generation of the appropriate tools to support the modelling language. Both projects use XMI as the common syntax for their models. Next we present the projects that cover the rest of the requirements namely constraint checking, model transformations and code generation. The entire set of core components are plug-ins integrated into the Eclipse platform something that preserves the stability and extensibility of the overall environment.

Atlas Transformation Language (ATL) [14] is a project developed at INRIA French National research institution and aims to provide model-to-model transformations. ATL is also an Eclipse plug-in that implements the Query/View/Transformation (QVT) language standard. ATL is actually a domain specific language build for transformations. Basically it allows defining model-to-model transformations with the use of appropriate editor tools. It must be denoted that the transformations are defined based on the meta-models. Currently ATL is adopted as the basic component, along with the QVT standard, of the Eclipse Model-to-Model transformation (M2M) project. There is a variety of defined transformations already available online onto the Eclipse ATL ZOO something that reveals the popularity of ATL as the major transformation language.

openArchitectureWare (oAW) [15] is a framework that provides a set of modelling tools integrated into a coherent model driven development environment. Careful study of the tools developed within this project reveals that it follows exactly the same guidelines and characteristics for working in the context of MDA. Additionally it provides the capability to choose selectively components from the overall framework since these are built as Eclipse plug-ins. Some of the components of the project, which perform specific tasks are not quite as powerful as their counterparts; EMF, GMF and ATL. Therefore these were not selected. oAW though contains other powerful tools with their accompanying languages that can assist in the complete and coherent integration of an MDA framework.

Foremost is the Xpand template language, an extract of which is shown onto Figure 5, which supports advanced features for building code generators in any programming language. It must be denoted that the environment provides an alternative code generation facility, which is EMF Java Emitter Templates (JET) [32], [33]. Although JET is very powerful itself and can be used to generate code in any language, it is more focused and best to use for generating Java code. Therefore Xpand template language is found to be more competent for text-based generation to any particular language.

Another component is the Check language, which is an OCL based language that allows definition of constraints onto the EMF meta-model and directly onto the models. oAW has strong support for EMF based models but can work also with other models (e.g. UML2). Additionally it even allows the definition of OCL constraints using Java. A core workflow engine controls the generator's workflow, as specified in an XML format. The workflow definition drives the execution by invoking the corresponding components for reading and instantiating models, checking for constraint violations and then finally, for generating code.

Fig. 5. Building code generators using XPand template language

5   Conclusions and Future Work

In this article we stress out the importance of tools for industrial use of meta-modelling frameworks. Such type of frameworks should provide the ability to define and generate modelling tools. Additionally they must comply with some other funda-mental requirements. There are various initiatives to formulate a coherent environ-ment and each of them comprise of some powerful tools. Study of those frameworks exposed that each initiative follows the same guidelines to deliver these essential fea-tures. Despite that fact none of them provides a complete solution to the problem. The commercial XMF-Mosaic covers most of the important aspects but it also lacks in terms of the generation of stable modelling editor tools using XTools.

IEME is our proposition of a framework that covers all these aspects by integration of the most powerful tools and languages. It must be denoted that there might be other dominant tools and languages that also fulfil their specific goals. The most important reason for the selection of these is their smooth ability to integrate as plug-ins to the extensible open source Eclipse platform. Eclipse platform provides the flexibility and the dynamics required by such an environment. A developer might require adding or altering a facility to suit its specific company requirements. It is no secret that major frameworks and industrial organisations use Eclipse as their development platform.

There are also other benefits provided by the integrated environment. These are namely its precise meta-meta language that is based on OMG MOF, its support for a common interchangeable syntax such as XMI. Someone might argue that there are so many versions of XMI that interoperability is not easy to achieve. The attempt though is to at least provide a common widely acceptable syntax for the models in order to be compliant with other frameworks that adopt this standard syntax. Furthermore EMF and GMF projects are now very mature offering remarkable capabilities for the gen-eration of stable and user friendly modelling tools with a simplistic procedure.

Constraint checking, transformations and code generation are covered in great depth by the appropriate projects.

An important aspect that was identified and remains to be tackled, as future work, is the configuration management when porting to newer versions of the modelling language. Transition to another meta-model by incarcerating new semantics requires adjusting the modelling language's editor tools. Therefore it can be realised that models designed using the new version of the language are dissimilar to previous models. The framework needs to provide the capability to convert the latter to reflect the improved modelling language. An initial consideration is the usage of the powerful ATL transformation language to define transformations between the different versions of the models. Such an improvement to the framework will be very beneficial reducing further transition costs.

The environment is an initial effort to provide a complete solution to the MDA paradigm, covering all necessary aspects. Further research and testing of the environment with examples and case studies will detect any deficiencies to further improve it. Since the environment is characterised by its extensibility and adaptability such alterations can be easily implemented. Finally another important aspect that remains open is the interoperability of IEME with the rest of the major frameworks presented in this article. MDA growth requires this interoperability amongst powerful frameworks since it will provide the ability to the developer to make use of the most appropriate tools to accomplish its objectives.

References

[1] The OSS through Java Initiative, [Online] Available: http://www.tmforum.org/browse.aspx?catID=2896

[2] The TeleManagement Forum, [Online] Available: http://www.tmforum.org

[3] Model Driven Architecture (MDA), Specification Guide V1.0.1, Object Management Group (OMG), [Online] Available: (June 2003), www.omg.org/docs/omg/03-06-01.pdf

[4] Object Constraint Language (OCL) Specification, version 2.0, Object Management Group (OMG), [Online] Available (June (2005), http://www.omg.org/docs/formal/06-05-01.pdf

[5] Ou, S., Georgalas, N., Azmoodeh, M., Yang, K., Sun, X.: A Model Driven Integration Architecture for Ontology-Based Context Modelling and Context-Aware Application Development. In: Rensink, A., Warmer, J. (eds.) ECMDA-FA 2006. LNCS, vol. 4066, Springer, Heidelberg (2006)

[6] Azmoodeh, M., Georgalas, N., Fisher, S.: Model-driven systems development and integration environment. In: BT Technology Journal, vol. 23(03), Springer, Berlin Heidelberg (2005)

[7] Georgalas, N., Azmoodeh, M., Ou, S.: Model Driven Integration of Standards Based OSS Components, In: Proceedings of the Eurescom Summit on Ubiquitous Services and Application, Heidelberg, Germany (2005)

[8] Georgalas, N., Azmoodeh, M., Clark, T., Evans, A., Sammut, P., Willans, J.: MDA-Driven Development of standard-compliant OSS components: the OSS/J Inventory Case-Study, In: Proceedings of the Second ECMDA with emphasis on Methodologies and Transformations, Canterbury, UK (September 2004)

[9] Georgalas, N.: NGOSS/MDA: Realising NGOSS as a Model Driven Approach, Catalyst project, TeleManagement World Conference, Nice, France (2005)

[10] Eclipse – an open development platform, [Online] Available: http://www.eclipse.org/
[11] The OpenOSS Programme, TeleManagement Forum, [Online] Available: http://www.tmforum.org/browse.aspx?catID=2602&linkID=31021
[12] Eclipse Foundation Inc. Eclipse Modelling Framework (EMF), [Online] Available: http://www.eclipse.org/emf/
[13] Eclipse Foundation Inc. Graphical Modelling Framework (GMF), [Online] Available: http://www.eclipse.org/gmf/
[14] INRIA Research Institution, Atlas Transformation Language (ATL), [Online] Available: http://www.eclipse.org/m2m/atl
[15] openArchitectureWare.org, openArchitectureWare (oAW), [Online] Available: http://www.eclipse.org/gmt/oaw
[16] Nytun, J.P., Prinz, A., Tveit, M.S.: Automatic Generation of Modelling Tools. In: ECMDA-FA: Proceedings of Second European Conference, pp. 268–283. Springer, Berlin/Heidelberg (2006)
[17] Greenfield, J., Short, K., with contributions by Cook, S., Kent, S.: Software Factories: Assembling Applications with Patterns, Frameworks, Model and Tools. John Willey and Sons, New York (2006)
[18] Unified Modelling Language (UML), version 2.0, Object Management Group (OMG), [Online] Available: (June 2004), http://www.omg.org/technology/documents/formal/uml.htm,
[19] Vanderbilt University, A Generic Modelling Environment, GME 5 User's Manual, [Online] Available: http://www.isis.vanderbilt.edu/projects/gme/GMEUMan.pdf
[20] Honeywell Labs, DOmain Modelling Environment (DOME), [Online] Available: http://www.htc.honeywell.com/dome/index.htm.
[21] Metacase, MetaEdit+ Version 4.5 User's Guide, [Online] Available (2006), http://www.metacase.com/support/45/manuals/meplus/Mp.html
[22] Xactium, Language Driven Development and XMF-Mosaic, White papers, [Online] Available: (March 2005)
     http://whitepapers.zdnet.co.uk/0,1000000651,260134763p,00.htm,
[23] AndroMDA.org, Open Source MDA Generator Framework, [Online] Available: http://www.andromda.org
[24] DSM Forum.org, [Online] Available: http://www.dsmforum.org/
[25] DSM Forum.org, DSM Case Studies and Examples, [Online] Available: http://www.dsmforum.org/cases
[26] Balasubramanian, K., Gokhale, A., Karsai, G., Sztipanovits, J., Neema, S.: Developing Applications Using Model-Driven Design Environments. IEEE Computer Society Journal, Vanderbilt University (2006)
[27] SourceForge.net, Generic Eclipse Modelling System (GEMS) User's Guide, [Online] Available: 540131&big_mirror=0 (1159), http://downloads.sourceforge.net/gems/gems_user_guide_2_0_5_01.pdf?modtime=,
[28] Honeywell Labs, DOME User's Guide V.5.2.2, [Online] Available (1999), http://www.htc.honeywell.com/dome/DOMEGuide.pdf
[29] Metacase, MetaEdit+ Version 4.5, The Graphical Metamodelling Example, [Online] Available (2006),
     http://www.metacase.com/support/45/manuals/Graphical%20Metamodelling.pdf
[30] Xactium, Applied Meta-modelling: A Foundation for Language Driven Development, Version 0.1, [Online] Available (2004), http://www.securewebonline.com/Services/AppliedMetamodellingV01.pdf

[31] Meta Object Facility (MOF) Core Specification, version 2.0, Object Management Group (OMG), [Online] Available (January 2005), http://www.omg.org/docs/formal/06-01-01.pdf
[32] Azzurri Ltd. JET Tutorial Part 1, [Online] Available: http://www.eclipse.org/articles/Article-JET/jet_tutorial1.html
[33] Azzurri Ltd. JET Tutorial Part 2, [Online] Available: http://www.eclipse.org/articles/Article-JET2/jet_tutorial2.html

Efficient Reasoning About Finite Satisfiability of UML Class Diagrams with Constrained Generalization Sets

Azzam Maraee[1] and Mira Balaban[2,*]

[1] Information Systems Engineering Department
[2] Computer Science Department
Ben-Gurion University of the Negev, Beer-Sheva 84105, Israel
mari@bgu.ac.il, mira@cs.bgu.ac.il

Abstract. UML class diagrams play a central role in the design and specification of software, databases and ontologies. The model driven architecture approach emphasizes the central role that models play, towards achieving reliable software. It is important that models are correct and that problems are detected as early as possible in the software design process. However, current case tools do not support reasoning tasks about class diagrams and enable the construction of erroneous models. There is an urgent need for methods for detecting analysis and design problems. In this paper, we present a linear programming based method for reasoning about finite satisfiability of UML class diagrams with constrained generalization sets. The method is simple and efficient and can be easily added to a case tool. It improves over existing methods that require exponential resources and extends them to new elements of class diagrams.

Keywords: UML class diagram, finite satisfiability, consistency, cardinality constraints, reasoning about class diagram, generalization set constraints, class hierarchy structure.

1 Introduction

The Unified Modeling Language (UML) is nowadays the industry standard modeling framework, including multiple visual modeling diagrams collectively, referred to as a UML model. Traditionally, UML models are used for analysis and design of complex systems. Their relevance has increased with the advent of the Model-Driven Development (MDD) approach, in which analysis and design models play an essential role in the process of software development. Recently, with the emergence of web-enabled agent technology, UML models are used also for ontology representation, and construction and extraction of ontologies [7].

In view of their wide popularity, it is highly important that UML models provide reliable support for the designed systems, and be subject to stringent

* Supported by the Lynn and William Frankel center for Computer Sciences.

D.H. Akehurst, R. Vogel, and R.F. Paige (Eds.): ECMDA-FA 2007, LNCS 4530, pp. 17–31, 2007.

quality assurance and quality control criteria [21]. Indeed, an extensive amount of research efforts is devoted to formalization of UML models, specification of their semantics, and development of reasoning and correctness checking methods [2, 16]. Moreover, with the prevalence of the Model Driven Engineering approach, it is expected that all information in a design model will be effective in its successive models.

Modeling problems usually arise when models are scaled to model large, distributed applications. A model may originate from different sources and a large number of designers can be involved in the modeling process. Designers are highly prone to making mistakes, and combining information from different sources gives rise to potential conflicts [3, 6, 10]. [14] shows that defects often remain undetected, even if the model is read attentively by practitioners.

It is highly important that models are tested for correctness, and that problems are detected as early as possible in the software design process. Nevertheless, current case tools do not support reasoning about UML models, and enable the construction of erroneous ones. Furthermore, implementation languages still do not enforce design level constraints. Hence, there is an urgent need for reasoning methods for detecting analysis and design problems.

Class Diagrams are probably the most important and best understood among all UML models. A Class Diagram provides a static description of system components. It describes systems structure in terms of classes, associations, and constraints imposed on classes and their inter-relationships. Constraints provide an essential means of knowledge engineering, since they extend the expressivity of diagrams. UML supports class diagram constraints such as cardinality constraints, class hierarchy constraints, and inter-association constraints. Example 1 below, presents a class diagram that includes cardinality and hierarchy constraints.

Example 1. Figure 1 presents a class diagram with three classes named *Academic*, *Graduate* and *FacultyMember*, one association *advisor-student* between instances of the *Academic* and the *Graduate* classes, with roles named *advisor* and *student*, respectively, a cardinality constraint that is imposed on this association, and a generalization set with a super-class *Academic* and sub-classes *Graduate* and *FacultyMember*. The cardinality constraint states that every *Graduate* student must be advised by exactly one *Academic*, while every *Academic* must advise exactly two *Graduate* students. The generalization set states that *Graduates* and *FacultyMembers* are *Academic* as well, implying that the *advisor* of a *Graduate* can be a *Graduate* or a *FacultyMember* or another *Academic*.

In the presence of constraints a class diagram may turn inconsistent, as it might impose constraints that cannot be finitely satisfied. Figure 1, presents a multiplicity constraint cycle that involves a compound class, *Graduate*, whose instances must be related to *Academic* instances. Therefore, the number of *student-advisor* links in every diagram instance must be both, $G \cdot 1$ and $A \cdot 2$, assuming that G and A are the number of graduates and academics, respectively. Therefore, the extensions of *Graduate* and *Academic* must satisfy $G = A \cdot 2$, while the *Graduate* extension is a subset of the *Academic* extension. This constraint can be

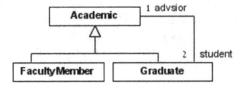

Fig. 1. A Class Diagram with a Finite Satisfiability Problem

satisfied only by empty or infinite extensions. Such problems are termed *finite satisfiability* problems.

The problem of finite satisfiability has been studied in the context of various kinds of conceptual schemata [1, 3, 5, 8, 10, 15, 20]. There are methods for testing finite satisfiability, for detecting causes for unsatisfiability, and for heuristic suggestions for diagram correction. Yet, no method provides a feasible solution for detecting lack of finite satisfiability for the combination of cardinality constraints, class hierarchy constraints, and generalization sets constraints.

In this paper, we present a linear programming based method for reasoning about finite satisfiability of UML class diagrams with constrained generalization sets. The method is based on a reduction to the algorithm of Lenzerini and Nobili [15] that was applied only to ER-diagrams without class hierarchies. It is simple and feasible since it adds in the worst case only a linear amount of entities to the original diagram. It improves over previous extensions of the Lenzerini and Nobili method that require the addition of an exponential number of new entities to the original diagram [5]. An implementation of our method within a UML case tool is currently under development.

The paper is organized as follows: Section 2 presents the finite satisfiability notion, summarizes relevant methods for detecting finite satisfiability problems in class diagrams, introduces the Generalization Set notion of UML2.0, and classifies different class hierarchy structures. Although this paper focuses only on finite satisfiability problems, for the sake of completeness we also introduce the consistency notion. Section 3 describes a polynomial time algorithm for testing finite satisfiability of UML class diagrams with unconstrained generalization sets. Section 4 extends the algorithm to operate on constrained generalization sets, and investigates the limits of this method. Section 5 is the conclusion and discussion of future work.

2 Background

The standard set theoretic semantics of class diagrams associates a class diagram with *class diagram instances* in which classes have extensions that are sets of objects that share structure and operations, and associations have extensions that are relationships among class extensions. We denote class symbols as C, association symbols as A, and role symbols as rn. Henceforth, we shorten expressions like "instance of an extension of C" by "instance of C" and "instance of an extension of A" by "instance of A".

A cardinality constraint (also termed multiplicity constraint) imposed on a binary association A between classes C_1 and C_2 with roles rn_1, rn_2, respectively, is symbolically denoted:

$$A(rn_1 : C_1[\ min_1,\ max_1], rn_2 : C_2[\ min_2,\ max_2]) \tag{1}$$

The multiplicity constraint $[min_1, max_1]$ that is visually written on the rn_1 end of the association line is actually a participation constraint on instances of C_2. It states that an instance of C_2 can be related via A to n instances of C_1, where n lies in the interval $[min_1, max_1]$. A class hierarchy constraint between a super class C_1 and a subclass C_2 is written $ISA(C_2, C_1)$ and called also *ISA constraint*. It states a subset relation between extensions of C_2 and C_1.

A *legal instance* of a class diagram is an instance where the class and association extensions satisfy all constraints in the diagram. Correctness of a class diagram involves consistency and satisfiability notions, that are discussed in [2, 5, 15, 20]. We further elaborate this terminology, and suggest additional notions, in order to facilitate a more accurate definition of correctness.

- **Consistency Notions:**
    1. A *class diagram is consistent (satisfiable)* if it has an instance with at-least one non-empty class extension. Otherwise, it is inconsistent.
    2. A *class C in a class diagram is consistent* if there is an instance I in which the extension of C is non-empty (C is said to be *consistent in* I). Otherwise, it is *inconsistent, (unsatisfiable)*.
    3. A *class diagram is all class consistent* if every class is consistent.
    4. A *class diagram is fully consistent* if it has an instance in which all classes are consistent.
- **Finite Satisfiability Notions:**
    1. A *class is finitely satisfiable* in a class diagram if there is a finite instance in which the class is consistent (A class diagram instance is finite if all class extensions are finite).
    2. A *class diagram is all class finitely satisfiable* if for every class there is a finite instance in which the class is consistent. Lenzerini and Nobili [15] used the notion of *strong satisfiability* for this term.
    3. A *class diagram is fully finitely satisfiable* if it has a finite instance in which all classes are consistent.

The important notions for consistency and finite satisfiability are those of *full consistency* and *full finite satisfiability*. [17] shows that full consistency is equivalent to all class consistency, and full finite satisfiability is equivalent to all class finite satisfiability. Inconsistency and lack of finite satisfiability are errors in design that might delay system development and increase its cost [13]. The first because an inconsistent class diagram does not have a non-empty extension, and the latter because there is no finite and non-empty extension [4]. The consistency problem is instigated in [2, 12].

2.1 Methods for Reasoning About Finite Satisfiability of UML Class Diagrams

The method of Lenzerini and Nobily is defined for *Entity-Relationship (ER)* diagrams that include *Entity Types (Classes)*, *Binary Relationships (Binary Associations)*, and *Cardinality Constraints*. The method consists of a transformation of the cardinality constraints into a set of linear inequalities whose size is polynomial in the size of the diagram. All class finite satisfiability of the ER diagram reduces to solution existence of the associated linear inequalities system. The linear inequalities system is defined as follow:

1. For each association $R(rn_1 : C_1[min_1, max_1], rn_2 : C_2[min_2, max_2])$ insert the following inequalities:
   - For $min_2 > 0$: $r \geq min_2 \cdot c_1$ and for $max_2 \neq *$: $r \leq max_2 \cdot c_1$.
   - For $min_1 > 0$: $r \geq min_1 \cdot c_2$ and for $max_1 \neq *$: $r \leq max_1 \cdot c_2$.
2. For every entity or association symbol T insert the inequality: $T > 0$.

Lenzerini and Nobili also present a method for identification of causes for non-satisfiability. This method is based on a transformation of the conceptual schema into a graph and identification of critical cycles. Similar approaches are introduced in [20, 8]. Hartman, in [9] further develops methods for handling finite satisfiability problems in the context of database key and functional dependency constraints. Heuristic methods for constraint corrections are presented in [10, 11].

Calvanese and Lenzerini, in [5], extend the inequalities based method of Lenzerini and Nobili [15] to apply to schemata with class hierarchy constraints. The expansion is based on the assumption that class extensions may overlap. They provide a two stage algorithm in which the finite satisfiability problem of a class diagram with *ISA* constraints is reduced into the finite satisfiability problem of a class diagram without *ISA* constraints. Then, similarly to [15], they check all class finite satisfiability of the new class diagram by deriving a special system of linear inequalities (different from that of [15]).

The class diagram transformation process of [5] is fairly complex, and might introduce, in the worst case, an exponential number, in terms of the input diagram size, of new classes and associations. The method was further simplified in [4], where class overlapping is restricted to class hierarchy alone. The simplification of [4] reduces the overall number of new classes and associations, but the worst case is still exponential. Example 2 presents the application of [4] to Figure 1.

Example 2. The application of the [4] method yields four classes and eight associations. Each class and association is represented by a variable in the resulting inequalities system. The variables are:

1. **Class variables:** a_1 for an *Academic* that is neither a *Graduate* nor a *FacultyMember*; a_2 for an *Academic* that is a *Graduate* but not a *FacultyMember*; a_3 for an *Academic* that is a *FacultyMember* but not a *Graduate*; a_4 for an *Academic* that is simultaneously a *Graduate* and a *FacultyMember*.

2. **Association variables:** $\{ad_{ij}|1 \leq i \leq 4 \wedge j \in \{2,4\}\}$. Every specialized association relates two new classes, one for the advisor role and the other for the *student* role. The indexes represent the indexes of the class variables. For example, the variable r_{12} represents the specialization of the *advisor-student* association to an association between *Academics* who are neither *Graduates* nor *FacultyMembers* (the a_1 variable) and *Academics* specialized to *Graduates* but not to *FacultyMembers* (the a_2 variable).

The inequalities system below results from application of the method of [4] to Figure 1. Equations 1-4 translate the 2..2 multiplicity, equations 5-6 translate the 1..1 multiplicity, and the inequalities in 7-9 represent the satisfiability conditions. The inequalities system is unsolvable, implying that the class diagram in Figure 1 is finitely unsatisfiable.

1. $2a_1 = ad_{12} + ad_{14}$.
2. $2a_2 = ad_{22} + ad_{24}$.
3. $2a_3 = ad_{32} + ad_{34}$.
4. $2a_4 = ad_{42} + ad_{44}$.
5. $a_2 = ad_{12} + ad_{22} + ad_{32} + ad_{42}$.
6. $a_4 = ad_{14} + ad_{24} + ad_{34} + ad_{44}$.
7. $a_1, a_2, a_3, a_4, ad_{12}, ad_{14}, ad_{22}, ad_{24}, ad_{32}, ad_{34}, ad_{42}, ad_{44} \geq 0$.
8. $a_1 + a_2 + a_3 + a_4 > 0$.
9. $ad_{12} + ad_{14} + ad_{22} + ad_{24} + ad_{32} + ad_{34} + ad_{42} + ad_{44} > 0$.

2.2   UML2.0 Class Hierarchy Concepts: Generalization Sets

In UML2.0 class hierarchy constraints are expressed using the *Generalization Set* (*GS*) concept, which is similar to the former class hierarchy grouping construct [18]. A *GS*s includes a superclass and a set of sub classes (different from the super class). The semantics is that the sub classes denote sub sets of the set denoted by the super class. *GS*s may be constrained as follows [18, 19]:

1. *complete* - An instance of the superclass is an instance of at least one subclass.
2. *incomplete*- There might be instances of the superclass of that are not instances of any subclass.
3. *disjoint*- Subclasses are mutually exclusive.
4. *overlapping* - Subclasses may overlap.

The *GS* constraints can be combined to form one of the following valid combination: {complete, disjoint}, {incomplete, disjoint}, {complete, overlapping}, {incomplete, overlapping}. Figure 2 shows a *disjoint* constraint.

2.3   Classification of Class Hierarchy Structures

Class hierarchy can arise in various structures that affect the finite satisfiability decision algorithm. We distinguish three parameters that determine the class hierarchy structures and content:

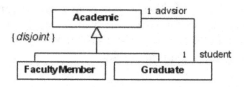

Fig. 2. Constrained Generalization Set

1. **ISA Graph Structure:** *ISA* constraints can form three kinds of graph structures:

   (a) **Tree Structure**, as in Figure 1: A subclass has a single super class.
   (b) **Acyclic Structure**: Multiple inheritance is allowed, but the undirected induced subgraph formed by the *ISA* constraints is acyclic. For example, in Figure 3-a, the hierarchy structure is not a tree, as F is a sub class of both C and D, but the undirected class hierarchy graph is acyclic. The acyclic structure prevents multiple inheritance with a common ancestor-class.

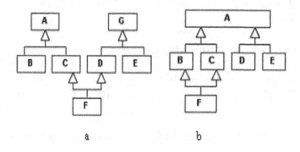

Fig. 3. Unconstrained Hierarchy Structures

   (c) **Graph Structure**, as in Figure 3-b: unrestricted multiple inheritance.
2. **Presence of *GS* Constraints.**
3. **Number of *GS*s per superclass**, as in Figure 3-b.

We use an abbreviated notation that specifies the value of these parameters. The *hierarchy structure* is denoted by one of {T,A,G}, standing for *Tree structure, Acyclic graph*, and *Graph*, respectively. The presence of *GS* constraints is denoted by C, and the presence of multiple *GS*s per superclass is denoted by M. The multiple *GS*s per superclass distinction is relevant only for tree structure hierarchies. For acyclic on graph hierarchies, multiple *GS*s per a single superclass are allowed by the graphical structure. The resulting hierarchy variants are: [T]-GS for tree structured unconstrained hierarchy with a single *GS* per superclass; [T-C]-GS for tree structured constrained *GS*s with a single *GS* per superclass; [T-M]-GS for tree structured unconstrained hierarchy with multiple

GSs per super class; [T-C-M]-GS for a constrained tree hierarchy with multiple GSs per super class; [A]-GS for an unconstrained acyclic hierarchy; [A-C]-GS for a constrained acyclic hierarchy; [G]-GS for unconstrained graph hierarchy; [G-C]-GS for a constrained graph hierarchy.

3   Reasoning About Finite Satisfiability of UML Class Diagrams with Unconstrained GSs

In this section, we present a method for reasoning about finite satisfiability of UML class diagrams with unconstrained GSs. We start with a tree structured hierarchy [T]-GS, and extend it to the hierarchical structures: {[T-M],[A],[G]}-GS.

The method builds on top of the Lenzerini and Nobili [15] algorithm described in Section 2. We reduce the *finite satisfiability* problem of a class diagram with *ISA* constraints, into the *finite satisfiability* problem of a class diagram that is handled by [15]. First, we state that *all class finite satisfiability* implies a *full finite satisfiability* The proof is similar to the proof for the case of the restricted ER diagrams, as presented in [15].

Theorem 1. *If a class diagram is all class finitely satisfiable then it is fully finitely satisfiable.*

Proof. (Sketched) The theorem is proved by the following argument: Every two disjoint instances can be combined into a single instance of the class diagram. The argument holds due to the special character of UML class diagram constraints, which are closed under disjoint instance combination. For full proof consult [17].

3.1   Testing the Finite Satisfiability of Class Diagrams with [T]-GS

Algorithm 1.

- **Input**: A class diagram CD that includes binary associations and [T]-GS.
- **Output**: True, if CD is *all class finitely satisfiable*; false otherwise.
- **Method**:
  1. Class diagram reduction - Create a new class diagram CD' as follows:
     (a) Initialize CD' by the input class diagram CD.
     (b) Remove from CD' all generalization set constructs.
     (c) For every removed generalization set construct create new binary associations between the superclass to the subclasses, with 1..1 participation constraint for the subclass (written on the super class edge in the diagram) and 0..1 participation constraint for the super class.
  2. Apply the Lenzerini and Nobili algorithm to CD'.

Example 3. Figure 4 is the reduced class diagram of Figure 1, following step 1 in the algorithm. Applying the inequalities method of [15] (step 2) yields the inequalities system below. We use the symbols *ad* for *Academic*, *g* for *Graduate*,

fm for *FacultyMember*, *as* for the *advisor-student* association, and isa_1, isa_2 for the new associations ISA_1 and ISA_2 respectively.

$$as \geq 2ad,\ as \leq 2ad,\ as \leq g,\ as \geq g,\ isa_1 \geq g,\ isa_1 \leq g,\ isa_1 \leq ad,\ isa_2 \geq fm,$$
$$isa_2 \leq fm,\ isa_2 \leq ad,\ \text{and}$$
$$as > 0,\ ad > 0,\ g > 0,\ fm > 0,\ isa_1 > 0,\ isa_2 > 0$$

This system has no solution and therefore the [15] algorithm returns False. The same result was obtained in Section 2 by applying the [5],[4] algorithm to Figure 1.

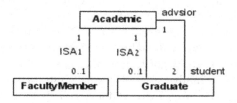

Fig. 4. The Reduced Class Diagram of Figure 1

Claim 1: [Correctness of Algorithm 1] Algorithm 1 tests for *all class finite satisfiability* of class diagrams with [T]-GS.

Proof. (sketched) the claim builds on showing that the translated class diagram CD' preserves the satisfiability of the input class diagram CD. Full proof appears in [17].

Claim 2: [Complexity of Algorithm 1] Algorithm 1 adds to the [15] method an $O(n)$ time complexity, where n is the size of the class diagram (including associations, classes and ISA constraints).

Proof. The additional work involves the class diagram reduction, which creates a class diagram with the same set of classes and one additional association that replaces every class hierarchy constraint. Since there is a linear additional work per ISA constraint, the overall additional work is a linear to the size of the class diagram.

3.2 Extensions for {[T-M], [A], [G]}-GS

Algorithm 1 applies properly to the other unconstrained structures: {[T-M], [A], [G]}-GS. The extensions preserve the correctness of the algorithm since the reduction of *all class finite satisfiability* of CD to that of CD' is still correct. The more complex structure does not break the reduction because as long as the GSs are not constrained, *ISA* constraints can be simulated by regular links between the involved classes. Different instances of a superclass C in CD' can be unified into a single instance of C in CD, without breaking any constraints.

4   Reasoning About Finite Satisfiability of UML Class Diagrams with Constrained Generalization Sets

Adding *GS*-constraints to the class diagram imposes additional requirements on its finite satisfiability problem. In order to test finite satisfiability under *GS*-constraints, the finite satisfiability problem of a class diagram *CD* with *ISA* constraints, is reduced into the finite satisfiability problem of a "constrained" class diagram *CD'* without class hierarchy. The additional constraints on *CD'* preserve the constraints on the *GS*s of *CD*. The inequalities system obtained by applying the method of [15] to *CD'* is expanded with new inequalities that reflect the *GS* constraints. This algorithm is first introduced for *single GS*-constraints, i.e., the four *GS*-constraints *disjoint, complete, incomplete, overlapping*, and then expanded for handling combinations of *pair GS*-constraints. We begin with an algorithm for deciding finite satisfiability of tree structured ([T-C]-GS) class diagrams. We show that the algorithm applies also to [T-C-M]-GS and to [A-C]-GS class diagrams. Finally we explore the limits of the algorithm for the [G-C]-GS class diagrams. We show that for graph structured class hierarchies, the algorithm can handle the *overlapping* and the *incomplete GS*-constraints, but falls short for deciding finite satisfiability for the *disjoint* and the *complete GS*-constraints.

The *incomplete* and the *overlapping* constraints of generalization sets have a "possibilistic" semantics: The first states that there might be direct instances of the superclass, and the second states that subclasses may overlap. Finite satisfiability for these constraints requires the realization of the possibilistic nature. That is, the *incomplete* constraint requires the existence of direct instances of the superclass, and the *overlapping* constraint requires the existence of common instances for subclasses. For the finite satisfiability problem, we require the existence of an instance in which incomplete super-classes have direct instances, and overlapping subclasses have common instances.

4.1   Testing Finite Satisfiability of Tree Structured ([T-C]-GS) Class Diagrams

Algorithm 2.

- **Input**: A class diagram *CD* that includes binary associations and [T-C]-GS.
- **Output**: True, if *CD* is *all class finitely satisfiable*; false otherwise.
- **Method**:
  1. Class diagram reduction:
     (a) Steps 1.a, 1.b, 1.c from Algorithm 1.
     (b) For every generalization set $C, C_1, ..., C_n$ in *CD*, add constraint *Const* on its classes as follows:
         for *disjoint/overlapping* constraint, *Const* is: "there is no/(at least one) instance of class C which is associated with more than one instance from $C_1, ... C_n$ via the *ISA* links";

for *complete/incomplete* constraint, *Const* is: "all/part of the instances of class C are associated with the instances of the classes $C_1, ..., C_n$ via the ISA links".

2. Inequalities system construction:
   (a) Create the inequalities system for CD' according to the Lenzerini and Nobili algorithm.
   (b) For every single constraint *Const* added in step 1b, extend the inequalities system, as follows:
      i. $Const = disjoint$: $C \geq \sum_{j=1}^{n} C_j$.
      ii. $Const = complete$: $C \leq \sum_{j=1}^{n} C_j$.
      iii. $Const = incomplete$: $\forall j \in [1, n].C > C_j$.
      iv. $Const = overlapping$: Without inequality.
   (c) For every pair of constraints added in step 1b, extend the inequalities system, as follows:
      i. *disjoint, incomplete*: $C > \sum_{j=1}^{n} C_j$.
      ii. *disjoint, complete*: $C = \sum_{j=1}^{n} C_j$.
      iii. *overlapping, complete*: $C < \sum_{j=1}^{n} C_j$.
      iv. *overlapping, incomplete*: $\forall j \in [1, n].C > C_j$.
3. Apply the Lenzerini and Nobili algorithm to CD'.

Example 4. Consider Figure 2. The interaction between the cardinality constraint, the hierarchy, and the GS constraints causes a finite satisfiability problem. Applying the method of [15] with the extension in Algorithm 2, step 2.b.i, to the reduced class diagram of Figure 2 yields the unsolvable inequalities system (same variables from Example 3) presented below, implying that the class diagram is finitely unsatisfiable.

$isa_1 = g$, $isa_1 \leq ad$, $isa_2 = fm$,$isa_2 \leq ad$, $as = ad$, $ad = g$, $ad > 0$, $as > 0$, $g > 0$,$fm > 0$, $isa_1 > 0$, $isa_2 > 0$, and the *disjoint* inequality: $ad \geq g + fm$

Comment: The inequalities that are used in step (2.b) for satisfying the single GS-constraints are not mutually exclusive. Indeed, there are solutions for the inequalities system that can imply finite satisfiability for several constraints. For example, a solution that yields equality in a *disjoint* inequality implies that the *disjoint* constraint can be replaced by a *complete* constraint, without affecting finite satisfiability, and vice versa. Step (2.c) handles pairs of GS- constraints that result from combinations of *disjoint / overlapping* with *complete / incomplete*. The single constraint inequalities are tightened so to meet the combined constraints.

Claim 3: [Correctness of Algorithm 2] Algorithm 2 tests for *all class finite satisfiability* of class diagrams with [T-C]-GS hierarchy structure.

Proof. (Sketched) The claim builds on showing that the translated class diagram CD' together with its associated constraints, preserves the *all class finite satisfiability* of the input class diagram CD. As for the second step of the algorithm, we show that for each constraint the additional inequality (or equality) provides a necessary and sufficient condition for the existence of a CD' instance that satisfies the generalization set constraint. For example, inequality [i] in step 2.b of Algorithm 2 characterizes the existence of a CD' instance that satisfies the referenced *disjoint* constraint. For full proof consult [17].

Claim 4: [Complexity of Algorithm 2] Algorithm 2 adds an $O(n)$ time complexity to the [15] method, where n is the size of the class diagram (including associations, classes and ISA constraints).

Proof. The additional work involves the class diagram reduction, which creates a class diagram with the same set of classes and one additional association that replaces every class hierarchy constraint. In addition, every GS constraint adds a single inequality. Since the work per generalization set is linear in its size, the overall additional work is linear in the size of the class diagram.

The inequalities of the pair GS-constraints are not exclusive. The first and second inequalities imply, each, the last. Therefore, finite satisfiability with the pair constraints {*disjoint, incomplete*}/ {*disjoint, complete*} implies finite satisfiability with the {*overlapping, incomplete*} constraints. This observation leads to the following conclusion:

Conclusion: If a tree structured class diagram CD is fully finitely satisfiable, then a class diagram CD' which is obtained from CD by replacing pairs of GC-constraints {*disjoint, incomplete*}/ {*disjoint, complete*} with {*overlapping, incomplete*} is also fully finitely satisfiable.

4.2   Extension of Algorithm 2 to {[T-C-M], [A-C], [G-C]}-GS Hierarchy Structure - Exploring the Limits of the Suggested Method

Algorithm 2 extends properly to the {[T-C-M], [A-C]}-GS hierarchy structures, but it does not extend to the full case of [G-C]-GS hierarchies. The single GS-constraints *incomplete* and *overlapping* cause no problems. But the presence of the *disjoint* or the *complete* constraints within cyclic class hierarchies fails the algorithm. The reason is that in general graph structured class hierarchies, these GS-constraints have an implicit global effect on other generalization sets in a cycle. We now demonstrate the problems, and explain why the method of Algorithm 2 cannot handle these cases.

Presence of a *disjoint* GS-Constraint in a [G-C]-GS class diagram: Consider the class diagram in Figure 5-a. The *disjoint* constraint imposed on the generalization set {A, B, C, D} implies that in every instance, the extension of E properly includes the extension of D. But, object members of class E are mapped in a 1:1 manner to members of D, implying that the sets have the same size. The only solution for proper set inclusion with equal size is that the sets are either empty or infinite. Therefore, the diagram is not fully finitely satisfiable.

Nevertheless, Algorithm 2 yields a solvable inequalities system as shown below. We use the symbols a, b, c, and e for the classes A, B, C, D and E respectively, isa_1, isa_2 isa_3 for the new associations between A to B, A to C

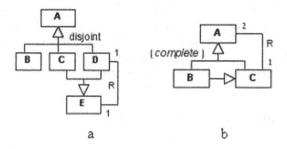

Fig. 5. Constrained Graph Hierarchy

and A to D respectively, isa_4, isa_5 for the new associations between E to C and E to D respectively and the symbol r for the R association.

1. **The Inequalities System produced by Algorithm 2 for Figure 5-a:**
   (a) **The Generalization Set $\{A,\ B,\ C,\ D\}$:**
      - $isa_1 = b,\ isa_1 \le a,\ isa_2 = c,\ isa_2 \le a,\ isa_3 = d,\ isa_3 \le a.$
      - The disjoint inequality: $a \ge b + c + d.$
   (b) **The Generalization Set $\{C,\ D,\ E\}$:**
      - $isa_4 = c,\ isa_4 \le e,\ isa_5 = d,\ isa_5 \le e, r = d,\ r = e.$
2. **A Possible Solution:** $a = 3,\ b = c = d = e = 1,\ , isa_1 = isa_2 = isa_3 = isa_4 = isa_5 = 1,\ and\ r = 1.$

The reason for the failure of Algorithm 2 to detect that the diagram in Figure 5-a is not fully finitely satisfiable is lies in the projection of the *disjoint* constraint from one generalization set to the other. The implied *disjoint* constraint on the lower generalization set is not recorded in the inequalities system.

Presence of a *complete* GS-Constraint in a [G-C]-GS class diagram: Consider the class diagram in Figure 5-b. The *complete* constraint states that the union of the extensions of classes B and C is the extension of class A. Yet, B is a subclass of C, implying that the extensions of C and A are equal. On other hand, the elements of class C are mapped in a $1 : 2$ manner to those of class A. The only solution for having a $1 : 2$, *onto* mapping from a set to itself is either empty or infinite. Therefore, the class diagram is not fully finitely satisfiable.

Nevertheless, Algorithm 2 yields a solvable inequalities system as shown below.

1. **The Inequalities System of Figure 5-b:**
   (a) $isa_1 = b,\ isa_1 \le a, isa_2 = c,\ isa_2 \le a, isa_3 = b,\ isa_3 \le c, r = 2c,\ r = a.$
   (b) The completeness inequality: $a \le b + c.$
2. **A Possible Solution:** $a = 2,\ b = c = 1,\ , isa_1 = isa_2 = isa_3 = 1, and\ r = 2.$

The reason for the failure of Algorithm 2 to detect that the diagram in Figure 5-b is not fully finitely satisfiable lies in the projection of the $\{B,\ C\}$ generalization set on the constraints imposed on the other generalization set. The implied constraint for the $\{A,\ B,\ C\}$ generalization set is *complete, overlapping*. The addition of this constraint yields an unsolvable inequalities system.

5   Conclusions and Future Work

In this paper, we have introduced a simple and effective method for deciding full finite satisfiability of class diagrams with constrained generalization sets. The advantage of this method lies in its simplicity and efficiency. The method applies to class diagram features that are not handled by other approaches, and improves the efficiency of existing methods.

We have studied the limits of this method with respect to the interaction between class hierarchy structure and the kind of *GS* constraints it includes. Yet, it seems that the combination of graph structured class hierarchies with the *disjoint* and *complete* *GS*-constraints does not occur that often. One possibility might be a combination of the expensive Calvanese-Lenzerini algorithm with our method. That is, apply our method in most cases, and resort to the inefficient method whenever our method does not apply. It is possible also that proper preprocessing of the *GS*-constraints in a class diagram, can strengthen our method.

In the future, we plan to explore the possible extension of the presented method for testing full finite satisfiability in the presence of n-ary association with complex cardinality constraints, qualifier constraints, association class constraints, and association constraints.

Another direction involves the possibility of expanding our method with heuristics for detecting and repairing finite satisfiability problems following the ideas of [10, 11]. The intention is to apply similar strategies for repairing finite satisfiability problems in UML2 class diagrams with class hierarchy constraints.

References

[1] Balaban, M., Shoval, P.: MEER-An EER Model Enhanced with Structure Methods. Information Systems, vol. 27(4) (2002)

[2] Berardi, D., Calvanese, D., Giacomo, D.: Reasoning on UML class diagrams. Artificial Intelligence (2005)

[3] Boufares, F., Bennaceur, H.: Consistency Problems in ER-schemas for Database Systems. Information Sciences, Issue 4 (2004)

[4] Cadoli, M., Calvanese, D., De Giacomo, G., Mancini, T.: Finite Satisfiability of UML Class Diagrams by Constraint Programming. In: Wallace, M. (ed.) CP 2004. LNCS, vol. 3258, Springer, Heidelberg (2004)

[5] Calvanese, D., Lenzerini, M.: On the Interaction between ISA and Cardinality Constraints. In: Proc. of the 10th IEEE Int. Conf. on Data Engineering (1994)

[6] Calvanese, D., De Giacomo, G., Lenzerini, M., Nardi, D., Rosati, R.: Description Logic Framework for Information Integration. In: Proceedings of the Sixth International Conference on the Principles of Knowledge Representation and Reasoning (KR'98), pp. 2–13 (1998)

[7] Guizzardi, G., Wagner, G., Guarino, N., van Sinderen, M.: An Ontologically well-Founded Profile for UML Conceptual Models. In: Persson, A., Stirna, J. (eds.) CAiSE 2004. LNCS, vol. 3084, Springer, Heidelberg (2004)

[8] Hartman, S.: Graph Theoretic Methods to Construct Entity-Relationship Databases. In: Nagl, M. (ed.) WG 1995. LNCS, vol. 1017, Springer, Heidelberg (1995)

[9] Hartman, S.: On the Implication Problem for Cardinality Constraints and Functional Dependencies. Ann.Math.Artificial Intelligence (2001)

[10] Hartman, S.: Coping with Inconsistent Constraint Specifications. In: Kunii, H.S., Jajodia, S., Sølvberg, A. (eds.) ER 2001. LNCS, vol. 2224, Springer, Heidelberg (2001)

[11] Hartman, S.: Soft Constraints and Heuristic Constraint Correction in Entity- Relationship Modeling. In: Bertossi, L., Katona, G.O.H., Schewe, K.-D., Thalheim, B. (eds.) Semantics in Databases. LNCS, vol. 2582, Springer, Heidelberg (2003)

[12] Kaneiwa, K., Satoh, S.: Consistency Checking Algorithms for Restricted UML Class Diagrams. In: Proceedings of the Fourth International Symposium on Foundations of Information and Knowledge Systems (2006)

[13] Kozlenkov, A., Zisman, A.: Discovering Recording, and Handling Inconsistencies in Software Specifications. Int. J. of Computer and Information Science 5(2) (2004)

[14] Lange, C., Chaudron, M., Muskens, J.: In Practice: UML Software Architecture and Design Description. IEEE Software, vol. 23(2) (2006)

[15] Lenzerini, M., Nobili, P.: On the Satisfiability of Dependency Constraints in Entity-Relationship Schemata. Information Systems, Vol. 15(4) (1990)

[16] Liang, P.: Formalization of Static and Dynamic UML Using Algebraic. Master's thesis, University of Brussel (2001)

[17] Maraee, A.: Efficient Methods for Solving Finite Satisfiability Problems in UML class Diagrams. Master' thesis, Ben-Gurion University of the Negev (2007)

[18] OMG.: UML 2.0 Superstructure Specification (2005)

[19] Rumbaugh, J., Jacobson, G., Booch, G.: The Unified Modeling Language Reference Manual Second Edition. Adison Wesley, London, UK (2004)

[20] Thalheim, B.: Entity Relationship Modeling, Foundation of Database Technology. Springer, Heidelberg (2000)

[21] Unhelkar, B.: Verification and Validation for Quality of UML 2.0 Models. Addison-Wesley, London, UK (2005)

A Practical Approach to Model Extension

Mikaël Barbero[1], Frédéric Jouault[1,2], Jeff Gray[2], and Jean Bézivin[1]

[1] ATLAS Group, INRIA and LINA,
University of Nantes, France
Firstname.Lastname@univ-nantes.fr
[2] Department of Computer and Information Sciences,
University of Alabama at Birmingham
Lastname@cis.uab.edu

Abstract. In object technology, reusability is achieved primarily through class inheritance. In model engineering, where reusability is also important, it should be possible to extend a modeling artifact in a similar manner to add new capabilities. This paper presents a conceptual and practical approach to model extensibility, in which new models are created as derivations from base models. There are several situations where such an extensibility mechanism is useful and essential (e.g., in the case of hierarchies of metamodels). In order to achieve the goal of model extension, a precise definition of the extension mechanism is needed, based on a strict model definition. After describing the context of model extension through a motivating example, the paper outlines a practical implementation with characterization of its main conceptual properties. The solution is being implemented as part of the AMMA model engineering platform under Eclipse.

1 Introduction

Model-Driven Engineering (MDE) offers an advantage due to its power in providing a homogeneous view of heterogeneous artifacts [1]. The main assumption leading to this power is summarized by "everything is a model"; i.e., models are considered as a unifying concept in software.

The work presented here is based on precise definitions of the principles of MDE given in [5] and [7]. According to these previous works, MDE relies on two main relations: *conformance* and *representation*. In this paper, we introduce a third relation called *extension*.

The *conformance* relation links one model to another model called its *reference model*. Throughout this paper, we abbreviate the conformance relation as *c2* (for "conforms to"). Figure 1 illustrates this definition.

Although this first definition allows an indefinite number of conformance layers, the layers must stop at some level for practical purposes. This is accomplished by giving the definitions of the three different kinds of models encountered in the OMG modeling stack:

1. A *metametamodel* is a model that is its own reference model (i.e., it conforms to itself),

D.H. Akehurst, R. Vogel, and R.F. Paige (Eds.): ECMDA-FA 2007, LNCS 4530, pp. 32–42, 2007.

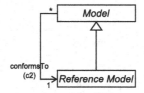

Fig. 1. Definition of a model and its reference model

2. A *metamodel* is a model such that its reference model is a metametamodel,
3. A *terminal model* is a model such that its reference model is a metamodel.

These definitions define a modeling architecture based on three levels, which is compatible with the OMG view.

The second foundational relation of MDE is called *representation*, which links terminal models to the systems they represent. This relation is abbreviated *repOf* (for "representation of") and satisfies the principle of substitutability[1] [8]. This relation is illustrated by Fig. 2. The conformance of a terminal model to its metamodel is also depicted.

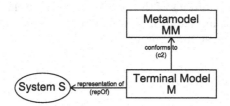

Fig. 2. Basic relations of *representation* and *conformance*

This paper is based on the existence of an additional relation between models called *extensionOf*. Let M_i be a core model representing most concepts for a kind of system. The extension model M_f is a model, defining some new concepts not in M_i but making references to existing M_i concepts. Figure 3 illustrates this relation between the two models M_i and M_f.

The composition of M_i with its extension model M_f leads to a new model M_r (see Fig. 4). M_r is the result model of the composition of initial model M_i and fragment model M_f. This composition does not need to be actually computed, it can be interpreted (i.e., queries over M_r are dynamically translated into queries over M_i and M_f). However, considering the model M_f as an extension of model M_i leads toward a consideration of model M_r.

This paper is organized as follows. Section 2 provides a motivating example. Section 3 describes a corresponding implementation in KM3 [5], and Section 4

---

[1] A model M is said to be a representation of a system S for a given set of questions Q if for each question of this set Q, the model M will provide the same answer that the system S would have provided in answering the same question.

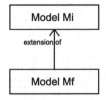

Fig. 3. Relation of extension between two models

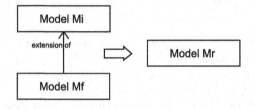

Fig. 4. Extension model and fragment model

gives the conceptual definitions of the model extension mechanism. Section 5 further characterizes this mechanism. Section 6 gives an overview of related works. Section 7 concludes and summarizes future work.

2   Motivating Example

Petri nets are a well-known formalism used to study communication between parallel systems [12]. A classical Petri net is a set of places and transitions linked by directed arcs. Arcs run from a place to a transition or from a transition to a place. The following Petri net (Fig. 5) has four places ($P1$, $P2$, $P3$, and $P4$) and two transitions ($T1$, and $T2$).

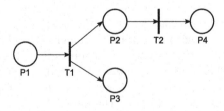

Fig. 5. A simple PetriNet

The metamodel depicted on Fig. 6 specifies all the concepts of a simple Petri net like the one on Fig. 5. This metamodel describes a Petri net as a set of *Arcs* and *Nodes*. A *Node* can be either a *Place* or a *Transition*.

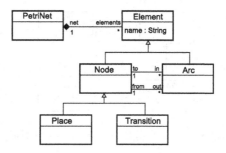

Fig. 6. PetriNet metamodel

From the Petri net of Fig. 5, an infinite number of executions can be launched. The metamodel does not allow the design of Petri nets with a specific execution state. To overcome this limitation, we can *extend* the previous metamodel with the concepts describing the state of a Petri net at a given time. Such a Petri net is said to be marked. A marked Petri net can be represented by attaching a set of *Token*s to some *Place*s. This addition does not affect the previously defined structure of the Petri net.

An initial simplified solution would add an integer attribute to class *Place*. This would give an initial marking by storing the number of tokens associated to a place. However, this would prevent more advanced representations like colored and value-based tokens. Therefore, our application of model extension enables the separate modeling of tokens. Figure 7 shows the same Petri net of Fig. 5 with tokens on places $P1$ and $P2$.

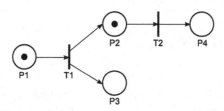

Fig. 7. A simple PetriNet at a given execution state

As we previously mentioned, the base structure of the Petri net with marking is not changed. The metamodel of the Petri net with marking is depicted on Fig. 8. It adds the concept of *Marking* as a set of *Token*s. Each *Token* is associated with a *Place*. The *Place* class comes from the first Petri net metamodel defined in Fig. 6.

This new metamodel is an extension of the original Petri net metamodel. The Petri net of Fig. 7 conforms to this extension. Actually, this Petri net is conforming to the combination of the initial metamodel with its extension, which is the metamodel given in Fig. 9. This combination merges the common concept of *Place* to build the complete metamodel.

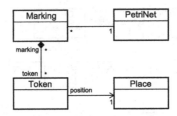

Fig. 8. Marking metamodel extension of PetriNet

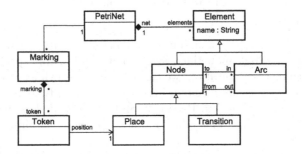

Fig. 9. Result of PetriNet metamodel and marking extension combination

There are many extensions to Petri nets (e.g., colored Petri nets, hierarchical Petri nets, timed Petri nets). The previous mechanism can be used to describe the metamodels of those extensions without having to start anew each time, but by extending the same base metamodel.

3   Implementation Support

In the previous section, an extension to a Petri net metamodel was introduced as a motivating example. This section provides the definition of those metamodels in KM3 [5] format. This format has been the foundation of a conceptual framework that will be described in the next section and extended to a formal definition of model extension.

The initial metamodel of PetriNet describes concepts of *Arcs*, *Places* and *Transitions*. The metamodel given in Fig. 10 is exactly the same as the one in Fig. 6, but represented using a different (textual) notation. Each concept is a named *Element* having a reference to its owning Petri net. *Places* and *Transitions* have some input and output *Arcs*. *Arcs* are linked to one source *Node*, and to one target *Node*.

The previous metamodel describes the concepts that are shared between all kinds of Petri nets. An extension of this metamodel has been defined to represent marked Petri nets and is given in Fig. 11. It is the same metamodel as the one presented in Fig. 8. All classes having the same name as one of the classes of

```
 1 package PetriNet {
 2   class PetriNet {
 3     reference elements[1-*] container : Element oppositeOf net;
 4   }
 5   abstract class Element {
 6     attribute name : String;
 7     reference net : PetriNet oppositeOf elements;
 8   }
 9   abstract class Node extends Element {
10     reference in[*] : Arc oppositeOf to;
11     reference out[*] : Arc oppositeOf from;
12   }
13   class Arc extends Element {
14     reference from : Node oppositeOf out;
15     reference to : Node oppositeOf in;
16   }
17   class Place extends Node {}
18   class Transition extends Node {}
19 }
```

Fig. 10. PetriNet metamodel in KM3

the initial metamodel actually correspond to the same classes. Previous features are not re-defined. For instance, the *PetriNet* class is present in both the initial metamodel and in the extension metamodel. Only the *markings* reference to *Marking* elements is added. The extension metamodel is also adding the concepts of *Marking* and *Token*. A *Marking* contains a set of *Token*s and a token is attached to a *Place*.

```
 1 package PetriNet {
 2   class PetriNet {
 3     reference markings[*] : Marking;
 4   }
 5   class Place {}
 6   class Marking {
 7     reference petrinet : PetriNet;
 8     reference tokens[*] container : Token;
 9   }
10   class Token {
11     reference position : Place;
12   }
13 }
```

Fig. 11. Marking metamodel extension of PetriNet in KM3

When the previous metamodel is used as an extension of the initial one, it can be described as the "composition" of those two metamodels into a single one. This "composed" metamodel is given in Fig 12. Each concept defined in one of the two previous metamodels is present in this new metamodel. When a concept exists in both previous metamodels (like *Place* and *PetriNet*), the result of the extension is the merging of elements from the initial metamodel and from its extension. For instance, we can see the *markings* reference that have been added within the *PetriNet* class or the *Token* class added within the *PetriNet* package. We are identifying common concepts in KM3 metamodels by using a

```
 1 package PetriNet {
 2   class PetriNet {
 3     reference elements[1-*] container : Element oppositeOf net;
 4     -- @begin extensionOf
 5     reference markings[*] : Marking;
 6     -- @end extensionOf
 7   }
 8   abstract class Element {
 9     attribute name : String;
10     reference net : PetriNet oppositeOf elements;
11   }
12   abstract class Node extends Element {
13     reference in[*] : Arc oppositeOf to;
14     reference out[*] : Arc oppositeOf from;
15   }
16   class Arc extends Element {
17     reference from : Node oppositeOf out;
18     reference to : Node oppositeOf in;
19   }
20   class Place extends Node {}
21   class Transition extends Node {}
22   -- @begin extensionOf
23   class Marking {
24     reference petrinet : PetriNet;
25     reference tokens[*] container : Token;
26   }
27   class Token {
28     reference position : Place;
29   }
30   -- @end extensionOf
31 }
```

Fig. 12. Result of PetriNet metamodel and marking extension combination in KM3

fully qualified name. The elements that are added by the extension metamodel are surrounded by the – *@begin extensionOf* and – *@end extensionOf* comments.

4   Conceptual Framework

The initial limitation of our implementation handled KM3 metamodel extension by concatenating the textual representation of the the participating metamodels. The new implementation of metamodel extension is focused on the abstract syntax and has been fully automated using model transformation. A first transformation matches model elements by name, and a second one uses this mapping as input to merge the initial and extension metamodels.

The motivating example introduced in the previous section described the concept of model extension informally. Some examples of implementation have then been given with the KM3 notation. This notation has been precisely defined within a conceptual framework in a previous work [5]. The first two following definitions come from this conceptual framework. They are repeated here for convenience. The last definition extends those two to describe model extension formally.

Definition 1. *A directed multigraph $G = (N_G, E_G, \Gamma_G)$ consists of a finite set of nodes N_G, a finite set of edges E_G, and a mapping function $\Gamma_G : E_G \rightarrow N_G \times N_G$ mapping edges to their source and target nodes.*

Definition 2. *A model $M = (G, \omega, \mu)$ is a triple where:*

- $G = (N_G, E_G, \Gamma_G)$ *is a directed multigraph,*
- ω *is itself a model (called the reference model of M) associated to a graph $G_\omega = (N_\omega, E_\omega, \Gamma_\omega)$,*
- $\mu : N_G \cup E_G \to N_\omega$ *is a function associating elements (nodes and edges) of G to nodes of G_ω.*

Definition 3. *Let M_i and M_f be two models conforming to the same reference model ω*

- $M_i = (G_i, \omega, \mu_i)$ *and* $G_i = (N_i, E_i, \Gamma_i)$
- $M_f = (G_f, \omega, \mu_f)$ *and* $G_f = (N_f, E_f, \Gamma_f)$
- $\omega = (G_\omega, \omega_\omega, \mu_\omega)$ *and* $G_\omega = (N_\omega, E_\omega, \Gamma_\omega)$

Let $\epsilon : N_f \to N_f \cup N_i$ be a mapping from nodes of M_f to nodes of M_f and nodes of M_i. ϵ maps each node from N_f to that same node or to a node from N_i:

$$\epsilon(x) = \begin{cases} x & if\ \forall v \in N_i, v \neq x\ or, \\ y & if\ \exists y \in N_i, y = x \end{cases}$$

Note: Node comparison operators $=$ and $\neq$ must be defined in a metamodel specific way. For instance, in Section 3, classes (KM3 specific concept) were compared according to their names. The definition of such operators is out of the scope of this paper. We are considering this comparison as a decidable and deterministic issue in the following definitions.

The extension $M_r = M_i \oplus_\epsilon M_f$ of model M_i by model M_f according to ϵ is the model M_r with

- $M_r = (G_r, \omega_r, \mu_r)$ *and* $G_r = (N_r, E_r, \Gamma_r)$
  - $N_r = N_i \cup \epsilon(N_f)$,
  - $E_r = E_i \cup E_f$,
  - $\Gamma_r(x) = \begin{cases} \Gamma_i(x) & if\ x \in E_i \\ \epsilon^{\{2\}}(\Gamma_f(x)) & if\ x \in E_f \end{cases}$,
  - $\mu_r(x) = \begin{cases} \mu_i(x) & if\ x \in N_i \cup E_i \\ \mu_f(x) & if\ x \in N_f \cup E_f \end{cases}$.

The function $\epsilon^{\{2\}} : N_f^2 \to (N_f \cup N_i)^2$ is the bidimensional version of $\epsilon : x \mapsto y$ defined as $\epsilon^{\{2\}} : (x, y) \mapsto (\epsilon(x), \epsilon(y))$

An illustration of model extension is given in Fig. 13. The initial model M_i containing four elements is extended by M_f containing three elements according to the ϵ mapping. ϵ maps the two lower nodes of M_f to themselves and the third one to a node of M_i. The result of the extension is M_r, which contains six nodes: all four from M_i and only two from M_f.

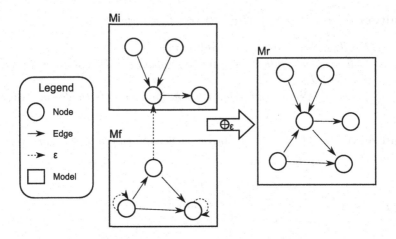

Fig. 13. Example of model extension

5 Characterization of Model Extension

From previous definitions, some characteristics of model extension may be leveraged. The following (non-exhaustive) list presents some of the characteristics of use for model extension.

– Fragment model has no dangling edges. A dangling edge is an edge linked to only one node. With this kind of structure, a fragment model would have been a special entity. Because there is no dangling edge, the fragment model is a "true" model conforming to a reference model.
– Models M_i, M_r and M_f conform to the same reference model. Even the fragment model M_f is a model conforming to the reference model. This result comes from the absence of a dangling edge.
– With our conceptual definitions, it is possible to define libraries of model extensions. These libraries should have a lattice structure. For instance, we could have a library of Petri net metamodels, with each metamodel capturing the concepts of each type of Petri net by extending another kind of Petri net metamodel.

6 Related Work

The problem of model extension is central to most practical model editing tasks. Many solutions have been found in specific contexts. For intance, in case one is dealing only with UML models (i.e., models conforming to the UML metamodel), then specific ad-hoc solutions based on profiles have been proposed [3].

There have been a lot of discussions comparing these ad-hoc UML profiling techniques and heavyweight metamodel based solutions considering MOF-conforming metamodels. According to the specific practical context, it has been found that one solution is better than the other for reasons of tool availability [13,14,11,4,6].

Considering model extension, there is a similar principle in the UML 2 Infrastructure specification [10] called package merge. This operation was defined to assist in modularizing the UML 2 metamodel. It also defines compliance levels regarding the packages that are merged. We chose not to follow this specification for several reasons. First, it is an UML-specific operation that is difficult to express for other kinds of metamodels. Second, the package merge operation has not been provided in a clearly defined conceptual framework. Finally, it has been shown that UML 2 package merge has many problems and can not be used in its present definition [15,16].

In this paper, we propose a more general approach. To this purpose, we have chosen the KM3 minimal notation to build a conceptual and practical solution. This has several advantages. First, since there are significant libraries of open source metamodels in KM3, this will allow direct experimentation on the basis of the available metamodels. Second, there are available bridges between KM3 and most popular metametamodels like MOF 1.4, MOF 2.0, Ecore, MetaGME, and Microsoft DSL Tools. As a consequence, the extensibility solution proposed here could be mapped to these other representation systems. Finally, since KM3 is a minimal metametamodel, this permits a basic conceptual solution that has more chances to be independent of implementation idiosyncrasies.

7   Conclusions and Future Work

This paper introduced the *extensionOf* relation between models. This relation has been formally defined within a conceptual framework. Definitions given in Section 4 are generic and do not rely on a specific metamodel. The solution introduced in this paper is being implemented as part of the AMMA model engineering platform under Eclipse. This approach will lead to capabilities that assist in the composition of models.

Metamodel extensibility is very important to define auto-adaptive tools by coupling a core metamodel extension and a set of base tool extensions. The Atlas Model Weaver [2] is already a proof of concept of this approach. It defines a core weaving metamodel and a generic editor. The editor auto-adapts itself depending on the metamodel extensions specified by the user. Moreover, it is also possible to define extensions to each editor part for a specific metamodel extension.

Finally, following the principles presented in [7], Domain-Specific Languages (DSLs) [9] extension could be based on model extension. We are considering a DSL as a set of coordinated models [7]: an abstract syntax, a concrete syntax, and a specification of the semantics. From a model-based point of view, the abstract syntax of a DSL is a metamodel. Thus, DSL concepts can be extended with the mechanism described in this paper. The study of how to extend the concrete syntax model and how it is related to grammar extension represents areas of future work.

Acknowledgements

This work has been partially supported by the ModelPlex European integrated project FP6-IP 034081 (Modeling Solutions for Complex Systems).

References

1. Bézivin, J.: On the Unification Power of Models. Software and Systems Modeling 4(2), 171–188 (2005)
2. Didonet Del Fabro, M., Bézivin, J., Valduriez, P.: Weaving Models with the Eclipse AMW plugin. In: Eclipse Modeling Symposium, Eclipse Summit Europe 2006, Esslingen, Germany (2006)
3. D'Souza, D., Sane, A., Birchenough, A.: First-Class Extensibility for UML Packaging of Profiles, Stereotypes, Patterns. In: France, R.B., Rumpe, B. (eds.) UML '99 - The Unified Modeling Language. Beyond the Standard. LNCS, vol. 1723, Springer, Heidelberg (1999)
4. Gitzel, R., Hildenbrand, T.: A taxonomy of Metamodel Hieriarchies, University of Mannheim (January 2005)
5. Jouault, F., Bézivin, J.: KM3: a DSL for Metamodel Specification. In: Gorrieri, R., Wehrheim, H. (eds.) FMOODS 2006. LNCS, vol. 4037, Springer, Heidelberg (2006)
6. Karsai, G., Maroti, M., Ledeczi, A., Gray, J., Sztipanovits, J.: Composition and Cloning in Modeling and Meta-Modeling Languages, IEEE Transactions on Control System Technology, special issue on Computer Automated Multi-Paradigm Modeling, 263–278 (March 2004)
7. Kurtev, I., Bézivin, J., Jouault, F., Valduriez, P.: Model-based DSL Frameworks. In: Companion to the 21st Annual ACM SIGPLAN Conference on Object-Oriented Programming, Systems, Languages, and Applications, OOPSLA, Portland, OR, USA (October 22-26, 2006) 602–616 (2006)
8. Liskov, B., Wing, J.: A Behavioral Notion of Subtyping. ACM Transactions on Programming Languages and Systems 16(6), 1811–1841 (1994)
9. Mernik, M., Heering, J., Sloane, A.M.: When and how to develop domain-specific languages. ACM Comput. Surv. 37(4), 316–344 (2005)
10. Object Management Group: Unified Modeling Language: Infrastructure, version 2.1.1, formal/07-02-06, http://www.omg.org/cgi-bin/doc?formal/07-02-06
11. Pérez-Martínez, J.E.: Heavyweight extensions to the UML metamodel to describe the C3 architectural style. ACM SIGSOFT Software Engineering Notes 28(3), 5 (2003)
12. Peterson, J.: Petri Nets, ACM Computing Surveys, 223–252 (September 1977)
13. Rötschke, T.: Adding Pluggable Meta Models to FUJABA, In: 2nd International Fujaba Days, 2004, 04-253, Universität Paderborn, 57–61 (2004)
14. Turki, S., Soriano, T.: A SysML Extension for Bond Graphs Support ICTA'05, 5th International Conference on Technology and Automation, Thessaloniki, Greece, 276–281 (October 2005)
15. Zito, A., Diskin, Z., Dingel, J.: Package Merge in UML 2: Practice vs. Theory?, Model Driven Engineering Languages and Systems, 185–199 (2006)
16. Zito, A., Dingel, J.: Modeling UML 2 Package Merge With Alloy, In: Proc. of the 1st Alloy Workshop (Alloy '06). Portland, Oregon, USA (November 2006)

Model Transformation from OWL-S to BPEL Via SiTra

Behzad Bordbar[1], Gareth Howells[2], Michael Evans[1], and Athanasios Staikopoulos[1]

[1] University of Birmingham, UK
{B.Bordbar,A.Staikopoulos,M.E.Evans}@cs.bham.ac.uk
[2] University of Kent, UK
W.G.J.Howells@kent.ac.uk

Abstract. Although there are a large number of academic and industrial model transformation frameworks available, allowing specification, implementation, maintenance and documentation of model transformations which provide a rich set of functionalities, such tools are inherently complex. In particular, for a newcomer to the field of model transformation and for researchers who are only interested in experimentation and creation of prototypes, the steep learning curve is a significant hurdle. There is thus a clear scope for the creation of model transformation frameworks that are both easy to use and able to conduct complex transformations. Simple Transformer (SiTra) is a model transformation framework, which was originally designed to be a "way in" for the experienced programmer, to start using the concepts of model transformation, and for academic researchers to experiment with the creation of prototypes of implementation of their transformations. The underlying idea of SiTra is to put less focus on the specification language, maintenance and documentation aspects of transformation, by focusing on the implementation of transformations. SiTra makes use of Java for the specification of transformations. This alleviates the need to learn a new specification language or get to grips with a new tool and development environment. SiTra is equipped with a strong transformation engine to execute the transformation behind the scenes. This paper reports on a case study involving transformations from Ontology Web Language-Service (OWL-S) to Business Process Execution Language (BPEL), demonstrating that SiTra can also be used to handle complex and large transformations.

1 Introduction

Model Driven Development (MDD) [1] is an emerging technology for software development, promoting the role of models and automatic creation of code by predefined model transformations. A variant of MDD suggested by the Object Management Group (OMG) is the Model Driven Architecture (MDA) [2, 3]. MDA provides an enabling infrastructure with standard specifications facilitating the definition and implementation of model transformations between Meta Object Facility (MOF) [4] compliant languages. The application of model transformations is expected to improve the software development process in many ways, as it enhances productivity, portability, interoperability, ease of use, maintenance and reusability [3, 5, 6].

D.H. Akehurst, R. Vogel, and R.F. Paige (Eds.): ECMDA-FA 2007, LNCS 4530, pp. 43–58, 2007.
© Springer-Verlag Berlin Heidelberg 2007

At the moment, there are many industrial [7-9] and academic [10, 11] model transformation tools available; for a detailed list refer to [12]. These tools bring enormous benefit to the developers. For example, they include repository of models for reuse. They also make use of high-level languages for defining transformation. For example, [7], [10] and [11] makes use of, scripting language JPython, ATL and Kermeta, respectively. However, model transformation frameworks are complex. For a newcomer to the field of model transformation learning a framework is a serious impediment. Simple Transformer (SiTra) [13] is a model transformation framework, which is designed to be a "way in" for experienced programmers, to start using the concepts of model transformation, and for academic researchers to experiment with the creation of prototypes of implementation of their transformations. SiTra, which is written in Java, also makes use of Java for specification of transformations. This alleviates the need to learn a new specification language or getting to grips with a new tool and development environment.

SiTra has been successfully applied to the bench mark example of [14] and is documented in [13]. In this paper, we shall further evaluate SiTra by conducting a case study involving transformations from Ontology Web Language for Services (OWL-S) [15] to Business Process Execution Language (BPEL) [16]. A copy of SiTra is available for free download at [17].

The structure of the paper is as follows: Section 2 provides an overview of the Web service and model transformation in the context of Web services. Section 3 briefly describes SiTra and its architecture. Section 4 presents the case study of transformation from OWL-S to BPEL and discusses various outcomes of the study. Finally, section 5 presents a conclusion and draws a summary.

2 Preliminaries

This section describes introductory notions used in this paper. Firstly, a short review of Web Service languages such as WSDL, BPEL and OWL-S will be presented. Secondly, a brief review of existing research on model transformation for Web Services will be given.

2.1 Web Services

Web service technology [18] promises to provide a new level of functionality on top of the existing Web infrastructure, allowing applications to share data and to benefit from the capabilities of other applications, independent of the platforms and languages used to build them. The technology aims to facilitate the composition of a number of Web services in order to create a single service with richer functionality than any of the constituent services. In order to achieve this, the creation of languages for describing services and their interactions has received considerable attention. This paper deals with three such languages; Web Service Description Language (WSDL), Business Process Execution Language (BPEL) and Ontology Web Language – Services (OWL-S).

2.1.1 Web Service Description Language

The Web Service Description Language (WSDL) [19] is an XML language for describing Web services, particularly as service interfaces. The description separates the abstracted functionality offered by a service from the concrete details of how and where that functionality is offered. Its role and purpose can be compared to that of IDLs in conventional middleware languages such as CORBA.

A WSDL file has an abstract part, which specifies information such as signatures of operations offered by the service, the messages that are exchanged between providers and requestors as input, output and fault parameters of these operations. The concrete part of a WSDL file defines the protocol bindings and location of such services [20].

A WSDL file provides all the necessary information to assess and invoke the operations of a service. However, WSDL files do not provide any additional (semantic) information indicating, for example, "what the service does" and "how it is to be employed". To include such information, languages such as OWL-S are used to capture the semantics of the Web service. WSDL documents provide a mechanism for expressing simple behaviour. However, describing complex interactions, such as business processes, require using other languages such as BPEL or WSCI [21].

2.1.2 Business Process Execution Language

The Business Process Execution Language for Web Services (BPEL) [16] provides an XML based-language for the formal specification of business processes and business interaction protocols. A BPEL file makes use of the WSDL file of involving services. Consequently, BPEL can be seen as an extension of WSDL [19] that provides basic one-way or request-response mechanisms for the Web service inter-communication. BPEL is designed for expressing processes in detail, allowing composition and coordination of activities such as for sequential, parallel, iterative, conditional, compensational and fault execution [21]. Hence, business process expressing interaction between services can be specified elegantly.

2.1.3 Ontology Web Language for Services

The Ontology Web Language for Services (OWL-S) [15] is also an XML based language, which facilitates capability-driven description of Web Services. It supports automatic Web service discovery, invocation, composition and interoperation based on the semantic descriptions of Web services (OWL Services Coalition [15]). An OWL-S service profile allows us to specify "who provides the service" and "what function is computed by the service". In addition, the profile contains an expandable list of service parameters, allowing the characteristics of the service to be described in detail.

OWL-S differs from other Web service languages (for example WSDL), which offers descriptions of the syntax of the messages used in accessing a service, exposing the operations and protocols it utilizes. An OWL-S service description permits the inclusion of machine-readable information, which describes the service's capabilities in terms of the function(s) it performs, the preconditions and effects of these functions and how the service relates to other Web services. These features support the representation of Web services on the (still somewhat conceptual) Semantic Web [22]. The computer-interpretable representation of a Web service that OWL-S enables provides the potential to develop software that can automatically create composite web services by selecting and composing existing services. Such software could represent savings in the time and effort expended by Web users in searching for appropriate services along with providing a method of selecting Web services which is much more efficient and effective than searching using existing engines.

In addition, OWL-S allows the definition of composite processes [15] which can be built from the basic atomic processes (grounded in WSDL) of a number of different services. Composite processes can be defined dynamically by an agent or statically as part of the description of some virtual Web service. They are realised by executing atomic processes in a structured way (in a predefined sequence, for example, or concurrently) and by passing the results of executions as inputs to other atomic processes.

2.2 Model Transformation in Web Services

Recently, application of model transformation techniques to the development of Web services has received considerable attention [23-26], among others. Bézivin et al [23] use the ATL [10] transformation language and ATLAS engine to generate Platform Specific models from UML class and EDOC models to three different target platforms namely Java, Web Services and Java Web Service Developer Pack (JWSDP). UML Activity diagrams are well suited for platform independent modeling of business processes. Transformation of such models to BPEL and WSCI are studied in [27] [25] and WSCI [28], respectively. Koehler et al [29] investigates model driven transformations based on graph-theoretic methods to define the mapping among models possessing formal semantics, which in turn are used to analyze and synthesize the business protocol specifications. Finally, [30] uses the YATL transformation language to map and apply transformations from EDOC models to Web services.

The focus of this paper is on model transformation techniques and challenges. However, another important focus for research is to develop tools for the transformation of OWL-S specifications to BPEL specifications; as these two languages provide complimentary capabilities. BPEL is well supported by the software vendors as the favorite choice for the execution of the web services. BPEL is not designed for addressing the challenges of the semantic web. On the other hand, OWL-S is not designed for execution. Mandell and McIlraith [31] provide an interesting investigation into this area, by attempting to adapt BPEL4WS for the Semantic Web. This paper presents an alternative approach by transferring OWL-S models to BPEL, so models of the semantics of the system are expressed in OWL-S the execution is conducted in BPEL, which provides better tool and support.

3 Simple Transformer (SiTra)

There are many industrial and academic case tools supporting model transformation [7-11]. It poses as a question: why to attempt introducing yet another model transformation framework? To answer this, it is crucial to notice that a model transformation consists of two major steps. The first step is to define and specify the model transformation. This is often a complex task involving significant domain knowledge and understanding of both the source and target model domains. For example, defining a model transformation from OWL-S to BPEL, not only requires understanding of both languages, but also requires an analytic approach to discover the correct mapping between the model elements. The second step is to execute the transformation. Currently, elegant execution of the specifications is still a research issue in many cases and may require significant manual intervention in order to provide a correct implementation. In a large project, it is possible to divide the specification and implementation between two different groups of people who have relevant skills. In the case of smaller groups of developers, newcomers to MDD, and budding academic researchers, the combined effort involved in becoming an expert in the two sets of skills described above is overwhelming. In particular, the steep learning curve associated with current MDD tools is an inhibitive factor in the adoption of MDD by even very experienced programmers. SiTra aims to address the above issues by proposing a simple Java library for supporting a programming approach to writing transformations, based on the following requirements:

Use of Java for writing transformations: This relinquishes the programmer from learning a new language for the specification of transformations

Minimal framework: To avoid the overhead of learning a new Java library, the presented method has a very small and simple API

3.1 Introducing SiTra

The architecture of SiTra is depicted in Fig.1. A transformation specifies how elements of the Metamodel of the source are mapped into the elements of the Metamodel of the destination. A transformation framework, creates a destination model, which is an instance of the destination metamodel, from a source model, which is an instance of the source metamodel. Because, SiTra uses Java, as depicted in the picture, Metamodels of the source/destination and the model of the source must be created in Java. These could be provided using a Java implementation of a MOF repository, or more usually by providing an implementation of the metamodel using Java classes. For smaller models these can be created manually. For larger models one of numerous existing UML to Java tools could be used.

As depicted in Fig.1, the transformation in SiTra is provided by a number of Java classes, each of which corresponds to a model transformation rule. These classes must implement the SiTra interface Rule. The SiTra class and corresponding interface Transform are used to execute the defined transformation on a particular source model. The two simple interfaces for supporting the implementation of transformation rules in Java are shown below. The Rule interfaces should be implemented for each transformation rule written. The Transformer interface is implemented by the transformation algorithm class, and is made available to the rule classes

```
interface Rule<S,T> {
  boolean check(S source);
  T build(S source, Transformer t);
  void setProperties(T target, S source, Transformer t);
}
interface Transformer {
  Object transform(Object source);
  List<Object> transformAll(List<Object> sourceObjects);
  <S,T> T transform(Class<Rule<S,T>> ruleType, S source);
  <S,T> List<T> transformAll(Class<Rule<S,T>>    ruleType,List<S> source);
}
```

3.2 Rules

A transformation problem is split up into multiple rules; the SiTra library facilitates
this, using the Rule interface. A class that implements this interface should be written
for each of the rules in the transformation. The methods of this interface are described
as follows:

1. The implementation of the check method should return a value of true if the rule is
   applicable to the source object. This is particularly important if multiple rules are
   applicable for objects of the same type. This method is used to distinguish which of
   multiple rules should be applied by the transformer.
2. The build method should construct a target object that the source object is to be
   mapped to. A recursive chain of rules must not be invoked within this method.
3. The setProperties method is used for setting properties of the target object (attributes or links to other objects). Setting the properties is split from constructing the
   target so that recursive calling of rules is possible when setting properties.

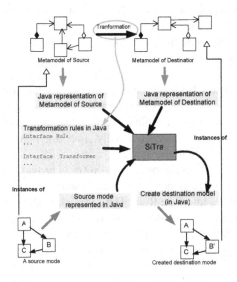

Fig. 1. An outline of the SiTra framework

If it is impossible to distinguish between multiple rules using the check method, explicit rule invocation must be used to transform objects for which multiple rules apply. Objects that are derived from properties of the source object should be converted to objects for properties of the target object by calling the transform method on the transformer. However, the power transformation algorithm of SiTra manages the details of the transformation automatically. For example, it keeps the track of the objects, which are already mapped.

3.3 Transformer

To instantiate a SiTra transformation, the rule classes must be added to an instance of the SimpleTransformer class. The transformation can then be executed by calling the transform method with the root object(s) of the source model. An abstraction of the transformation algorithm is as follows:

```
FOR EACH rule
  IF rule.check(source) THEN
    IF notRecorded(source, rule) THEN
      target = rule.build(source, this)
      record(source, target, rule)
          rule.setProperties(source, this)
```

The algorithm runs through all rules in order to check which rule can be applied to a source objects. We are only interested in the source object which are not transformed yet, this is checked via the method notRecorded(). For such objects, the method build is applied which results in the creation of a target object. To ensure that a source object is not transformed more than once, the method record captures the correspondence between the source, target and rule. Finally, the method setProperties is invoked to assign further properties and attributes to the source object.

4 Case Study: Transformation from OWL-S to BPEL

In this section we shall present our case study of applying SiTra to transformation of the models from OWL-S to BPEL. We shall start by presenting metamodels of OWL-S and BPEL in the next two sections.

4.1 Metamodel of OWL-S

Fig.2 presents a metamodel of the OWL-S following [15]. We shall explain some of the model elements. An OWL-S process is a specification of the ways a client may interact with a service. A process gives a detailed perspective on how to interact with a service. Fig.2 depicts various attributes of OWL-S process. For example, a process will not execute properly unless its preconditions are true. Preconditions are logical statement representing Conditions. The attribute has Precondition specifies one of the preconditions of the service and ranges over a Precondition instance defined according to the schema in the Process ontology.

An Atomicprocess is a (process) description of a service that expects one (possibly complex) message and returns one (possibly complex) message in response. In contrast, a composite process (not depicted in Fig.2, due to space limitations) is one that maintains some state; each message the client sends advances it through the process.

OWL-S makes use of WsdlGrounding for referring to WSDL constructs. Each WsdlGrounding instance, in turn, contains a list of WsdlAtomicProcessGrounding instances. A WsdlAtomicProcessGrounding instance refers to specific elements within the WSDL specification, using the properties such as wsdlService, wsdlPort, wsdlInputMessage as depicted in Fig.2. For example, wsdlService, wsdlPort present the URI of a WSDL service (or port) that offers the given operation. For further details on OWL-S we refer the reader to [15].

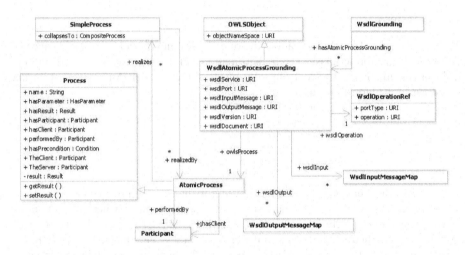

Fig. 2. A portion of OWL-S metamodel

4.2 Metamodel for BPEL

The BPEL specification can be represented by an equivalent MOF compliant metamodel, as the one depicted in Fig.3. As such, the metamodel specifies a number of

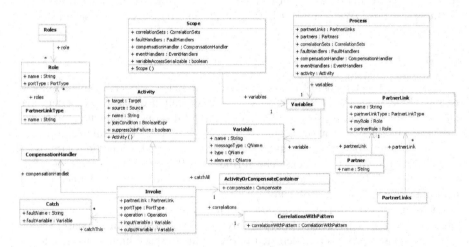

Fig. 3. A (partial) BPEL Metamodel

model elements that are equivalent to XML constructs, defining various activity types, which allow sequential, parallel, conditional or repetitive processing of actions. In addition it defines a number of other features, such as variables, execution context (scope) and exceptions, allowing the creation of complicated and realistic processes, performing various invocation styles and data manipulations in an algorithmic manner. For description of BPEL metamodel see [23] and [27].

4.3 Mapping of Elements

The following tables depict the correspondence between some of the model elements of OWL-S processes. For example, AtomicProcess in OWL-S, the element representing the most basic class of Web service processes, is mapped to a BPEL Process. The mapping also requires the creation of a number of other BPEL and WSDL elements so that the meaning of the output model corresponds entirely to that of the input. In addition to the main Process element, a PortType, an Operation, a PartnerLinkType, an Invoke and a Role must be created. The properties of these model elements must correspond to those of the source OWL-S AtomicProcess. From the collection of inputs belonging to an AtomicProcess, a single BPEL Input can be created, along with an associated Message and Variable. Each of the OWL-S Inputs corresponds to a single Part in the BPEL Message. OWL-S outputs can be converted to BPEL in an identical manner.

There are several examples in the table in which the OWL-S Process model element does not map to anything in BPEL or WSDL. For example, OWL-S precondition and result elements are used to incorporate semantic information regarding the change of state that occurs when the process is executed. Such notions have no equivalent in BPEL, hence it is not possible to map them to BPEL. BPEL does not support the representation of information of this nature, and thus no mapping exists for these elements.

A key set of mappings from OWL-S to BPEL involves OWL-S ControlConstruct elements. These, in general, correspond to BPEL Activity objects and are used to describe the nature in which the components of a Web service process are executed. Both OWL-S and BPEL provide similar constructs for this purpose. For example, both languages contain a Sequence element, indicating that any processes contained within should be executed strictly in order. An OWL-S Sequence maps directly to a BPEL Sequence. Some of the other ControlConstructs map to BPEL elements in a similar fashion. However, some of the OWL-S ControlConstructs have no corresponding BPEL Activity. For example, the OWL-S AnyOrder construct indicates that its component processes should all be executed, but in no particular order. BPEL has no corresponding construct. It is possible, though, to model OWL-S AnyOrder elements as BPEL Sequence elements without affecting the functionality of the output BPEL model (this may affect the efficiency of its execution, however). Therefore, the following table 1 shows the corresponding BPEL element for an OWL-S AnyOrder to be a Sequence. A similar situation arises around OWL-S Choice constructs.

Table 1. Equivenlent mapping of OWL-S Process and BPEL elements

OWL-S Process	BPEL
\<Process\>	\<Process\>
\<AtomicProcess\>	\<Process\> + \<PortType\> + \<Operation\> + \<PartnerLinkType\> + \<Role\> + \<invoke\> Operation + PortType names must be consistent with the created WSDL file. **Note:** require an \<invoke\> call within \<Process\> tags and Operation + PortType names must be consistent with the created WSDL file.
[\<input\>]* (of Atomic Process)	\<input\> + \<message\> + \<variable\>
\<input\>	\<part\> (of the \<message\> created for all inputs)
[\<outputs\>]* (of Atomic Process)	\<output\> + \<message\> + \<variable\>
\<output\>	\<part\> (of the \<message\> created for all outputs).
\<precondition\>	**Note:** This does not really map, due to complicated representation of Preconditions in OWL-S.
\<result\>	**Note:** This contains semantic information about the output of a process and does not map usefully to any BPEL class. The \<with-Output\> property will be covered by the mappings described above.
\<participant\>, \<SimpleProcess\>, \<CompositeProcess\>	\<partner\>
[\<input\>]* of Composite Process	\<message\> + \<variable\>
\<input\>	\<part\> (of the message created for all inputs)
[\<outputs\>]*of Composite Process	\<message\> + \<variable\>
\<output\>	\<part\> (of the message created for all outputs).
\<ControlConstruct\>	\<Activity\> (See below)
\<sequence\>	\<sequence\>
\<Iterate\>, \<RepeatUntil\>, \<RepeatWhile\>	\<while\>
\<AnyOrder\>	Model as \<sequence\>
\<Split\>	\<flow\>
\<Choice\>	Model as \<switch\>
\<IfThenElse\>	\<switch\>
\<components\> of a sequence, split... etc.	See below...

Table 1. *{Continued}*

<Binding> (as in <hasDataFrom> property) toParam, valueSource, theVar, fromProcess	<variable> (or part thereof) corresponding to that generated for the given process and parameter.
<valueSpecifier>, <SplitJoin>, <Perform>, <Produce>	-

The OWL-S Profile [15] of a Web service contains semantic information regarding what functionality the service offers, who is likely to use the service and what properties it shares with other similar services. BPEL provides no means of representing such information and therefore, there is no mapping between the OWL-S Profile and BPEL. However, some of the elements contained in the OWL-S Profile can be converted into useful human-readable information. Where possible, the transformation between OWL-S and BPEL should support the conversion into text of such elements along with their inclusion in the output BPEL file(s). The following table 2 shows examples where text conversion may be useful.

Table 2. Equivenlent mapping of OWL-S Profile and BPEL elements

OWL-S Profile	BPEL
<input>, <output>	See Process Section
<profile>, serviceName, textDescription contactInformation	Incorporate into process name(s). Include as plain text.
<precondition>, <result>, <parameter>, <ServiceParameter>, <ServiceCategory>, <ServiceClassification>, <ServiceProduct>.	-

The Grounding section [15] of an OWL-S service model contains pointers to a WSDL file in which details of how to access the real Web service processes that make up an OWL-S process are given. The mapping between the OWL-S Grounding and WSDL is, therefore, trivial, with the names of OWL-S elements corresponding directly to elements in BPEL. The following table 3 shows this mapping in full.

Table 3. Equivenlent mapping of OWL-S Grounding and WSDL/BPEL elements

OWL-S (Grounding)	WSDL/BPEL
<owlsProcess>	Mapping to BPEL dealt with by Process Model.
<wsdlOperation>	<wsdl:Operation>
URI: wsdlPortType	<wsdl:PortType>
URI: wsdlService	<wsdl:Service>
URI: wsdlPort	<wsdl:Port>

Table 3. *{Continued}*

URI: wsdlInputMessage	<wsdl:Message>
<wsdlGrounding>, <wsdlInputMessageMap>, URI:owlsParameter, URI: xsltTransformation	-
URI: wsdlMessagePart	<wsdl:Part>
URI: wsdlVersion	(<wsdl version="...">)
URI: wsdlDocument	Name of wsdl doc/target namespace.

4.4 Model Transformation

This section will describe examples of transformation from OWL-S to BPEL. For an elaborate list, see [32]. Consider transforming the model element WsdlAtomicProcess-Grounding (for short WAPG), described briefly in section 4.1 to Business Process (for short BPELProcess). The WAPG correspond to an operation related to a given atomic process. The following snippet of code depicts a QVT-like rule for the transformation:

```
1   rule WAPG2BPELProcess
2     wapg:WsdlAtomicProcessGroundin
3     proc:Process [
4       vairable = Sequence{v1,v2},
5       partnerLink = Sequence{pl1}
6       activity = act
7     ]

8   when {
9     WAPG2InputVariable(wapg,v1)
10    WAPG2OutputVariable(wapg,v2)
11    WAPG2PartnerLink(wapg,pl1)
12    WAPG2Invoke(wapg,act)
13  }

15  rule WAPG2InputVariable
16    wapg:WsdlAtomicProcessGrounding [
17      wsdlInputMessage=mt, owlsProcess.name=n
18    ]
19    var:Variable [
20      name=n+'OWLSInputVariable', messageType=mt
21    ]
```

Fig. 4. QVT like rules

It can be seen that, the above snippet (Fig.4) contains two rules: The first rule, WAPG2BPELProcess, is implemented by calling four rules described in lines 9-12 within the when clause. It uses two variables v1 and v2 that correspond to InputVariable and OutputVariable accordingly of the Invoke operation of the atomic process, triggered by the PartnerLink p1. The snippet also describes the rule WAPG2InputVariable, which maps and modifies the variable's name and messageType. The equivalent SiTra code written in Java is depicted in Fig.5.

The QVT-like specification of the transformation rules map quite cleanly into Java Classes that implements the SiTra Rule interface. The build method for each rule can be seen to construct a new object of the appropriate target class. The check method in these examples simply returns a value of true as we do not need to perform any specific checks. The main work in these classes is performed within the setProperties method. This method sets the properties of the newly constructed target object according to

```
public class WAPG2BPELProcess
  implements Rule<WsdlAtomicProcessGrounding, Process> {
    public boolean check(WsdlAtomicProcessGrounding source) {
      return true;
    }
    public Process build( WsdlAtomicProcessGrounding source,
                          Transformer t) {
      return new Process();
    }
    public void setProperties( Process proc,
                               WsdlAtomicProcessGrounding wapg,
                               Transformer t) {
      Variable v1 = t.transform(WAPG2InputVariable.class, wapg);
      Variable v2 = t.transform(WAPG2InputVariable.class, wapg);
      PartnerLink p1 = t.transform(WAPG2PartnerLink.class, wapg);
      Invoke act = t.transform(WAPG2Invoke.class, wapg);
      proc.variables = new Variable[] { v1,v2 };
      proc.partnerLink = new PartnerLink[] { p1 };
      proc.activity = new Activity[] { act };
    }
}
```

```
public class WAPG2InputVariable
  implements Rule<WsdlAtomicProcessGrounding, Variable> {
    public boolean check( WsdlAtomicProcessGrounding source) {
      return true;
    }
    public Variable build( WsdlAtomicProcessGrounding source,
                           Transformer t) {
      return new Variable();
    }
    public void setProperties( Variable var,
                               WsdlAtomicProcessGrounding wapg,
                               Transformer t) {
      String n = wapg.owlsProcess.name;
      URI mt = wapg.wsdlInputMessage;
      var.name = n+"OWLSInputVariable";
      var.messageType = mt;
    }
}
```

Fig. 5. SiTra Code

either: properties of the source object as can be seen in the WAPG2InputVariable rule; or according to transformations of properties of the source object as illustrated by the WAPG2BPELProcess rule.

5 Discussion and Related Work

One of the important lessons learned from this case study is that the difficulty of writing transformation is independent of the choice of transformation framework. As explained in section 4.3, identifying correct mappings between elements is a challenging task, as it requires an understanding of the semantics of elements between two different domains. In this paper, as the main focus is on exploring the limitations and capabilities of SiTra, finding precise mapping of elements was of secondary importance. For example, we have decided to map the <AnyOrder> to <sequence>, forcing an order on a set of events. However, after making this decision, SiTra has helped us to write and implement the transformation in simple way. As result, the "difficulties of identifying correct transformations (whatever the language) and difficulties of writing transformation in SiTra (or other transformation frameworks) are different things". SiTra does not make the design part of creating a good set of transformation simple, it just provide and easier route to the implementation. The primary purpose of SiTra is to be simple. We strongly resisted the temptation of extending the transformer interface to overcome some limitations. We feel that this would violate our primary objective of a "simple" transformation approach. This of course has a cost, specifically that there are limitations in that we cannot tackle some of the more complex transformation problems easily. For example, a general limitations regards a situation in which there is more than one rule that should map to the same target object. There is no way to determine, using SiTra, which of the rules should construct the target object. It is necessary for the designer of the transformation to decide which rule should construct the object, to avoid such non-determinisms.

Another limitation discovered as the result of conducting the case study is regarding the recursive invocation of rules. We facilitate this by splitting the construction and setting properties of a target object. However, there is no means to enforce this, and there are potential design issues regarding situations in which some properties may need to be set in the build() method and some not (handled via setProperties() method). Identifying advantages and disadvantages of each of the two is a subject for future studies.

The graph transformation approaches [33, 34] have many merits with respect to formalism and a long history of use. However, they require a significant amount of new material to be learnt for novice users and also require significant libraries and development environments in terms of supporting framework. The source and target models are expressed using the notion of graphs, where as with SiTra, the source and target models are simple Java objects. The transformation specifications use similar concepts of rules but require a new language to be learnt for writing them, rather than the SiTra approach of using a programming language directly.

The declarative rule based approaches [35-37] suffer many of the same problems. They all require a specific model transformation specification language to be leant. Tefkat [37] and ATL [36] are both supported by a transformation engine and environment similar in concept to our Transformer implementation class (as the engine) and a Java IDE (as the environment), although in a much more heavyweight manner than SiTra.

Our Java based environment does not of course provide any specific support for debugging transformations; debugging has to be done via Java debugging tools, which are sufficient, however do make debugging a little more complex as one has to debug the rules via the internal workings of the Transformer class.

The imperative approaches such as [38] are perhaps the most similar to SiTra in terms of the style of writing a transformation rule. However, they too, all expect the transformation writer to learn a new language, and require use of a bespoke environment in which to execute the transformations.

As stated in the introduction, the SiTra library described in this paper is not intended as a replacement for a full Model Transformation Framework or as a model transformation specification language, rather it is intended as a "way in" for experienced programmers to start using the concepts of transformations rules, without the need to learn a new language, or get to grips with a new framework of tools and development environments.

Given this purpose it can be argued that a comparison between SiTra and the existing transformation languages and frameworks is not really appropriate. However, it is interesting to note what can and can't be achieved with SiTra in relation to these other approaches.

6 Conclusions

In Model Driven Development, a fundamental idea is to automatically transform models from one modelling domain to another. Consequently, providing suitable model transformation frameworks to support such transformations is of paramount importance. This paper has reported on a case study involving transformation of models in OWL-S to BPEL, via our lightweight modelling transformation framework called SiTra. SiTra uses Java for the specification of the transformation rules, significantly eliminating the need to learn any new model transformation languages or to master complex model transformation frameworks. SiTra masks the details of the execution from the user by providing a powerful execution engine to implement the transformations. The paper has presented a mapping of important model elements from OWL-S to BPEL and describes samples of transformation rules written in QVT-like language and their equivalent in SiTra. The case study demonstrates that the method adopted by SiTra is powerful enough to handle even large and complex transformations.

Some of the concepts in OWL-S have no corresponding concepts in BPEL. As a result, elements modelling such concepts cannot be mapped to BPEL. Identifying correct transformation between two modelling domain is a challenging task. Indeed, we have come to the conclusion that model transformation frameworks, including SiTra, do not make the design part of creating a good set of transformations simple. However, SiTra provides an easier route to the implementation. This is crucial, as easier routes to implementation open opportunities for better adoption of the MDD.

Acknowledgement

The authors wish to express their gratitude to David Akehurst for his assistance with this project.

References

1. Stahl, T., Volter, M.: Model Driven Software Development; technology engineering management. Wiley, Chichester (2006)
2. Frankel, D.S.: Model Driven Architecture: Applying MDA to Enterprise Computing. OMG Press (2003)
3. MDA: Model Driven Architecture, Object Management Group (2005), www.omg.org/mda/
4. MOF: Meta Object Facility (MOF) 2.0 Core Spec.: Available (2004), at http://www.omg.org
5. Kleppe, A.W., Jos & Bast, W.: MDA Explained: The Model Driven Architecture–Practice and Promise. Addison-Wesley, London, UK (2003)
6. Denno, P., Steves, M.P., Libes, D., Barkmeyer, E.J.: Model-Driven Integration Using Existing Models. In: IEEE Software, vol. 20, pp. 59–63. IEEE computer Society, Los Alamitos, CA (2003)
7. Arcstyler: Arcstyler 5.0- Interactive Objects (2005)
8. OptimalJ: Compuware Software coporation (2005)
9. XMF-Mosaic: xactium (2005), http://www.xactium.com/
10. ATLAS: ATLAS, Université de Nantes (2005)
11. kermeta: Triskell Metamodelling Kernel (2005)
12. Planetmde: Planet MDE (2005), http://www.planetmde.org
13. Akehurst, D.H., Bordbar, B., Evans, M.J., Howells, W.G.J., McDonald-Maier, K.D.: SiTra: Simple Transformations in Java. ACM/IEEE 9TH International Conference on Model Driven Engineering Languages and Systems, Vol. 4199, pp. 351–364 (2006)
14. Bezivin, J., Rumpe, B., Schurr, A., Tratt, L.: A bench mark for model tranformation, see the Call for Papers at sosym.dcs.kcl.ac.uk/events/mtip05/long_cfp.pdf. Model Transformations in Practice Workshop, part of MoDELS 2005 (2005)
15. OWL-S: OWL Services Coalition (2004), OWL-S: Semantic Markup for Web Services. (2004), http://www.daml.org/services/owl-s/1.1
16. BEA, IBM, Microsoft, SAP, A., Systems, S.: Business Process Execution Language for Web Services. Version 1.1. (2003)
17. SiTra: Simple Transformer (SiTra): an MDE tool http://www.cs.bham.ac.uk/bxb/SiTra.html
18. W3C: Web Services Architecture (2004)
19. Chinnici, R., Moreau, J.-J., Ryman, A., Weerawarana, S.: Web Services Description Language (WSDL) Version 2.0, W3C (2006), http://www.w3.org/TR/wsdl20/

20. Alonso, G., Casati, F., Kuno, H., Machiraju, V.: Web Services. Springer, Berlin (2004)

21. W3C: Web Service Choreography Interface (WSCI) 1.0, W3C Note (2002)

22. Berners-Lee, T., Hendler, J., Lassila, O.: The Semantic Web: A new form of web content that is meaningful to computers will unleash a revolution of new possibilities. Scientific American (2001)

23. Bézivin, J., Hammoudi, S., Lopes, D., Jouault, F.: An Experiment in Mapping Web Services to Implementation Platforms. Technical report: 04.01. LINA, University of Nantes, Nantes, France (2004)

24. Bordbar, B., Staikopoulos, A.: On Behavioural Model Transformation in Web Services. In: Wang, S., Tanaka, K., Zhou, S., Ling, T.-W., Guan, J., Yang, D.-q., Grandi, F., Mangina, E.E., Song, I.-Y., Mayr, H.C. (eds.) Conceptual Modeling for Advanced Application Domains. LNCS, vol. 3289, Springer, Heidelberg (2004)

25. Gardner, T.: UML modelling of automated business processes with a mapping to BPEL4WS. In: 17th European Conference on Object Oriented Programming (ECOOP) (2005)

26. Bordbar, B., Staikopoulos, A.: Modelling and Transfomation of Behavioural aspects of Web Services. In: 3rd Workshop in Software Model Engineering - WiSME2004, UML 2004, Lisbon, Portugal (2004)

27. Bordbar, B., Staikopoulos, A.: On Behavioural Model Transformation in Web Services. Conceptual Modelling for Advanced Application Domain (eCOMO), China, pp. 667–678 (2004)

28. Bordbar, B., Staikopoulos, A.: Modelling and transforming the behavioural aspects of web services Third Workshop in Software Model Engineering (WiSME) at UML, Portugal (2004)

29. Koehler, J., Hauser, R., Kapoor, S., Wu, F.Y., Kumaran, S.: A model-driven transformation method. In: Seventh IEEE International Enterprise Distributed Object Computing Conference, Brisbane, Australia, pp. 186–197 (2003)

30. Patrascoiu, O.: Mapping edoc to web services using yatl. Eighth IEEE International Enterprise Distributed Object Computing, pp. 289–297 (2004)

31. Mandell, D.J., McIlraith, S.A.: Adapting BPEL4WS for the semantic web: The bottom-up approach to web service interoperation. In: Fensel, D., Sycara, K.P., Mylopoulos, J. (eds.) ISWC 2003. LNCS, vol. 2870, Springer, Heidelberg (2003)

32. SiTra: Simple Transformer (SiTra): an MDE tool (2006)

33. Konigs, A.: Model Transformations with Tripple Graph Grammars. Model Transformations in Practice Workshop at MoDELS 2005. In: Briand, L.C., Williams, C. (eds.) MoDELS 2005. LNCS, vol. 3713, Springer, Heidelberg (2005)

34. Taentzer, G., Ehrig, K., Guerra, E., Lara, J., Lengyel, L., Levendovszky, T., Prange, U., Varro, D., Varro-Gyapay, S.: Model Transformations by Graph Transformations: A Comparative Study. Model Transformations in Practice Workshop at MoDELS 2005. In: Briand, L.C., Williams, C. (eds.) MoDELS 2005. LNCS, vol. 3713, Springer, Heidelberg (2005)

35. Akehurst, D.H., Howells, W.G., McDonald-Maier, K.D.: Kent Model Transformation Language. Model Transformations in Practice Workshop, part of MoDELS 2005. In: Briand, L.C., Williams, C. (eds.) MoDELS 2005. LNCS, vol. 3713, Springer, Heidelberg (2005)

36. Jouault, F., Kurtev, I.: Transforming Models with ATL Model Transformations in Practice Workshop at MoDELS. In: Briand, L.C., Williams, C. (eds.) MoDELS 2005. LNCS, vol. 3713, Springer, Heidelberg (2005)

37. Lawley, M., Steel, J.: Practical Declarative Model Transformation With Tefkat. Model Transformations in Practice Workshop at MoDELS 2005. In: Briand, L.C., Williams, C. (eds.) MoDELS 2005. LNCS, vol. 3713, Springer, Heidelberg (2005)

38. Kalnins, A., Celms, E., Sostaks, A.: Model Transformation Approach Based on MOLA. Model Transformations in Practice Workshop at MoDELS 2005. In: Briand, L.C., Williams, C. (eds.) MoDELS 2005. LNCS, vol. 3713, Springer, Heidelberg (2005)

Improving the Interoperability of Automotive Tools by Raising the Abstraction from Legacy XML Formats to Standardized Metamodels

Mark Brörkens and Matthias Köster

Carmeq GmbH, Carnotstr. 4, 10587 Berlin, Germany
{mark.broerkens,matthias.koester}@carmeq.com

Abstract. Automotive system design demands frequent exchange of data between different parties and tools. In order to improve the interoperability, standardization bodies and partnerships have put high effort in defining XML based languages for system descriptions.

However, the mere existence of a standardized XML based data exchange format doesn't guarantee seamless interoperability. The validation possibilities given by XML DTD or Schema are not sufficient. Additionally, the maintenance of XML formats for the growing complexity of today's systems is an increasing challenge.

This paper describes the experiences with the model-driven approach taken by the automotive initiative AUTOSAR. It illustrates the limitations of designing data exchange formats in XML and shows how a higher level of abstraction increases the interoperability between tools. A powerful concept for mapping a metamodel to XML schema allows for integrating legacy XML formats.

Furthermore, current activities on improving interoperability by automatically generating a tool framework for AUTOSAR and other automotive tools are explained.

1   Introduction

The development of an automotive electric/electronic system is distributed over many parties. Whenever information is exchanged, the involved parties need to agree on common syntax and semantics. While exchanging data via informal documents often was sufficient in the past, the complexity of todays automotive systems [1][2] requires a more formal machine readable exchange of information.

An important step for improving the interoperability between different parties is to standardize a common domain-specific language including its syntax and semantics. Since all involved tools must be able to read and write this language, using XML (eXtensible Markup Language)[3][4] is a good idea: Tool vendors can use high quality off-the-shelf XML libraries for XML processing and validation.

The automotive initiative AUTOSAR (AUTomotive Open System ARchitecture) [5] has started to standardize a data exchange format that covers several steps in automotive system development including abstract description of

D.H. Akehurst, R. Vogel, and R.F. Paige (Eds.): ECMDA-FA 2007, LNCS 4530, pp. 59–67, 2007.
© Springer-Verlag Berlin Heidelberg 2007

software components as well as fine-grained mapping of bits to frames on communication networks. Section 2 describes the (meta)model based approach for designing and generating the AUTOSAR XML schema.

For a seamless interoperability between tools, additional consistency checks that exceed the expressive power of W3C XML schema [4] and alternative XML schema languages such as W3C DTD [3] or RELAX NG [6] are required. These constraints are often defined informally and therefore are likely to be interpreted differently by various tool vendors.

Section 3 describes the layered architecture for tool interoperability defined by AUTOSAR. This architecture defines a hierarchy of abstraction levels and their impact on tool interoperability.

The metamodel developed by AUTOSAR can not only be used to generate the XML schema or documentation, it can also be used as a source for the generation of a tool platform. Since AUTOSAR itself is not developing tools, some AUTOSAR members have formed the informal OTF for Automotive [1] initiative. This initiative plans to develop an open platform that can be used by any tool vendor. The current status of that initiative is presented in section 4.

2   Improving Interoperability by Standardization of Data Exchange Formats

2.1   Standardisation on XML Level

Standardization bodies and partnerships have put high effort in defining XML based data exchange formats for specific use cases. Some examples are:

- ASAM FIBEX [7] (Field Bus Exchange Format) focuses on message-oriented bus communication systems. It allows to describe bus configuration, parameterization, design, monitoring and simulation.
- MSR SW [8] focuses on the description of automotive software

Those data exchange formats usually are defined by a formal XML DTD or XML Schema and informal descriptions of constraints which exceed the expressive power of generic XML validation techniques.

The XML DTDs or XML schema specified in these standards are created manually or are assembled semi-automatically out of several XML fragments for better maintainability. The availability of these XML formats highly improves the interoperability and reduces development costs of tools: Generic off-the-shelf XML libraries can be used to parse and validate XML descriptions. However, this manual approach of creating a XML-based data exchange format is not sufficient for the needs within the AUTOSAR development partnership:

- Complex interlinked structures are very *hard to understand and maintain* at the XML level.

---

[1] Open Tool Framework for Automotive.

- Conceptual discussions on the AUTOSAR language are often interrupted by *discussions on how to implement the concepts in a XML schema language.*
- The *expressive power* of XML schema languages such as XML DTD or XML schema is *not sufficient* for seamless tool interoperability. Additional constraints need to be defined separately and are (if not defined using a formal unambiguous language) a potential risk for misinterpretations and therefore are a risk for limited interoperability.

For reasons mentioned before, AUTOSAR decided not to create the XML-based exchange format by directly editing XML schema descriptions. Instead, the implementation of the language in XML was de-coupled from discussions on the actual content. This was achieved by raising the abstraction from XML to a metamodel.

2.2   Standardization on Metamodel Level

AUTOSAR started modeling the AUTOSAR language using class diagrams. The increasing number of developers and growing complexity of the model required a modeling guide. As described in "Definition and Generation of Data Exchange Formats in AUTOSAR" [9] , the focus of that modeling guide is to support the automotive experts in modeling their domain knowledge in the AUTOSAR metamodel. Individual developers do not need to delve into UML modeling techniques. This approach has the following advantages:

- The graphical representation allows for quickly getting a good overview, even over highly interlinked information.
- The experts can concentrate on their domain knowledge and do not need to care about the implementation in an XML schema language
- The replica mechanism of the UML tool Enterprise Architect [10] allowed for distributed development of several experts on the same model.

AUTOSAR delegated the implementation of its XML schema to a small group of modeling and XML experts. This group defined powerful rules for mapping the AUTOSAR metamodel to XML schema. These mapping rules had to fulfill the following requirements:

- Allow for strong validation using standard XML parsers
- Ability to reproduce existing XML structures and patterns that are well established in the automotive domain. (See for example [11]).
- Configuration of mapping rules based on tagged values in the metamodel

Even though the AUTOSAR language is modeled using UML class diagrams, some constraints can't be expressed: A more powerful constraint language is required.

Example for a Model Constraint. In the AUTOSAR metamodel, the class ElectricalRange represents an electrical range for different applications. This class has attributes `minVoltage` and `maxVoltage` that specify the range in voltage (see figure 1 for details). It also has the attribute `typicalVoltage`, which must be a voltage in the specified range. This constraint can't be expressed with XML schema. But it can be expressed easily with an OCL constraint (Object Constraint Language) [12]:

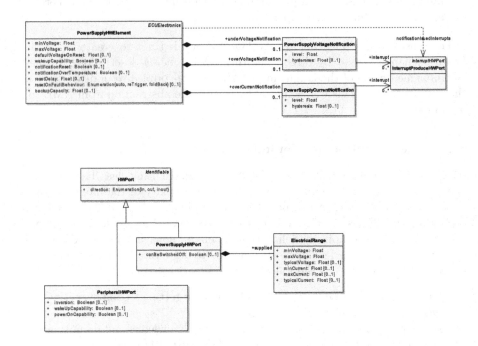

Fig. 1. AUTOSAR 2.0 metamodel for classes `ElectricalRange` and `PowerSupplyHWPort`

```
context ElectricalRange

inv self.minVoltage <= self.typicalVoltage and
   self.typicalVoltage <= self.maxVoltage
```

Elaborating the example above, the class `PowerSupplyHWPort` describes power supplying and consuming hardware ports. If the `direction` attribute is set to `in`, the port is a power supplier. If `direction` is set to `out`, the port consumes power. A `PowerSupplyHWPort` has a pin of type `HWPin`, which can be connected via a `PinHWConnection` with another port. Connecting two such pins requires that an out and an in pin are connected and that both have a compatible electrical range. This can be checked with the following OCL constraint:

```
context PowerSupplyHWPort

let out =
 PinHWConnection.allInstances()
   ->select(conn | conn.connectedPin->includes(self.pin))
    .connectedPin->excluding(self.pin).port

inv self.pin.direction = 'in' implies
 out.direction = 'out'
 and
 self.electricalRange.minVoltage = out.electricalRange.minVoltage
 and
 self.electricalRange.maxVoltage = out.electricalRange.maxVoltage
```

Breaking these constraints can cause severe damage, thus it's especially important for an OEM (Original Equipment Manufacture) to ensure that the AUTOSAR XML descriptions from different suppliers describe a consistent system. This can be reached by adding these constraints to the metamodel and validating them when assembling the system description from different suppliers.

Although AUTOSAR has started using OCL for formal descriptions of constraints in the metamodel most constraints are still described informally. A more extensive use of OCL instead of informal descriptions would help to increase the interoperability.

3   Layered Architecture for Tool Interoperabilty

Figure 2 shows a layered architecture for tool interoperability. On the first layer, files are used to exchange data between different tools. On the next layer the data format is specified. Using XML as the file format allows easy exchange of data, but doesn't ensure the referential integrity of the data. On the next layer the content can be accessed as interlinked data structures and referential integrity can be reached, but the semantic consistency of the data can't be easily expressed or checked. On top of the content layer is the semantic layer, where the data consistency can be checked by validating constraints on the content. Applications built on top of this layer can assume that the data, on which they operate, is consistent. Regardless of the intended use all tools must implement the lower four layers.

The upper-most levels focus on how tools present information to the users and how the business logic is implemented. Those levels are highly dependent on the intended use and therefore are only mentioned for the sake of completeness.

The base for any AUTOSAR tool is its ability to persist data as XML files. Working with XML makes it possible to use generic XML validation techniques.

Representing the data as instances of metamodels (content layer) supports the use of standard model APIs (Application Programming Interface) to access and query the data. Rather than working with XML and textual links between

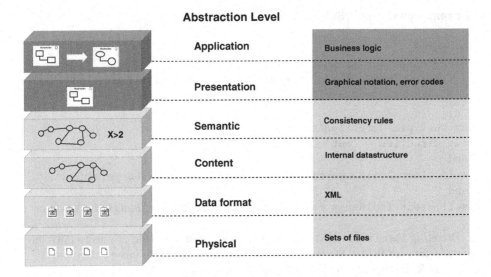

Abstraction Level

Application	Business logic
Presentation	Graphical notation, error codes
Semantic	Consistency rules
Content	Internal datastructure
Data format	XML
Physical	Sets of files

Fig. 2. Layered architecture for tool interoperability

XML elements, we are now working with references and links between classes and objects. This makes it much easier to ensure the referential integrity of the data. A higher level of abstraction is reached, making it easier to access and manipulate the data.

Using a reflective standard model API makes it is possible to build a generic validation layer on top of the model layer. This enables us to leverage the full power of model based validation techniques (e.g. OCL[12]).

4   OTF – A Layered Framework for Tool Interoperability

The Open Tool Framework (OTF) is an implementation of the layered architecture as described in the previous section. OTF is realized as a set of Eclipse plug-ins and uses the Eclipse Modeling Framework (EMF) [13] as its foundation. EMF is an open source implementation of the OMG EMOF 2.0 standard [14] and defines a mapping from EMOF to Java. This mapping can be used to generate a metamodel specific API, but EMF also provides a reflective model API. Other frameworks can use the reflective model API to provide generic services on top of EMF. A transaction layer and several OCL validation engines are available as open source.

EMF also provides an extensible framework for loading and saving models. This framework is based on the concept of resources, which consist of a set of model elements that should be stored at the same physical location. To specify the physical location of a resource, a Universal Resource Identifier (URI) is used. This rather abstract and generic approach allows support for a lot of different storage system. EMF provides persistence to XMI (XML Metadata Interchange)

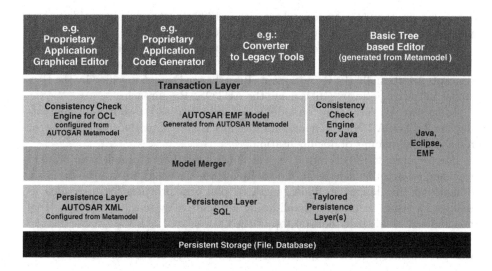

Fig. 3. OTF: a layered framework for tool interoperability

[15] and XML file formats, but other open source frameworks are available that provide persistence to RDBMS (Relational Database Management System).

EMF provides extension points to add custom resource implementations. This mechanism allows for integrating custom resources for the AUTOSAR XML format. The rules for mapping between AUTOSAR XML and the AUTOSAR metamodel are defined in the AUTOSAR "Model Persistence Rules for XML" [5] specification and are implemented by the OTF persistence layer. Since we extended the standard EMF resource mechanism, all available frameworks based on EMF and its resource system can be leveraged.

Figure 3 shows the architecture of the OTF framework. The lower three levels of tool interoperability are realized by the persistence layers and the model merger. The persistence layers transform AUTOSAR data from various representations into an instance of the AUTOSAR metamodel. The model merger merges data from several sources and detects redundant or conflicting information. Consistency checks are supported using the EMF validation mechanism. Constraints can either be defined as OCL expressions which are interpreted by the EMF OCL validation engine or by Java classes which navigate over the AUTOSAR EMF model. Read and write requests from application plugins (e.g. graphical editors, code generators, converters) are coordinated by the transaction layer.

5   Summary and Outlook

The model-driven approach for designing and generating the AUTOSAR XML schema was very successful. More than 30 domain experts have been actively working on the AUTOSAR metamodel in the last 3 years. Today the metamodel contains more than 600 classes and more than 1300 structural features. This complexity would not have been possible by manually creating a XML schema. Other automotive standardization organizations are already adopting this model-based approach. Future versions of the MSR Software [8] are likely to use the AUTOSAR concept. Additionally the Requirements Interchange Format specified by the Hersteller Initiative Software [16] is using the AUTOSAR approach.

Today the AUTOSAR metamodel is not only used as the source for generating the AUTOSAR XML schema, additionally it is used as the single source for a substantial amount of documentation.

Furthermore, the OTF initiative has shown that the metamodel can be used to generate an implementation of a tool platform that conforms to the designed domain specific language. This generated platform provides features such as reading, writing, merging and validating automotive system descriptions. Tool vendors can build their tools on top of the OTF.

We hope that more standardisation bodies will use the approach outlined in this paper, since this can improve the interoperability of tools dramatically.

References

1. AUTOSAR: Media release. (2006), `http://www.autosar.org/download/AUTOSAR_long_en.pdf`
2. Fennel, H., et al.: Achievements and exploitation of the AUTOSAR development partnership. (2006), `http://www.autosar.org/download/AUTOSAR_Paper_Convergence_2006.pdf`
3. W3C: Extensible markup language (xml) 1.1 (2 edn.). (September 2006), `http://www.w3.org/TR/2006/REC-xml11-20060816/`
4. W3C: Xml schema part1: Structures second edition. (October 2004), `http://www.w3.org/TR/xmlschema-1/`
5. AUTOSAR: Official website of the autosar development partnership. (2006), `http://www.autosar.org`
6. ISO: ISO/IEC FDIS 19757-2 document schema definition language (dsdl) – part 2: Regular-grammar-based validation – relax ng. (December 2002), `http://www.relaxng.org/#specs`
7. ASAM: FBX, FIBEX - field bus exchange format, version 2.0. (June 2006), `http://www.asam.net/03_standards_06.php`
8. ASAM: MSRSW, MSR software, version 2.3. (June 2005), `http://www.asam.net/03_standards_10.php`
9. Pagel, M., Brörkens, M.: Definition and generation of data exchange formats definition and generation of data exchange formats in autosar. In: Rensink, A., Warmer, J. (eds.) ECMDA-FA 2006. LNCS, vol. 4066, pp. 52–65. Springer, Heidelberg (2006)
10. Sparx Systems: Enterprise architect product page. (2006), `http://www.sparxsystems.com.au, http://www.sparxsystems.com.au/`
11. ASAM: HDO, harmonized data objects, version 1.0. (July 2004), `http://www.asam.net/03_standards_09.php`
12. OMG: UML OCL specification version 2.0. (June 2005), `http://www.omg.org/cgi-bin/doc?ptc/2005-06-06`
13. Eclipse Foundation: Website of the EMF eclipse project. (2006), `http://www.eclipse.org/emf`

14. OMG: Meta Object Facility (MOF) specification version 2.0. (January 2006), http://www.omg.org/cgi-bin/doc?formal/2006-01-01
15. OMG: XML Metadata Interchange (XMI) specification version 2.1 (September 2005)
16. Automotive HIS: Requirements interchange format, version 1.0a. (November 2005), http://www.automotive-his.de/simutool.htm

Templatable Metamodels for Semantic Variation Points

Arnaud Cuccuru, Chokri Mraidha, François Terrier, and Sébastien Gérard

CEA, LIST, Gif-sur-Yvette, F-91191, France
{arnaud.cuccuru,chokri.mraidha,francois.terrier,sebastien.gerard}@cea.fr

Abstract. In the field of Domain Languages Engineering, Semantic Variation Points are an important issue. This crucial information is often related to the dynamic semantics of systems. Identifying and understanding it is a requisite for all model-based activities (design, simulation, test, formal verification, etc.). Most of the time, semantic variation points are only informally identified in a documentation associated with a metamodel: they are not part of the metamodel itself, and there is currently no mechanism to capture them explicitly. We propose a template-based notation enabling semantic variation points to be clearly and explicitly identified within the metamodel, using template parameter definitions. Semantic variation points can then be intuitively fixed by parameter binding at both model and metamodel levels. We illustrate our proposal with a templated version of the UML 2 state machine metamodel. Finally, we describe a prototype implementation of our mechanisms in the context of the Eclipse Modeling Framework. [1]

1   Introduction

Metamodels, models and model transformations are the key elements of the Model Driven Architecture [11]. For a given domain, a metamodel offers a means for capturing commonly handled concepts, their connoted meaning and the relationships existing between them. For example, a metamodel can be used to specify an abstract syntax for a Domain Specific Modeling Language (DSML), thus providing a kind of grammar and lexicon to which a model must conform to comply with its reference metamodel. Transformation rules can then be expressed at the metamodel level, and applied to models that comply with their respective metamodels.

The predominance of metamodels in model driven approaches raises the issue of their potential reuse. Indeed, the ability to reuse and/or specialize (parts of) existing metamodels is crucial in order to avoid developing new metamodels

[1] This work has been performed in the context of the Usine Logicielle project (www.usine-logicielle.org) of the System@tic Paris Region Cluster. This project is partially funded by the "Direction Générale des Entreprises of the French administration", the "Conseil Régional d'Île de France", the "Conseil Général des Yvelines", the "Conseil Général de l'Essonne" and the "Conseil Général des Hauts de Seine".

D.H. Akehurst, R. Vogel, and R.F. Paige (Eds.): ECMDA-FA 2007, LNCS 4530, pp. 68–82, 2007.

from scratch. To do so, MOF [12] (OMG standard for metamodeling) provides constructs inspired by object-oriented techniques such as import, inheritance or package merge which is developed in section 2.3. Since Simula-67 and the early days of Objects, object-oriented languages have evolved beyond what are usually considered to be the fundamentals of the Object paradigm: objects, classes, encapsulation, inheritance and polymorphism. For reusability and capitalization purposes, some object-oriented languages (like C++ or Java) have integrated Genericity – a mechanism appearing in Ada 83 – which makes elements easier to reuse and specialize by affording generic definitions based on template parameters. Generic behaviors can then be expressed (quasi-) independently of the actual type of these generic parameters. We believe that the MOF would benefit from following the same type of evolution, especially at a time where the Model Driven Engineering (MDE) community recognizes a need for behaviored and executable metamodels [4]. This assertion is particularly true for DSMLs, which are an increasingly fundamental activity around model driven engineering.

In a DSML, the concepts handled typically go beyond the traditional use of MOF as a way to specify a "metadata repository". These metamodels are usually specified with a dynamic context in mind, where manifestations of the concepts identified in the metamodel carry dynamic semantics and are assumed to play a role in the context of an execution. If MOF could support behavioral descriptions, the metamodel of a DSML would typically embed operational semantics, so that models conforming to this metamodel could be executed. The reuse/specialization issue mentioned in the previous paragraph is at least as crucial for DSMLs. A metamodel specifications for state-based languages is a typical case where reuse and specialization mechanisms are needed. As illustrated in [10], state-based languages (i.e. languages using state machines as a way to specify behaviors) share common concepts (statemachines, states, transitions, guards, etc) and structural relationships between these concepts. They only vary in the interpretation that can be made from a program specified with one of these languages. In the UML 2 specification [14], these various potential interpretations are called "Semantic Variation Points", and we will be using this convenient expression throughout our paper. For metamodel reuse/specialization purposes, one might wish to capture these common properties in a generic metamodel. New specialized metamodels could then be specified from this common generic metamodel using traditional MOF specialization mechanisms, or even through the profiling mechanism proposed by the UML 2 Infrastructure[13]. The semantic variation points would then be fixed where needed through specialization of the different concepts. More generally in the field of domain languages engineering, semantic variation points are an important issue. This crucial information is often related to the dynamic semantics of systems. Identifying and understanding them is a requisite for all model-based activities (design, simulation, test, formal verification, etc.). However, MOF does not provide a way to explicitly declare (and fix) the semantic variation points of the generic metamodel. This information is accessible to users only through the associated documentation (most of the time written in natural language, such as in the case of the UML 2 metamodel), or is hidden in the behavioral description if the metamodel embeds operational semantics (in the same way as in [2]. We will give a more detailed description of this work in section 2). To fill the currently existing "gap", we propose to introduce the ability to define template parameters at the metamodel level, where parameters can be bound either at the model level or at the metamodel level.

In section 2, we examine how standard OMG mechanisms are limited for addressing the semantic variation points issue. In section 3, we then see how templateable metamodels could help us to explicitly and intuitively identify and fix semantic variation points. To illustrate our discussion, we propose a definition of a behaviored and parameterized version of the UML 2 StateMachine metamodel. To prove the feasability of our approach, section 4 briefly describes a prototype integration of a template support mechanism (largely inspired by UML 2 templates) as an extension of Ecore, an implementation of EMOF for the Eclipse IDE. In our conclusion, we discuss how the mechanisms we propose could be integrated into traditional model driven tool chains.

Note: Devising a formalism for behavioral description falls outside the scope of this paper. The template mechanism proposed here makes very few assumptions about the kind of formalism used to describe behaviors. The only assumption made is that behaviors are encapsulated in operations, and triggered by operation calls. This assumption is reasonable according to the object orientation of MOF. Even though the behavioral aspect of metamodels is not credited by the current MOF definition (in which descriptions are purely structural, and potential behaviors only identified through operation declarations on classes), several environments already offer a support for behavioral descriptions. This is namely the case of the Eclipse Modeling Framework [1] (via basic Java instructions) or Kermeta [7] (with an higher level action language completed with OCL like queries).

2   Standard Mechanisms for Metamodel Specialization

The MOF and the UML 2 Infrastructure provide mechanisms for specializing an existing metamodel. As we explained in our introduction, specializations are required to fix the semantic variation points identified in the semantic description of a metamodel. More precisely, the semantic description associated with the specializations of a generic metamodel will serve to fix its semantic variation points, so that specialized metamodels can be interpreted without ambiguity. To illustrate how the mechanisms provided by these two OMG standards can be applied, we have used a simplified version of the UML 2 state machine metamodel (Fig.1).

2.1   UML 2 State Machines

In UML, state machines are mainly used to describe the behavior associated with instances of active classes. A state machine owns one or more regions, which in turn own vertices (pseudo states and states) and transitions that relate vertices. Transitions are guarded by a constraint, and fired according to certain triggers referencing a firing event. Firing a transition results in the execution of the potentially associated effect behavior, and an evolution of the region's current state from the source vertex to the target vertex of the fired transition. To simplify our presentation, we consider that a state machine contains only one region.

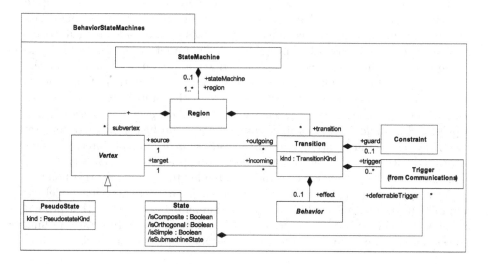

Fig. 1. Simplified UML 2 StateMachine Metamodel

At execution time, the state machine accesses an event pool that is managed by the context object owning this state machine. The context object interacts with its environment, and updates the content of the event pool according to certain event occurrences (reception of an operation call, a signal, etc.). The state machine takes, dispatches and processes events from the pool only once the previous event occurrence has been fully processed. This event processing policy is called "run-to-completion semantics". On the base of this simple dynamic semantics, many semantic variation points are identified in the UML 2 Superstructure. The event selection and transition selection policies are simple ones that we will focus on.

According to the current state of the state machine and the set of relevant events contained in the pool (i.e. those that can trigger a transition from the current state), the event selection policy determines an event dequeuing order, and leaves open the possibility of modeling different priority-based schemes. In the following sections, we consider the simple Lifo and Fifo policies as possible concrete semantics for the event selection policy. When "highest priority events" have been selected according to a concrete event selection policy, the transition selection policy determines the transition to be fired in the case where several events have the same priority level. In the following paragraphs, we consider a Random policy and a Stochastic policy as concrete semantics for the transition selection policy.

2.2   Specialization by Profiling

Profiling is a specialization mechanism provided by the UML 2 Infrastructure. A profile specializes metaclasses from an existing metamodel in order to adapt them for particular purposes. Basically, stereotypes can be defined to annotate particular metaclasses, so that the basic semantics of the targeted metaclass can be specialized. A stereotype embeds properties usually called tagged values, representing annotations to be interpreted for the targeted domain. In Fig.2, we define a profile that fixes the two identified semantic variation points for the UML state machines. This simple profile contains the definition of the *UnambiguousStateMachine* stereotype, that applies to the StateMachine metaclass. This stereotype embeds two tagged values: *eventPolicy* and *transitionPolicy*, typed by *EventSelectionPolicy* and *TransitionSelectionPolicy* enumerations respectively. These enumerations contain identifiers for the possible interpretations associated with the semantic variation points identified in the source state machine metamodel. Note that they could be extended to account for other policies. With an appropriate semantic description, a particular state machine model annotated with this profile could be interpreted unambiguously. Note that profiles are almost exclusively used to specialize UML 2 metamodel. However, nothing prevents users from defining profiles that specialize other metamodels.

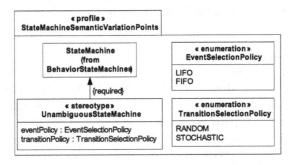

Fig. 2. Specialization by Profiling

2.3   Specialization by Generalization and Package Merge

The MOF provides several mechanisms to enable reuse and/or specialization of (parts of) existing metamodels. With **PackageImport**, the elements of an imported package are made visible to the elements contained in the importing Package. The UML 2 Infrastructure pragmatically defines the PackageImport concept as "a relationship that allows the use of unqualified names to refer to package members from other namespaces". It enables the names of the elements contained in the imported package to be added in some way to the importing package. Once these elements are imported into (i.e. made visible in) a package, they can be specialized by means of a **Generalization** relationship. Generalization is the MOF manifestation of the classical Inheritance capability of the Object paradigm. Imported elements are indeed reused as a basis for building a refined or specialized element. In Fig.3, the *UnambiguousBehavioredStateMachines* package imports the content of the *BehavioredStateMachines* package, so that the *StateMachine* metaclass is made visible for elements of the receiving package. The *SpecializedStateMachineA* and *SpecializedStateMachineB* metaclasses then specialize the *StateMachine* metaclass through a Generalization relationship. The semantic descriptions associated with the specialized metaclasses subsequently fix the semantic variation points of the *StateMachine* metaclass.

This solution is rather naive (one specialized metaclass for one particular interpretation) and is proposed here only for illustration purpose. In [2], the authors also use the Generalization relationship in the context of the Kermeta framework, albeit with a more modular solution. In Kermeta, metamodel designers can enrich the traditional structural part of a metamodel with an integrated operational semantics. Kermeta indeed provides an action language (supplemented by OCL-like queries) to encapsulate a behavioral description into metaclass operations. The modular solution is then to apply the Strategy design pattern [8], and exploiting the polymorphism of the action language. In the strategy design pattern, a "strategy class" embeds only one operation and is used as a server. A client class then embeds several operations, in which the behavior of each operation is expressed as a call for a strategy class operation. In the state machine example, the StateMachine metaclass acts as a client with two operations: *selectEvents()* and *selectTransition()*. Each of these operations in turn calls the operations of two abstract strategy classes: *EventSelectionPolicy* (with a *selectEvents()* operation) and *TransitionSelectionPolicy* (with a *selectTransitions()* operation). Several specializations, each implementing a different interpretation for the corresponding semantic variation point, can then be proposed for the strategy classes (i.e. LIFO, FIFO, etc).

An alternative metamodel specialization solution afforded by the MOF is the **PackageMerge** relationship. According to [15] this relationship is partially inspired from the combination of the "and" and "join" mechanisms of the Catalysis approach [5]. This relationship expresses how the contents of two packages are combined. It is similar to the Generalization relationship since it specifies that the contents of a merged package is extended in some way by the content of a receiving package. When an element of the receiving package has the same name as an element of the merged package, the characteristics of the receiving element are extended by the characteristics of the merged element. The result is an element that combines all their characteristics. The PackageMerge relationship is often used to provide several levels of detail for the definition of an element having different uses. The UML 2 superstructure, for example, makes extensive use of this mechanism to structure the specification with different levels of compliance for the various concepts considered. In Fig.4, we use this mechanism to build

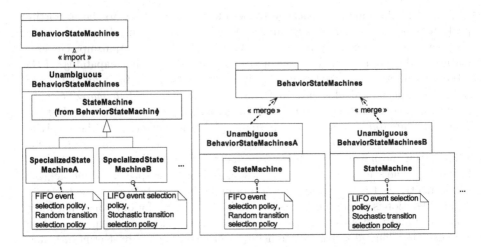

Fig. 3. Specialization by Pack-   **Fig. 4.** Specialization by PackageMerge
ageImport/Generalization

the specialized packages *UnambiguousBehaviorStateMachineA* and *UnambiguousBehaviorStateMachineB* from the general *BehaviorStateMachines* package, whereby the semantic description associated with each *StateMachine* metaclass of the receiving packages fixes semantic variation points for the *StateMachine* metaclass defined in the merged package.

2.4   Evaluation of Standard Mechanisms

All these specialization mechanisms are virtually equivalent, and the choice of one or the other is a matter of taste. In all cases, the semantic variation points are fixed by the semantic description associated with each specialized metaclass. For the specialization part of the semantic variation point issue, these mechanisms provide an effective solution. The main limitation of MOF concerns identification of the semantic variation points: a metamodel alone is not enough to confirm that they exist. This information is only and necessarily available in the textual semantic description associated with the metamodel. For behaviored metamodels (such as in Kermeta), it exists in the metamodel, but is hidden in the behavioral description (e.g. when operations on abstract metaclasses are called). We believe that use of template parameters would be an elegant and intuitive way to identify semantic variation points in a metamodel. Parameter binding would then be the natural way to specialize metamodels and intuitively fix semantic variation points.

3   Templateable Metamodels

3.1   Related Works

The potential benefits of templatable metamodels have already been partially explored by the MDE community. The authors of [6] propose to integrate a template based mechanism into GME (Generic Modeling Environment), which is a metamodeling environment for the definition of DSMLs. Their main reason for doing so is that recurrent structural modeling patterns appear when defining DSMLs. Designers thus need a way to capture recurrent patterns in a generic way, and templated metamodels are an obvious solution. Template parameters namely enable clear identification of roles in the patterns, and specify how an actual metamodel is derived from one or several pattern metamodels through parameter/role binding. The generic metamodeling design patterns can then be instantiated, composed, and specialized as needed to produce new metamodels. The authors identify such design patterns, either ones specific to DSML such as state charts or data flow modeling style patterns, or more general ones such as the composite structure design pattern. A similar but more general (i.e. less DSML-oriented) approach has been proposed in [3]. This also focuses on use of templatable metamodels to clearly specify and identify design patterns roles as template parameters.

These approaches share the idea that template parameters are a powerful tool for metamodel designers and can be efficiently combined with traditional MOF inheritance-like mechanisms (i.e. Generalization and PackageMerge) to meet the "design for reuse" criterion. The benefits identified by the authors concern mainly architectural aspect of metamodeling. We also share this analysis and we think that these works support genericity expression in the large, but we believe that benefits of templatable metamodels go beyond architectural/structural aspects. The next section of our article shows that templatization can also impact the semantic aspects of metamodeling and solve the semantic variation points issue. Outside of the MDE community, use of template parameters for fixing semantic variation points has already been investigated. In [10], the authors indeed describe the structural part of state machines as tuples, whose execution can be parameterized by functions and predicates. The philosophy of our proposal is similar, but is better adapted to common metamodeling practices. We provide a methodology that addresses the issue of explicitly denoting semantic variation points in DSML metamodels.

3.2   A Templated Version of the UML 2 State Machine Metamodel

Fig.5 illustrates how the UML 2 StateMachine metamodel can be parameterized using the default UML notation for templates. The PackageMerge relationship between the *TemplatedBehaviorStateMachine* and *BehaviorStateMachine* is not a requisite. We use it here only to show how an existing, unparameterized metamodel could be templated (the UML 2 metamodel is of course a good candidate for such templatization). A complete view of the *TemplatedBehaviorStateMachine* package obtained by merging is shown in Fig.6.

In the *TemplatedBehaviorStateMachine* package (Fig.5), the elements shown are those that were specialized or added (based on the metamodel defined in the merged package). To reflect the dynamic aspect of an execution, we added some

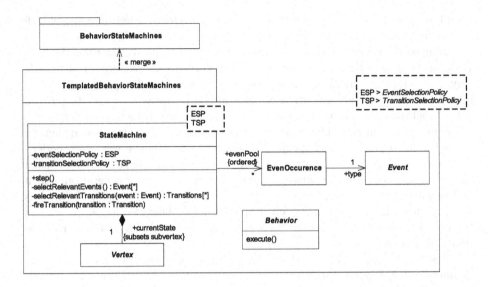

Fig. 5. UML 2 StateMachine Metamodel with Template Parameters

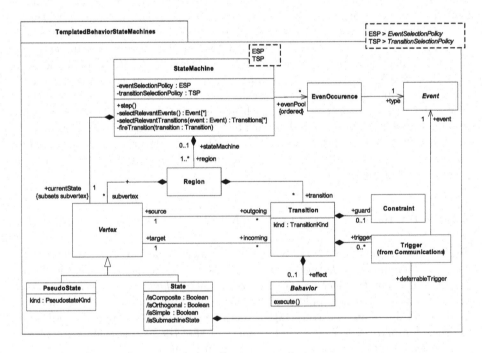

Fig. 6. Full view of the templated package resulting from the package merge

associations (*currentState* of a *StateMachine*), created some metaclasses (*EventOccurence*), and declared some operations on metaclasses, to reflect a behavior based on operation calls.

Let us now examine how an anonymous (but perceptive) reader would react to this diagram. Two template parameters are defined for the *TemplatedBehaviorStateMachine* package. They are ESP (a type that must comply with the *EventSelectionPolicy* abstract metaclass) and TSP (complying with the *TransitionSelectionPolicy* abstract metaclass), which are in turn referenced by the *StateMachine* metaclass. The *EventSelectionPolicy* and *TransitionSelectionPolicy* metaclasses own operations which indicate that potential behaviors are encapsulated in these metaclasses. Intuitively, our perceptive reader understands that the behavior associated with the parameters will impact the behavior of the parameterized *StateMachine* metaclass. The two template parameters provide him with a means for varying the operational semantics of the *StateMachine*. In other words, these parameters explicitly identify the points at which the semantics of a UML state machine can vary: Its semantic variations points have thus been explicitly and clearly identified. This intuition can be easily confirmed if we encapsulate an operational semantics (expressed here with a java-like syntax) in the *step* operation of the *StateMachine* generic metaclass, in which explicit references are made to the parameter behaviors through operation calls (selectEventToHandle and selectTransitionToFire):

```
public void step() {
  // local variable declarations
  Event[*] relevantEvents ;
  Event selectedEvent ;
  Transition[*] relevantTransitions ;
  Transition selectedTransition ;

  // selection of the event to handle
  relevantEvents := this.selectRelevantEvents() ;
  selectedEvent := eventSelectionPolicy.
                        selectEventToHandle(relevantEvents) ;

  // selection of the transition to fire
  relevantTransitions := selectRelevantTransitions(selectedEvent) ;
  selectedTransition := transitionSelectionPolicy.
                        selectTransitionToFire(relevantTransitions) ;

  // the selected transition is fired
  fireTransition(selectedTransitions) ;
}
```

Sometimes, dynamic aspects in metamodeling are defined using a separate model of values which is linked with the abstract syntax model via some kind of evaluation objects. In that case our approach could be applied in a similar way by defining template parameters on the model of values specifying the dynamic aspects.

Once the semantic variation points have been identified by template parameter definitions, the most natural way to fix them is to bind the parameters to concrete values (i.e. the types actually handled). In Fig.7 and 8, we illustrate how semantic variation points can be fixed both at the metamodel level and the model level. At the metamodel level, a new package can be defined from an existing templated package through the Bind relationship. In the resulting metamodel, references to template parameters are resolved and are replaced by the concrete values bound to the parameters. Using this mechanism, we create a *FIFO_Random_StateMachines* package in which the state machines select events according to a "FIFO" event selection policy, and transitions according to a "random" transition selection policy. At the model level, we declare a state machine with the same semantics, but binding takes place directly in the declaration of the generic metaclass instance.

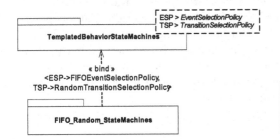

Fig. 7. Semantic Variation Points fixed at the Metamodel Level (M2)

Fig. 8. Semantic Variation Points fixed at the Model Level (M1)

4   Implementation for Ecore

In order to study the feasibility of our approach, we are currently developing an Eclipse[2] plug-in supporting the template mechanism we have illustrated in the previous section. The first step of this implementation is to extend the definition of Ecore (the Eclipse implementation of EMOF) used as a base for EMF. Ecore is itself described by an Ecore metamodel (in the same way that MOF is defined by a MOF metamodel). Extending the metamodeling capabilities of Ecore to support template expressions thus requires an extension of the Ecore metamodel. We base the description of the extensions we propose on the simplified view of the Ecore metamodel illustrated in Fig.9.

The extensions integrated in the Ecore metamodel are inspired by the UML 2 metamodel subset concerning templates. Our proposal is however simplified and adapted to metamodeling requirements, but we keep as much as possible the UML 2 vocabulary (and the meaning associated with each identified concept) in order to prevent UML 2 users from confusion.

---

[2] http://www.eclipse.org

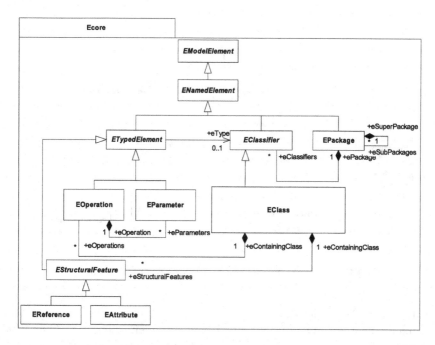

Fig. 9. Simplified Ecore Metamodel

4.1 Extensions for Template Declarations

Fig.10 illustrates the extensions we integrate in the Ecore metamodel in order to support template declarations. A *TemplateableElement* is an element that can optionally be defined as a template (i.e. an element that defines some formal template parameters) and/or bound to other templates (i.e. the definition of the element relies on the definition of another templateable element, and binds its formal parameters). A templateable element may own a *Template-Signature*, which in turn references a set of *TemplateParameter* elements. These *TemplateParameter* elements identify the formal parameters of the template. A *ParameterableElement* represents an element that can be bound as an actual value for a formal template parameter. TemplateableElement, TemplateParameter and ParameterableElement abstract metaclasses are then specialized for specific uses. Concretely, all TemplateableElement sub-classes will be able to embed template parameter definitions. TemplateParameter sub-classes will then be defined if necessary for each ParameterableElement specialization. In our proposal, EPackage and EClassifier specialize TemplateableElement, Classifier-TemplateParameter specializes TemplateParemeter, and EClassifier specializes ParameterableElement. The *ETypedElement* Ecore metaclass is also extended with an association to ClassifierTemplateParameter (*eGenericType* role). This association enables EOperation, EParameter and EStructuralFeature (i.e. sub-classes of the abstract TypedElement metaclass) to be typed by a classifier template parameter.

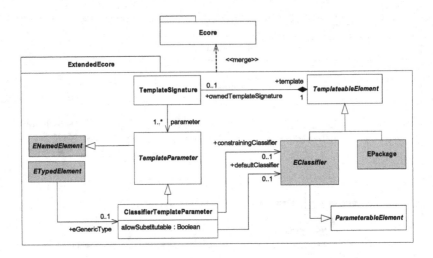

Fig. 10. Ecore Extensions for Template Declarations

Note that UML 2 goes further, and identifies other specializations for TemplateableElement (i.e. Operation) and ParameterableElement (i.e. Operation, Property and ValueSpecification). The implementation we describe here is only a prototype version, and we only keep for the moment specializations that are useful to support a template declaration similar to the one illustrated in Fig.5.

4.2   Extensions for Template Parameters Binding

Fig.11 illustrates the Ecore extensions we integrate to support binding of template parameters at the metamodel level[3]. A templateable element may own a set of *TemplateBinding* elements. A TemplateBinding is a relationship describing that the definition of the templateable element relies on the definition of

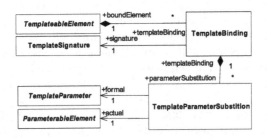

Fig. 11. Ecore Extensions for Template Parameters Binding

---

[3] Binding at the model level is not yet supported by the prototype, and requires further investigations.

another templateable element, and binds its formal parameters. The Template-Binding relationship references the template signature of the target template. It owns a set of *TemplateParameterSubstitution*, where each substitution relates a TemplateParameter (a formal parameter of the signature) to a ParameterableElement (the actual value bound to the formal parameter).

5   Conclusion

MOF does not provide standard mechanisms for identifying and fixing the semantic variation points of a metamodel, and works related to this issue do not provide satisfactory solutions. We have proposed a solution based on template definitions. We have shown how templateable metamodels could help us to explicitly and intuitively identify and fix semantic variation points, where a given point can be identified by a template parameter definition, and fixed by a parameter binding. Using the UML 2 syntax, we have illustrated the use of these mechanisms with the definition of a parameterized version of the UML 2 state machine metamodel. To show how templates could be supported by a metamodeling environment, we have also described a prototype version of an Eclipse plugin we are currently developing. For the implementation part of this work, we have mainly focused on how the Ecore metamodel could be extended to support template definitions and template binding. However, we have not discussed yet how templateable metamodels and the underlying tool support could be integrated in traditional model driven tool chains.

In the ideal case, the OMG would recognize the need for templated metamodels, and would submit a new Request For Proposal for a major revision of MOF. "Template support" would be an explicit requirement of this request for proposal. However, even in this ideal case, such standardized mechanisms would not be available before several years. As we (and readers?) are of course convinced by the usefulness of templates in metamodeling, we adopt a pragmatic position while waiting for a potential standardization. The implementation we have described in section 4 is the first step of the solution. The second one is to provide a plug-in used as an additional layer over traditional Ecore model driven tool chains. Our idea is that a traditional Ecore metamodel (i.e. without template parameters and binding) can be easily generated from a templated metamodel where parameters are bound. Indeed, Bertrand Meyer has already demonstrated in [9] that everything that can be be expressed using genericity and templates can also be expressed in some way with inheritance mechanisms. In that perspective it would be useful to study the impact to Ecore in terms of the memory and efficiency cost of our extensions.

Template support could be used as a useful tool for reasoning about models. The identification of semantic variation points is the benefit we have focused on, but the works described in section 3.1 have also identified other benefits (metamodel composition, metamodeling design patterns,etc.). Then, the model transformation rules we are developing could be applied, so that bound parameters of a templated metamodel would be actually replaced by concrete values in the resulting metamodel, using generalization relationships where needed to cope with semantic variations and specializations.

References

1. Budinsky, F., Steinberg, D., Merks, E., Ellersick, R., Grose, T.J.: Eclipse Modeling Framework. Addison-Wesley, London, UK (2003)
2. Chauvel, F., Jezequel, J.M.: Code generation from UML models with semantic variation points. In: Briand, L.C., Williams, C. (eds.) MoDELS 2005. LNCS, vol. 3713, Springer, Heidelberg (2005)
3. Clark, T., Evans, A., Kent, S.: Engineering Modelling Languages: A Precise Meta-modelling Approach. In: FASE, Fundamental Approaches to Software Engineering: 5th International Conference, Grenoble, France (2002)
4. Clark, T., Evans, A., Sammut, P., Willans, J.: An eXecutable Metamodeling Facility for Domain Specific Language Design. In: 4th OOPSLA Workshop on Domain-Specific Modeling, DSM, Vancouver, Canada (2004)
5. D'Souza, D.F., Wills, A.C.: Objects, components, and frameworks with UML: the catalysis approach. Addison-Wesley Longman Publishing Co., Inc, Boston, MA, USA (1999)
6. Emerson, M., Sztipanovits, J.: Techniques for metamodel composition. In: OOPSLA, 6th Workshop on Domain-Specific Modeling, Portland, Oregon, USA (2006)
7. Fleurey, F., Drey, Z., Vojtisek, D., Faucher, C.: Kermeta Language Reference Manual
8. Gamma, E., Helm, R., Johnson, R., Vlissides, J.: Design patterns: Abstraction and reuse of object-oriented design. In: Nierstrasz, O. (ed.) ECOOP 1993. LNCS, vol. 707, pp. 406–431. Springer, Heidelberg (1993)
9. Meyer, B.: Genericity versus inheritance. In: OOPSLA 86 Conference Proceedings, Portland, Oregon, USA (1986)
10. Niu, J., Atlee, J.M., Day, N.A.: Template Semantics for Model-Based Notations. In: IEEE Transactions on Software Engineering, pages vol. 29(10), pp. 866–882 (2003)
11. OMG. MDA Guide Version 1.0.1 (2003)
12. OMG. Meta Object Facility (MOF) 2.0 Core Specification (2004)
13. OMG. Unified Modeling Language: Infrastructure (2005)
14. OMG. Unified Modeling Language: Superstructure (2005)
15. Zito, A., Diskin, Z., Dingel, J.: Package merge in uml 2: Practice vs. theory? Model Driven Engineering Languages and Systems, pp. 185–199 (2006)

Execution of Aspect Oriented UML Models*

Lidia Fuentes and Pablo Sánchez

Dpto. de Lenguajes y Ciencias de la Computación
University of Málaga, Málaga, Spain
{lff,pablo}@lcc.uma.es

Abstract. The creation of precise, complete, platform independent models, whose implementation code can be fully generated for different target platforms, is often considered a key factor in Model-Driven Architecture (MDA). The execution of UML models is already a reality, mainly due to the adoption of the *Action Semantics*. However, UML and its action language are object-oriented based and certain concerns, called crosscutting concerns (e.g., encryption), can not be adequately encapsulated in single design modules. Such concerns result in scattered and tangled representations, which hinder system development, maintenance and evolution as well as the reusability of individual design modules. Aspect-Oriented Software Development (AOSD) has proven in recent years to be a useful technology for alleviating these shortcomings of object-orientation. This paper presents an extension to current Executable UML practice for the construction and execution of Aspect-Oriented UML models.

1 Introduction

The possibility of constructing models with a precise, complete and platform-independent behaviour specification, which even allows generation of 100% of the application code for several target platforms, has been considered as a crucial factor for the success of MDA [1–3]. The benefits of this approach go beyond simply reducing or skipping the coding stage. This kind of executable model helps to ensure platform independence, avoids obsolescence (programming languages may change, but models would stay), and, more importantly, allows verification of the models by means of its execution. Hence, inaccuracies inherent in a design can then be detected during the model execution, before moving on to implementation. Resolving such inaccuracies at design time is cheaper, faster and more desirable than carrying out necessary code modifications later on-the fly.

The execution of UML models, thanks to the adoption of an action language, is already a reality and several tools (Rhapsody, TAU G2, Nucleus BridgePoint or Kennedy Carter iUML) exist with such capabilities. However, UML and its action language are Object-Oriented, and consequently, some concerns, such as

---

* This work has been supported by MCYT Project TIN2005-09405-C02-01 and EC Grants IST-2-004349-NOE and the AMPLE IST-033710.

D.H. Akehurst, R. Vogel, and R.F. Paige (Eds.): ECMDA-FA 2007, LNCS 4530, pp. 83–98, 2007.

synchronisation, scheduling, persistence or encryption, cannot be adequately encapsulated into single design modules (i.e., classes), crosscutting application design modules [4]. This hampers model development, maintenance and evolution and at the same time it decreases the reusability of individual elements.

Aspect-Oriented Software Development (AOSD) has proven in recent years to be an appropriate technology for encapsulating crosscutting concerns in special units, named aspects, and providing mechanisms to compose them with the software modules they crosscut. This improves software system modularisation, and consequently, the maintenance, evolution and reusability of individual elements is easier [5].

The purpose of this work is to extend executable UML principles in order to support aspect-orientation. Our aim is twofold: (1) To improve the current modularisation of UML executable models; and (2) To bring the benefits of executable models to the Aspect-Oriented community. In order to achieve this goal, this paper presents two elements: (1) A UML 2.0 Profile for precise aspect-oriented behaviour modelling, which extends the Action Semantics when needed; and (2) A model weaver for aspect-oriented models that conforms the previous Profile. This *weaver* is required in order to be able to execute aspect-oriented models.

An Online Book Store System (OBS), taken from the existing literature [1] about executable modeling, has been used as an example to illustrate our approach throughout this paper. It has been refactored with aspects when required.

Following this introduction, the paper is structured as follows: Section 2 provides some background on Aspect-Oriented Software Development. Section 3 gives an overview of the approach. Section 4 presents the Online Book Store System. Section 5 outlines the principles for executing UML models. Section 6 describes the UML 2.0 Profile for AO executable modelling. Section 7 contains the description of a static and a dynamic model weaver. Section 8 focuses on the current tool support for our approach and the experiments carried out. Section 9 comments on related work, and finally, Section 10 outlines conclusions and future work.

2   Aspect-Oriented Software Development

Aspect-Oriented Software Development aims to overcome the shortcomings of traditional software decomposition techniques, such as Object-Oriented (OO) or Component-Based, regarding the encapsulation and composition of crosscutting concerns such as security, monitoring or persistence.

Aspect-orientation (AO) improves the separation of concerns providing the mechanisms for encapsulating each crosscutting concern appropriately in a single module, called *aspect*, and then specifying how this aspect must be composed with the software modules it crosscuts. AO principles are described below, together with the aspect-oriented terminology, shown in bold:

1. Software **base modules** (e.g., objects or components) do not contain any reference or code related to crosscutting concerns (e.g., persistence).

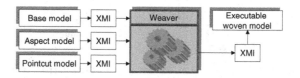

Fig. 1. Aspect-Oriented Executable UML Scenario

2. Crosscutting concerns are encapsulated in special modules, named **aspects**. Aspects contain special methods, called **advices**, which expose the crosscutting concern functionality.
3. Each software module permits the injection of crosscutting concerns at specific points, called **joinpoints**, of their execution flows (e.g., after they have executed a method).
4. Special composition rules, named **pointcuts**, specify those joinpoints of software modules where crosscutting concerns must be injected (e.g., after the execution of all the methods called foo()).
5. It is the task of each AO language or platform to compose the whole system, injecting the crosscutting concerns on the joinpoints according to the pointcuts. This composition process, known as **weaving**, can be performed at compile time (called *static weaving*) or at load or even runtime (called *dynamic weaving*). In the latter case, the weaver may allow us to add and remove aspects at runtime.

3   Our Approach

This section contains a general overview of our approach. Our goal is to obtain AO models that can be executed. It is also our intention to use well-known and widely used standards whenever possible, in order to obtain vendor-independent solutions and avoid the need for learning new notations and languages. Hence, UML is the most widely known and used software modelling language, there is a wide range of tools available that support it and the execution of UML models is already a reality.

In this paper we define a process for the construction of AO UML executable models. This process relies on the existence of two elements: (1) a UML 2.0 Profile for the specification of AO executable models, which is called AOEM (Aspect-Oriented Executable Modelling); and (2) a model weaver for AO models that conforms to the AOEM profile. Using both elements, such a process is defined (See Figure 1) as follows:

1. First of all, a common UML executable model is constructed for modelling all the non-crosscutting concerns. The *base model* is obtained.
2. Crosscutting concerns, including their precise and complete behaviour, are modelled as aspects using the AOEM Profile. This produces the *aspect model*.
3. The way in which crosscutting concerns must be composed with the concerns they crosscut is specified by means of a *pointcut model*. The rules for modelling pointcuts are also part of the AOEM Profile.

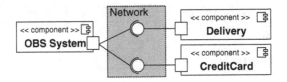

Fig. 2. Excerpt of the OnLine Book Store System architecture

4. The base and aspect models are composed together automatically, which produces the *woven model*. This woven model is a common UML executable model.
5. Finally, to execute the complete AO model, the woven model is imported into a UML tool with executing capabilities (e.g., Rhapsody).

To perform the weaving and to export/import models from/into UML tools, the UML models must be available in a standard and interoperable format. This is possible nowadays using the XMI (XML Metadata Interchange) standard for serialising UML models in XML documents. The model weaver presented in this paper takes as input the XMI representations of the base, aspect and pointcut models and produces an XMI representation of a model of the woven system as output. The steps of this process are illustrated in the following sections using the OBS example.

4   The Online Book Store System

An Online Book Store System(OBS), taken from the executable modeling literature [1], is used as an example to illustrate our approach. The Online Book Store has to provide a way for customers to place orders for books. From the set of use cases presented in [1], we focus in this paper on the ordering of books, which is specified as follows:

1. A customer starts a new order by selecting a book and the required quantity.
2. The customer can continue adding more books to the order.
3. Once the customer is satisfied with his selections, the order goes to the check out stage. A message is sent to the credit card company to process the payment.
4. If the payment is approved, a shipping order is created. A message is sent to the delivery company to inform that a new order is ready.

Additionally, two global requirements must be observed:(1) Each time an order changes, it must be persisted; (2) All the network communications have to be secure. Persistence and Encryption are easily identified as crosscutting concerns in the system.

Figure 2 shows an excerpt of the OBS system architecture, which is comprised of several components: the OBS System component, which is responsible for the OBS core functionality; and the external Credit Card and Delivery services. The communication between the OBS System and the external services is performed through a public network, and therefore, the messages sent over it must be encrypted.

Our intention is to construct an AO executable model of the OBS system, where Persistence and Encryption are well-modularised as aspects, without hampering system maintenance, evolution or reusability.

5 Executable UML Models

In order to execute a model, two basic elements are required: (1) an *actions language*, which contains the atomic platform-independent actions the models can carry out; and (2) an *operational semantics*, which specifies how models and the actions must be interpreted. Both elements in the UML standard are described below.

5.1 Operational Semantics

The operational semantics of UML is still in the process of standardisation. Nevertheless, several tools (e.g., Rhapsody, TAU G2 or Kennedy Carter iUML) implementing non-standard operational semantics for UML models already exist. The corresponding tool vendors are leading the creation of the official OMG standard, thus it is reasonable to suppose that it will be similar to current versions.

Fortunately, as the ideas behind them are quite similar it can be assumed that the final adopted standard will also be similar to the current practice. The process of constructing a UML executable model using these tools can be generalised and summarised as follows: Firstly, the system is decomposed into a set of components. Then, the structure of each component is detailed by means of class diagrams. The behaviour of each class is specified using a protocol state machine, whose transitions and states may have associated procedures (sets of actions), which model behaviours. Procedures are specified using an action language.

The OBS System component (see Figure 2) is modelled using these principles as follows: First of all, a class diagram (Figure 3 (left)) detailing component internals is constructed. Basically, the OBS System contains a System class to register/deregister users and to enter the application; at least one Book; some Customer data and Clerks to pack the orders. A ShoppingCart is used to store customers orders while they navigate the system.

Subsequently, the behaviour of each class is specified by means of a state machine. Figure 3 (right) shows the state machine for the ShoppingCart class. The shopping cart is initially empty, until an event for adding a book arrives. Subsequently, it shifts to the ItemsAdded state, where more events for adding a book can be received. When the customer performs a checkOut operation, the ItemsAdded state is left, and the ShoppingCart enters an orthogonal state with two concurrent substates: WaitingForDeliveryConfirmation and WaitingForCreditConfirmation. If the actions carried out in both finish successfully, a confirmation message is sent to the customer, otherwise, he/she is informed of the error.

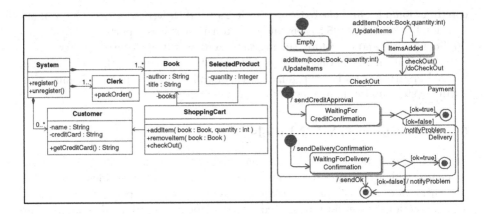

Fig. 3. Class diagram for the OBS System internals (left) Protocol State Machine for the ShoppingCart class

Table 1. UML actions used to model the OBS example

ReadSelf	Returns a reference to the object where it is executed
CreateLinkObject	Creates an association class between two objects
WriteStructuralFeature	Writes a value in an attribute of an object
CallBehavior	Invokes a procedure (another activity diagram)
CallOperation	Invokes an object method
SendSignal	Sends a signal to a target object passed as parameter

5.2   The Action Semantics

As commented before, the precise behaviour of each procedure is specified by means of an action language. UML defines, as part of the standard, its own action language. It defines operations that support the manipulation of objects and the logical constructs for the specification of algorithms. The specific set of actions used in this paper are explained in Table 1.

Intentionally, the UML action language does not enforce any notation for drawing actions. Thus, each tool defines its own notation. To avoid the use of notations that work specifically for proprietary tools, we have developed a UML Profile, following the ideas presented in [6]. It is compatible with any UML tool supporting activity diagrams and abstract actions, which is a common case. This Profile works as follows: Procedures are represented by means of UML activity diagrams. Actions are nodes of activity diagrams. An action is depicted using the general action symbol (a round cornered rectangle) stereotyped with its name (e.g., ≪ReadSelf≫). Inputs and outputs are depicted as pins. Additionally, each

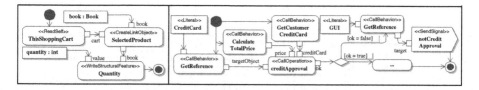

Fig. 4. Procedures for: addItem (left) doCheckOut (right)

specific action must have the same number of input/output pins as specified in the standard, which is ensured by means of OCL constraints.

Figure 4 (left) shows the behaviour of the ShoppingCart object after receiving an addItem event, modelled according to the UML Action language. This procedure has two parameters, the selected book and the required quantity. The procedure creates a new association link object of the SelectedProduct association class (see Figure 3 (left)), between the ShoppingCart that hosts the behaviour (returned by the ReadSelf action), and the selected book. The required quantity is finally written in the corresponding attribute (structural feature) of the created link object.

Figure 4 (right) illustrates the doCheckOut behaviour, which is executed after a ShoppingCart object receives a checkOut event. In this case, the object calculates the total price of the order, recovers customer credit card data, and obtains a reference to the CreditCard service. With these parameters, it requests a creditApproval from the CreditCard service. If the service confirms the transaction, the check out process continues; if the transaction is not approved, a message communicating the error is shown to the user. In this latter case, we used a behaviour defined by ourselves (e.g., a subroutine) called GetReference, which serves to get references to relevant components of the application, such as the GUI (Graphical User Interface) or the CreditCard and Delivery external services.

The procedures modelled in Figure 4 are not complete as they do not observe Persistence and Encryption, which are added using aspects in the next section.

6   Aspect-Oriented Modelling

This section describes how the OBS crosscutting concerns are added to the OBS model as aspects, achieving better modularisation. To support the construction of AO executable models, this paper presents the AOEM (Aspect-Oriented Executable Modeling) UML 2.0 Profile. This is integrated with the principles of Executable UML and its action language.

In agreement with [7], the AOEM Profile is specified through the definition of three elements: (1) The joinpoint model; (2) How aspects and their associated elements, such as advices, are modelled; and (3) The modelling of the rules, i.e., the pointcuts, that inject aspects into the modules they crosscut. Each of these elements is described in the following subsections.

Table 2. Aspect-oriented actions

GetMessName	Returns the name of the intercepted message
GetMessArgs	Returns an ordered collection with the message arguments
GetTarget	Returns a reference to the target of the message
GetSource	Returns a reference to the source of the message
Proceed	Executes the intercepted behaviour

6.1   Joinpoint Model

In an AO approach, the joinpoint model defines the points of the base modules where aspects (crosscutting concerns) can be injected. The AOEM Profile only allows observable execution points of classes/components to be intercepted: (1) object creation and destruction; (2) the sending and receiving of a message/method; (3) the throwing of an event; and (4) the raising of an exception. This non-invasive joinpoint model is suitable for use with black-box software modules, such as third-party components or legacy systems. Aspect advices can be executed *before, after* or *around* (in substitution of) the execution of the intercepted joinpoints. This paper will focus on the joinpoints related to the sending and receiving of a message, as the other cases, at modelling level, can be considered special cases of sending/receiving joinpoints (e.g., the raising of an exception can be handled as the sending of a special message).

6.2   Aspect Modelling

An aspect is modelled as a common class with special operations which model *advices*. Advices differ from common operations in that they are never invoked explicitly and they are executed by the AO weaver without the knowledge of the base class designer. For this reason, advices do not have parameters. Consequently, each aspect-orientated language has to provide mechanisms to allow advices to retrieve the information related to the intercepted joinpoint (e.g., the arguments of a message) that they might need. A subset of the AO actions provided by the AOEM Profile to access the joinpoint context is shown in Table 2.

Thus, advices are modelled as activity diagrams (common procedures) without input objects. They can have one or more output pins, in order to be able to modify values of the intercepted object flow. For instance, if an advice is executed before a message is sent, this could modify the value of message arguments. The update values would be placed as output values of the activity diagram representing the advice. In the particular case of advices executed *around* a joinpoint, the advice and the intercepted message should have the same number and kind of output objects.

To introduce Persistence and Encryption into the OBS system, two aspects are created. They are associated with the PersistentStore and Encrypter common classes. These classes have methods to persist objects and handle encrypted communications, respectively. On the joinpoints, the task of the advices is to

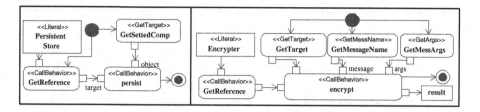

Fig. 5. Advices for: Persistence (left) Encryption (right)

collect the required data to invoke the appropriate PersistentStore or Encrypter methods.

Figure 5 (left) shows the advice for persistence. It recovers a reference to the object to be persisted and calls the persist(object) method of the PersistentStore class with this data. Figure 5 (right) depicts the advice for encryption. It relies on the Object[] encrypt(target:Object, method:String, arg:Object[]) method of the Encrypter. This method sends an encrypted request to the target object for executing method with arg as arguments. It returns the collection of (decrypted) values resulting from executing the method. Thus, the task of the encryption advice (Figure 5 (right)) is to extract from the intercepted joinpoint (the sending of a message) the target object, the message name and the arguments of the message, and, with these values, to invoke the encrypt method of the Encrypter class. The advice returns the values (decrypted) which result from executing the method.

6.3 Pointcut Modelling

Finally, to complete our aspect-oriented model, we need to specify the rules, pointcuts in AO terms, that establish where Persistence and Encryption must be injected. A pointcut expression is a pattern that matches several join points and associates them with one or more aspect advices. At modeling level, the common practice for specifying pointcuts is to use UML diagrams with wildcards [7, 8]. As we are interested in intercepting interactions between objects (message sending/receiving), sequence diagrams are selected because they are the main element in UML used to represent object interactions.

Using the AOEM Profile, a pointcut is expressed by means of a sequence diagram, stereotyped as «pointcut». This stereotype has a tagged value called advice: an ordered collection of aspect advices, which will be executed on the joinpoints selected by the pointcut.

The specific message inside the sequence diagram that must be intercepted is stereotyped as «joinpoint». This stereotype has two tagged values: (1)point, which indicates whether the joinpoint is either the sending (SEND) or the reception (RECEIVE) of the message; and (2) time, which specifies when the advice must be executed in relation to the joinpoint (BEFORE, AFTER, AROUND). Wildcards are allowed in class and method names: "*" represents any sequence of characters and ".." any sequence of arguments.

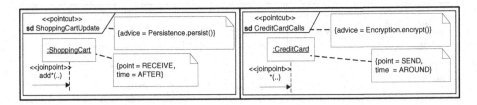

Fig. 6. Pointcuts for: Persistence (left) Encryption (right)

The pointcuts for adding persistence to the ShoppingCart objects and the encryption of all the messages sent to the CreditCard service are shown in Figure 6. Figure 6 (left) indicates the persist advice must be executed after the reception (i.e. after the method execution) of any message starting with "add" and with any number and kind of arguments. This message can come from any source, as this is not specified. Figure 6 (right) specifies that around sending any message ("*(..)" wildcard combination) from any source (not specified) to the CreditCard service, the encrypt advice must be executed.

In addition, a pointcut may express some constraints (e.g. the joinpoint has to be in a specific execution flow or a specific state) that must be satisfied in order to execute the associated advices. More powerful and complex pointcuts than those shown in Figure 6 can be expressed in the AOEM Profile. However, they are not included in this paper in order to avoid overwhelming the reader with too many AO details[1].

7   A Weaver for Executable Models

Finally, before executing the model, aspect behaviour must be added to the modules they crosscut according to the pointcut specifications, i.e. the *weaving* process has to be executed. The ultimate behaviour of common classes and aspects is expressed by means of activity diagrams. Therefore, the problem of weaving executable models can be reduced to the problem of weaving activity diagrams. This section describes a static weaver for AO models that conforms to the AOEM Profile. A dynamic weaving strategy is briefly outlined.

7.1   Static Weaving

The static weaver is responsible for adding the advice behaviours into the places (joinpoints) indicated by the pointcut specifications. This is achieved in two phases: joinpoint selection and aspect injection.

First of all, the *joinpoint selector* searches all the joinpoints that are selected by the pointcuts. Each of them is marked as ≪selected joinpoint≫. This stereotype has as tagged values the advice that must be added and the advice execution

---

[1] Interested readers can find further information of the AOEM Profile in http://www.lcc.uma.es/~pablo/ECMDA07

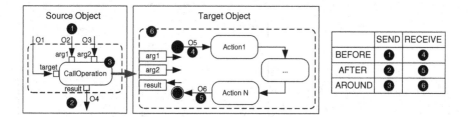

Fig. 7. Advice injection places

time. These data will be used later by the aspect injector. As the model weaver takes as input the XMI representation (an XML document) of the models, it allows us to use XPath expressions [9] to search the selected joinpoints. An XPath expression specifies a pattern that matches several XML tags within an XML document. Hence, the pattern specified by a pointcut is automatically transformed by the model weaver (using a model to text transformation) into a set of XPath expressions, which select all the XML tags corresponding to joinpoints selected by such pointcut.

The second step is to inject the aspect advices into the selected joinpoints (call actions and activities representing procedures in our particular case). Depending on the kind of joinpoint and the execution time of the advice, it can be injected into six different places, as illustrated in Figure 7. For instance, if an advice has to be executed BEFORE SEND a method, it is added between the call action and the actions that precede it (Figure 7, label 1). If it has to be executed AROUND SEND or AROUND RECEIVE, the corresponding call action (Figure 7, label 3) or activity (Figure 7, label 6), respectively, are substituted by the advice.

Aspect advices are injected as structured activities inside the procedures they crosscut (See Figure 8, grey background). Each structured activity has the same behaviour as the advice it represents. The AO actions of the original advice are appropriately transformed to common UML actions in the structured activity. The advice injection plus action transformation requires updating the object and control flows of the original procedures in order to ensure the correctness of the composition. How this is performed is outlined using the injection of the persist and encrypt advices (Figure 5) into the base OBS model as an example.

Figure 8 (left) shows the injection of the persist advice into the addItem procedure (Figure 4 (left)). It is injected just before the final node of the addItem procedure (an AFTER RECEIVE case (Figure 7, label 5)). The original control flow that went from the WriteQuantity action to the final node is removed; and the new control flows C1 and C2 are created. The GetTarget action of the original advice ((Figure 5 (left))) is replaced by a ReadSelf action, because the advice is injected into the target object.

The injection of the encrypt advice around the doCheckOut procedure (Figure 4 (right)) is illustrated in Figure 8 (right). As it is an AROUND SEND case (Figure 7, label 3), the original call action is substituted by an structued activity representing the encrypt advice. An input parameter in such activity is created

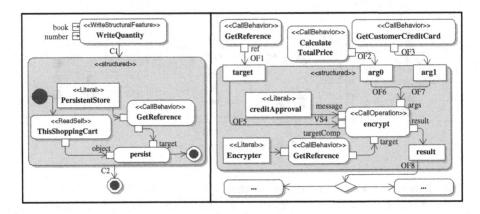

Fig. 8. addItem (left) and doCheckOut (right) procedures after weaving

by each argument of the substituted call action (arg0 and arg1). An additional input parameter (target) is also introduced to collect the target object of the call action. An output parameter (result) holds the return value of the substituted call action. In order to appropriately link adequately the structured activity with the preceding and succeeding actions, the object flows OF1, OF2, OF3 and OF8 are generated. OF1, OF2 and OF3 supply the input parameters and the target object to the structured activity input objects. OF8 passes the advice return value to the following actions. The AO actions of the original encrypt advice (Figure 4 (right)) are transformed as follows: (1) GetArgs originates the object flows OF6 and OF7; (2)GetMessName produces the literal creditApproval which feeds the message value pin; and (3) the GetTarget action gives rise to the object flow OF5.

We would like to point out that the transformation of AO actions, the advice injection and the object/control flows updating involve many special cases which are not mentioned here for the sake of brevity and simplicity[2]. As output of the weaving process, a common UML model, with the crosscutting concerns added where indicated, is obtained. This model can be executed in currently available UML tools.

7.2 Dynamic Weaving

In the case of dynamic weaving, pointcuts can be added, removed or updated at runtime and, consequently, aspect advices are woven/unwoven at runtime, by a dynamic weaving platform (DWP).

In this case, it is not possible to know whether a join point will trigger an advice until just before its execution. For this reason, each potential joinpoint is not directly executed by objects. Instead, a call to the DWP is performed, requesting the execution of the joinpoint. Then, the DWP checks if any advice

---

[2] Interested readers can find further information of the AOEM model weaver in http://www.lcc.uma.es/~pablo/ECMDA07

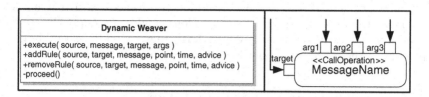

Fig. 9. Dynamic weaver interface (left) Call action problem (right)

has to be executed on such joinpoint. If it is so, the advice and the joinpoint are executed as it is specified in the pointcuts currently active.

The interface of the DWP is shown in Figure 9 (left). It has methods for loading/unloading pointcuts (addRule and removeRule, respectively). A pointcut is stored as a ((source,method,target,args),(advice,point,time)) tuple in the DWP. According to the joinpoint model of the AOEM Profile, each time an object needs to execute a call action, it will delegate such action to the DWP, using the execute(source, operation, target, args) method. Subsequently, the DWP searches for all the tuples (source,operation,target,args) matching with the current joinpoint. For each match found, the corresponding advice is executed at the specified point and time.

Before starting the execution of an AO model with dynamic weaving, the model must be preprocessed in order to prepare it, according to the following process:

1. The model of the DWP is added to the base model. The DWP must be a common UML executable model.
2. All potential joinpoints (e.g., the calls to methods) are replaced by requests to the execute method of the DWP.
3. The information specified in the pointcuts is loaded into the DWP.
4. The aspect model is added to the base model. The AO actions of the advices are transformed into common UML actions. All the information in the joinpoint context is stored in the DWP, thus each AO action (e.g., GetSource) is substituted by actions that read these values from the DWP. In the case of the proceed action, this is substituted by a call to the DWP.Proceed method, which executes the original call action.

With the current UML Action language, the execution of the delegated call action by the DWP is limited. This issue is illustrated in Figure 9 (right). The target object name and the method arguments are provided to the call action at runtime, but the message name and the number of input pins must be statically specified at modeling time (i.e. hard-coded in the action), so the complete call action can not be composed at runtime. An ad-hoc solution would be to hard-code all possible method calls to in the DWP during the preprocessing phase, but this has an obvious shortcoming related to scalability. This issue could be easily resolved using reflection mechanisms, not currently supported by the UML Action language. However, it is not complicated technically to implement the set of reflective actions we need. As UML models are executed by parsing XML documents, the implementation of these actions would only imply changing the appropriate values in the corresponding XML tags. A UML execution engine supporting some reflective actions is part of our ongoing work.

8   Tool Support and Experimentation

This section describes the experiments carried out to test our approach and the tools required to reproduce our experiments. When selecting tools, the best choice would be to find one that supports UML executable modeling and full XMI import/export capabilities. Unfortunately, at the present time there is no tool in existence which satisfies both requirements at the same time. The tools that have full XMI import/export facilities, do not simulate UML models; and the UML tools that are able to simulate models, do not export the models to XMI fully. Thus, we had to use different tools to test this approach.

UML modeling was done using the UML2 plugin for Eclipse[3], which is the most complete implementation of the UML 2.0 metamodel, including the whole UML Action language. It also offers full XMI export/import capabilities. MagicDraw[4] was used to draw the UML diagrams.

The implementation of the static weaver is tedious but simple, since we only have to manipulate XMI files (XML trees) following the rules of section 7. This can be implemented in any language with XML facilities. We have developed an small prototype, as proof of concept, of the static weaver using Java and DOM.

Finally, the woven model is simulated. There is no simulation tool that supports fully XMI importing capabilities. Several tools, such as Rhapsody or TAU, claim to offer such import/export capabilities, but the exportation is often partial, and most of the information regarding UML actions is often lost. In the same way, these tools are not able to import the information regarding to actions, when this is stored in an XMI file. Therefore, the solution adopted was to import the model "manually" into a simulation tool in order to check the correctness of the generated woven models. Telelogic Rhapsody was the tool selected for simulation.

It is evident that there is a clear lack of effective and seamless tool support for our approach. Consequently we are now developing a UML execution engine, which will be able to execute the UML Action language from its XMI 2.0 representation. In addition, this tool will have some reflective properties, making the development of dynamic weavers easier.

9   Related Work

There is some preliminary work about AO and executable modelling in the literature. It is described in this section.

---

[3] http://www.eclipse.org/uml2/

[4] http://www.magicdraw.org

Sunyé et al. [10] presented a framework for modeling aspect-oriented applications. It serves to construct aspect-oriented executable models, but the weaving is postponed until the implementation phase and thus, the execution of the complete (woven) model, including aspects, is not possible at modeling time.

Theme/UML [11] is an extension of UML for AO modelling. Theme/UML supports all the UML 2.0 diagrams. Therefore, using Theme/UML we should be able to weave UML executable models. However, although Theme/UML specifies the weaving semantics of the approach, until now the weaving must be done manually, since no tool support is available. Additionally, Theme/UML is not compatible with current UML tools, and a Theme/UML tool is still not available[5]. We tried to implement a Theme/UML weaver, but without fruitful results since it is quite complex and it is not precisely defined beyond sequence and class diagrams.

Cottenier et al. [12] present an idea very similar to this paper, but based on the Telelogic TAU G2 implementation of the Executable UML principles. They defined an AO Profile that extends the Telelogic SDL metamodel. SDL is not compatible at all with the current UML Action language and introduces some proprietary features that obviously can not be exported adequately to XMI. The weaver is implemented as a Telelogic TAU G2 add-in [12], therefore it is not portable and tool-independent. Additionally, the weaving process is not clearly described in their work.

Additionally, none of the previous work considers dynamic weavers. Both weavers can be used with any UML tool able to import/export UML models to XMI, avoiding the necessity to purchase expensive proprietary tools.

10   Conclusions and Future Work

This paper has described how to construct and execute AO models, relying on two elements, presented by this work: a UML 2.0 Profile, called AOEM, which supports precise modeling of aspect behaviour, and two AO model weavers. Both weavers produce a common UML executable model as a result. This model can be simulated using currently available tools. As the models are aspect-oriented, the modularisation of crosscutting concerns is improved, which makes system maintenance, development and evolution easier.

As this woven model, in the static weaving case, is a common UML executable model, 100% of code can be automatically generated (this feature is currently supported by some tools, such as Rhapsody and TAU G2). As the generated code is non aspect-oriented, it allows development teams to use AO at modeling level without AO support from the target programming language. In the dynamic weaving case, the execution is more interactive, as the aspect execution can be more clearly visualised. Different alternatives can be tested by simply updating pointcuts at runtime, without requiring to re-weave the model.

Readers familiar with AO may miss some AO features in the AOEM Profile, such as cflow, withincode constraints for pointcuts, inter type declarations

---

[5] See http://www.thethemeapproach.com/downloads.html

or mechanisms to deal with aspect-interaction, like weaving precedence rules. These features are contained in the AOME Profile, but are left out of this paper for the sake of brevity and in order to avoid overwhelming non AO readers with a lot of new concepts and terminology. However, as future work we intend to replace the current pointcut specification by Jointpoint Designation Diagrams (JPDD's) [8], which allow the specification of more expressive pointcuts. We will also investigate more flexible ways of accessing joinpoint context.

Additionally, the current implementation of the static weaving has some limitations due to the technology employed: Java, DOM and XPath. These technologies imply the direct manipulation of XMI files, which lead to cumbersome and difficult to maintain implementations. Using the same concepts and ideas as presented in this paper, we are developing a new version of the static model weaver using model transformations implemented in the ATL[6] language.

References

1. Mellor, S., Balcer, M.: Executable UML: A Foundation for Model Driven Architecture. Addison-Wesley, London, UK (2002)
2. Raistrick, C., et al.: Model Driven Architecture with Executable UML. Cambridge University Press, Cambridge (2004)
3. Starr, L.: Executable UML: The Models Are the Code. Model Integration Llc (2001)
4. Tarr, P., et al.: N degrees of separation: Multi-dimensional separation of concerns. In: Filman, R.E., et al. (ed.) Aspect-Oriented Software Development, pp. 37–61. Addison-Wesley, London, UK (2004)
5. Parnas, D.L.: On the criteria to be used in decomposing systems into modules. Communications of the ACM 15(12), 1053–1058 (1972)
6. Bock, C.: UML 2 Activity and Action Models. Journal of Object Technology 2(4), 43–53 (2003)
7. Fuentes, L., Sánchez, P.: Elaborating UML 2.0 Profiles for AO Design. In: 8th Workshop on AOM, 5th AOSD Conference (2006)
8. Stein, D., Hanenberg, S., Unland, R.: Expressing different conceptual models of join point selections in aspect-oriented design. In: Proc. of the 5th AOSD (2006)
9. World Wide Web Consortium (W3C): XML Path Language (XPath) Version 1.0 (1999), http://www.w3.org/TR/xpath.
10. Sunyé, G. et al.: Using uml action semantics for executable modeling and beyond. In: Proc. of the 13th CAiSE (2001)
11. Clarke, S., Baniassad, E.: Aspect-Oriented Analysis and Design: The Theme Approach. Addison-Wesley, London, UK (2005)
12. Cottenier, T., van den Berg, A., Elrad, T.: Motorola weavr: Model weaving in a large industrial context. In: Proceedings of the 6th AOSD Industry Track. (2007) Available at http://www.iit.edu/c̄oncur/weavr/papers/

---

[6] http://www.eclipse.org/m2m/atl/

An Algebraic View on the Semantics of Model Composition

Christoph Herrmann, Holger Krahn, Bernhard Rumpe, Martin Schindler,
and Steven Völkel

Institute for Software Systems Engineering, Braunschweig University of Technology,
Mühlenpfordtstraße 23
38106 Braunschweig, Germany
{herrmann,krahn,rumpe,m.schindler,voelkel}@sse.cs.tu-bs.de

Abstract. Due to the increased complexity of software development projects more and more systems are described by models. The sheer size makes it impractical to describe these systems by a single model. Instead many models are developed that provide several complementary views on the system to be developed. This however leads to a need for compositional models. This paper describes a foundational theory of model composition in form of an algebra to explicitly clarify different variants and uses of composition, their interplay with the semantics of the involved models and their composition operators.

Keywords: Model composition, Model merging, Semantics.

1 Model Composition

The complexity of software products and therefore of their development projects is steadily increasing. To handle this complexity models are used as an intermediate result to raise the level of abstraction, to enhance the understanding, and to simplify analysis and prediction of properties of the system under development. Nowadays modeling languages like the UML (Unified Modeling Language) and an increasing number of DSLs (Domain Specific Languages) are used for planning, architecting, developing, coding, deploying, and documentation purposes. Based on these languages a number of development approaches like OMG's Model Driven Architecture can be classified as "Model Driven Engineering" (MDE).

In any complex software system, mastering complexity means using a variety of semantically and syntactically precise [1,2] models to describe different aspects and views of the software system. Therefore it is essential to understand how these different models fit together and complement each other. For an integrated understanding, a clear definition of what composition of models means is necessary.

Model composition has impacts on at least three different levels:

- Syntactic level: the way the composition between models can explicitly be expressed as a new model in an appropriate modeling language.

D.H. Akehurst, R. Vogel, and R.F. Paige (Eds.): ECMDA-FA 2007, LNCS 4530, pp. 99–113, 2007.

- Semantic level: the meaning of the composed models as a unit in terms of semantics of the modeling languages involved.
- Methodic level: the integration of model composition techniques in software development processes and tools.

A clear explanation of a composition mechanism of models on each of these dimensions is necessary to facilitate a "compositional" use of models in development projects. E.g., for an integrated understanding of some models describing aspects of the same system it is not necessary to provide a syntactic composition operator that explicitly produces an integrated model. Instead it is essential to understand the meaning of "composition" using a semantic composition. For code generation purposes it is however often necessary to explicitly calculate the integrated model, because only from there it is possible to start the generator. This is a pity, because already in 1972 Parnas introduced modularity in his article [3] as an important requisite for independent understanding, development, and compilation – something we have achieved on code level, but not on model level so far. It therefore depends on the form of use which properties a model composition operator must have.

In contrast to concrete model composition techniques [4, 5, 6] we examine in this paper syntactic and specifically semantic properties of model composition as basis for a methodical discussion and therefore regard this paper as a first contribution to a wider discussion on compositionality of models.

The rest of the paper is structured as follows. Section 2 gives a compact recapitulation and introduction to our understanding of syntax and semantics of a modeling language. Section 3 describes the properties of model composition in algebraic terms. We derive requirements for well-defined model composition operators and give a first classification of possible operators. Section 4 describes related work, followed by a conclusion in Section 5.

2 Syntax and Semantics of Models

In software engineering we are basically concerned with graphical or textual languages to describe structure, behavior, or interaction of systems, interfaces etc. As these models shall usually be understood by tools, e.g., for code generation and test case definition there must be a clear definition of what the language concepts are. This is in sharp contrast to many other forms of models, where there is no formal and explicit definition of the modeling language used (see, e.g., architectural or medical models).

Formally, a modeling language M is a set of well-formed models. So a model $m \in M$ is syntactically well-formed, both by context-free syntax as well as conforming to all context-conditions. Each of these models gets a semantics by mapping it from the language to a well-known semantic domain [1, 7]. This principle is well understood in the field of programming languages, where each syntactic construct has a well defined meaning that describes its effects in terms of operational or denotational semantics.

Although standardization bodies have not yet been able to define a commonly accepted, formal semantics, e.g., for the UML as yet, we here assume such a semantic definition would be given. See [7] for a deeper discussion on semantic issues. To understand the meaning of composition, it is evident that the meaning / semantics of the involved models needs to be understood.

2.1 Semantic Domain and Mapping

Given a language M of models, the meaning of each element is usually given by explaining it in a well-known domain D, the semantic domain. This semantic domain describes which artifacts and concepts exist and must be well understood by both the language designer and the language users [7]. This principle is rather general, even so the details of the semantic domain as well as the form of representation vary. E.g., denotational as well as operational semantics can be subsumed under this form of approach using an abstract set of models resp. an abstract machine as semantic domain.

Examples for a semantic domain are the System Model [8], Abstract State Machines [9], or pure mathematics [2].

Given the modeling language M and the semantic domain D each model $m \in M$ must be mapped to D. As explained earlier, it is important to define the meaning (semantics) of models explicitly. So an explicit formal definition of the mapping is a function from M to D:

$$sm: M \rightarrow D \qquad (1)$$

Benefits of a formal mapping function are that we are able to reason about the mapping and thus, about the language and the instances itself.

2.2 Set-Valued Semantics

A general problem of the semantics definition of a model is that models should be useable in early phases of development. In early phases models are usually underspecified and somewhat abstract. Therefore, there is usually not a single system that realizes a model, but a larger set of realizations. Thus, the mapping of an underspecified diagram to program code or any other deterministic realization would result in either incomplete code or code that incorporates decisions not present in the model. These decisions done by the translation algorithm, however, are critical for the model understanding, as they may not intend the developers view. Currently many tools help themselves, by disallowing ambiguity and thus preventing underspecification. A mapping to code, therefore, for principal reasons cannot serve as a semantics definition. To adequately handle underspecification the semantics of languages like Spectrum [10] or Z [11] is described as a set of systems having the given properties instead of a single system [12]. Such specification oriented set-valued semantics allow us to describe and understand important properties of modeling languages. Thus we use set-valued semantics as a basis for further investigation into a model composition theory.

The basic idea is to map any model $m \in M$ to all systems which obey the constraints that the model imposes. Denoting the set of all systems with S the semantic domain is then the power set $D = \wp(S)$ and each instance $m \in M$ will be mapped by sm to the largest set of systems which fulfill the constraints.

$$sm: M \rightarrow \wp(S) \qquad (2)$$

We do not need to further investigate into the details of S, but understand that it captures the relevant properties of a system. These are usually structural properties (objects, their values and linkage) as well as behavioral and interaction properties (traces of interactions, etc.).

As an illustrative example for set-valued semantics covering underspecification consider a simple class diagram with one class "Person" having a String attribute "name". What do we know about the system described?

1. There is a class "Person"
2. All instances of the class "Person" and all instances of subclasses have an attribute "name" whose type is "String"
3. No more information can be inferred.

The real semantics of this model must be given as the set of all systems obeying 1 and 2. Usually these systems have other classes and possibly the class "Person" contains more attributes than "name", but in our set-valued semantics those systems still fulfill the constraints defined by the model. Furthermore, it is not given that there will ever be an instance of class Person at all. Instead the class Person may also be abstract.

This approach is called a "loose semantics" [10] and is very helpful in capturing underspecification. Today many developers and especially tools assume some kind of "completeness" of their models, which is quite conflicting with the possibility to compose models.

Set-valued semantics allows to state some important properties with respect to the semantic mapping sm:

- A model $m \in M$ is **consistent** exactly if $sm(m) \neq \varnothing$, which means that there is at least one system that obeys the instance's properties. Otherwise, there are some contradicting constraints in the model m itself.
- A model $m \in M$ does not contain information if $sm(m)=S$. Then any system can serve as an implementation.
- A model m_2 **refines** another model m_1 exactly if $sm(m_2) \subseteq sm(m_1)$. So, if we add more data to the model m_2, it further constraints the resulting set of systems, which therefore will become smaller.

The loose approach has an interesting aspect: the more we know, thus the more information is present in a model, the fewer implementations are possible. This is why m_2 has more information and thus refines m_1 exactly if $sm(m_2) \subseteq sm(m_1)$.

It is noteworthy that the "loose semantics" approach we use is loose on the behavioral as well as on the structural level. For existing behavioral elements, such as methods, their behavior may vary and additional structural elements (such as attributes, classes etc.) are possible.

Besides set-valued semantics for some forms of models and especially for executable languages an "initial" or a "minimal" semantics can be given. These forms of semantics correspond to the idea that there is a unique realization in the set mentioned above with minimalistic properties. Informally spoken, such a unique element can be characterized by assumptions like "everything explicitly defined is present, but nothing more". Class diagrams, e.g., lead to a canonical implementation through code generation and deterministic, completely defined state machines do have one single execution. Having both, a set-valued semantics for the specification of a system and an initial semantics, e.g., for test purposes or executable models, seems to be appropriate. For specification purposes, we concentrate on the set valued semantics.

3   An Algebraic View on Model Composition

When models are developed and composed, the developers as well as the tools always deal with their syntactic representation. But doing so, developers want to compose the meaning underlying these models. Thus, one goal of our algebraic theory is to clarify the relationships between composition on the syntactic and on the semantic level. Beyond that, another interesting issue consists in the question which basic requirements for a composition operator on the one hand and for composition tools on the other exist.

3.1   Model Composition

Model composition in its simplest form refers to the mechanism of combining two models into a new one. Without further information or requirements the definition of model composition is quite abstract. Denoting the universe of models with M we get the following definition of model composition operators:

Definition 1. Model composition operator
A model composition operator $\otimes$ is a function with two models as input, which produces a composed model as output: $\otimes: M \times M \rightarrow M$.

Given the semantics of models, we can infer properties of the semantics of a composition operator $\otimes$ by relating the semantics on its source and resulting model.

Definition 2. Property preserving (PP) composition operator
A composition operator $\otimes: M \times M \rightarrow M$ is property preserving on the left argument, if for any $m_1, m_2 \in M$ it holds: $sm(m_1 \otimes m_2) \subseteq sm(m_1)$. Analogously, it is property preserving on the right argument, iff $sm(m_1 \otimes m_2) \subseteq sm(m_2)$ and **property preserving (PP)** if both properties hold.

The simple example shown in Figure 1 serves as basis for further explanations.

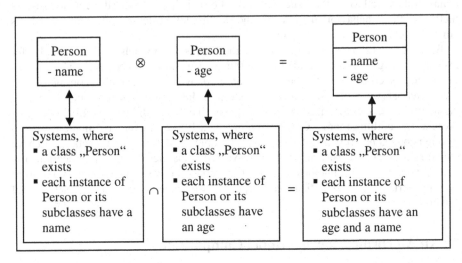

Fig. 1. Example for composition on models and semantics

Property preservation is important for a composition operator, as it ensures that no information and thus, no design decisions that were present in a source model are lost in the composition. We can infer that property preservation is equivalent to:

$$\forall \, m_1, m_2 \in M: \; sm(m_1 \otimes m_2) \subseteq sm(m_1) \cap sm(m_2) \tag{3}$$

Please note that this need not be equality, as the composition operator may be allowed to add further information that was not present in any of the models before. This can be useful, especially if there are decisions on unifications to make that are not unique. E.g., unnamed associations between the same classes can be identified, but need not.

Definition 3. Fully property preserving (FPP) composition operator
A composition operator $\otimes: M \times M \to M$ is **fully property preserving**, iff

$$\forall \, m_1, m_2 \in M: \; sm(m_1 \otimes m_2) = sm(m_1) \cap sm(m_2) \tag{4}$$

The most important consequence of FPP is that it allows us to separately analyze and understand the source models and their properties individually and to trace properties (as well as errors) of the composed model back to the input models. Furthermore, with a PP composition a model developer can be sure that the requirements defined in his models are preserved in the implementation. And third, a PP operator makes model composition understandable: changes in one input model have an impact on the composed model within a localized, clearly identifiable area, but do not affect properties defined in the other models.

A FPP composition operator neither adds nor forgets information. Unfortunately, we will have to live with the situation, that there are modeling languages, where there is no composed model that exhibits the desired properties. E.g., composing flat automata is not necessarily fully property preserving (depends on the assumed communication between these automata). In this case, emerging properties of the composition cannot necessarily be traced back to the original, but may result from the composition operator itself, which in fact is a composition and an additional refinement. However, adding wrong information through a composition operator may lead to an inconsistent result ($sm(m_1 \otimes m_2) = \varnothing$) even though the models originally where not inconsistent with each other ($sm(m_1) \cap sm(m_2) \neq \varnothing$). We therefore demand that composition preserves consistency:

Definition 4. Consistency preserving (CP) composition operator
A composition operator $\otimes: M \times M \rightarrow M$ is **consistency preserving (CP)**, iff

$$\forall\, m_1, m_2 \in M:\ sm(m_1) \cap sm(m_2) \neq \varnothing \ \Rightarrow\ sm(m_1 \otimes m_2) \neq \varnothing \qquad (5)$$

Corollary. A FPP composition operator is consistency preserving.

Proof: by definition.

In general as well as in the remainder of this paper we assume model composition to be property preserving as well as consistency preserving (but not in all cases fully property preserving).

3.2   A Generalization for Semantic Composition Operators

We have explained the desired properties of a composition operator using set-valued semantics. This technique can be generalized, assuming there is a composition operator $\oplus$ available on the semantic domain. Intersection $\cap$ as used above is such an operator.

Definition 5. General Semantic Composition Operator
The semantic composition operator $\oplus$ is a function with two sets of systems as input which produces a set of systems as output: $\oplus: D \times D \rightarrow D$.

Given these operators on both levels, the semantic composition operator $\oplus$ can be understood as semantics of the syntactic operator $\otimes$ if the diagram in Figure 2 commutes.

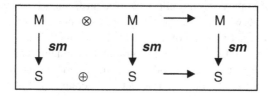

Fig. 2. Relationship between composition operators

We say the diagram commutes iff

$$\forall\ m_1, m_2 \in M:\ sm(m_1 \otimes m_2) = sm(m_1) \oplus sm(m_2) \tag{6}$$

A commuting diagram corresponds to a fully property preserving composition as defined above and exhibits the same advantages as discussed above. We therefore impose the requirement that the diagram in Fig. 2 should always commute. If not, at least the relaxed version must be considered:

$$\forall\ m_1, m_2 \in M:\ sm(m_1 \otimes m_2) \subseteq sm(m_1) \oplus sm(m_2) \tag{7}$$

Therefore, the syntactic operator $\otimes$ reflects the semantic composition $\oplus$ and an additional refinement. However, in the following we use intersection as semantic composition only.

3.3 Syntax-Based Properties of Composition

Examining properties of the syntactic composition $\otimes$, we find that there may be absorbing or neutral elements. In a first attempt, we may call a model $m \in M$ right-neutral, iff

$$\forall\ m_1 \in M: m_1 \otimes m = m_1 \tag{8}$$

A model $m \in M$ is called right-absorbing, iff

$$\forall\ m_1 \in M: m_1 \otimes m = m \tag{9}$$

Left-neutral and left-absorbing is defined analogously and **neutral** respectively **absorbing** is the combination of both sides. Furthermore, we might call a composition operator $\otimes$ **commutative** iff

$$\forall\ m_1, m_2 \in M: m_1 \otimes m_2 = m_2 \otimes m_1 \tag{10}$$

and **associative** iff

$$\forall\ m_1, m_2, m_3 \in M: (m_1 \otimes m_2) \otimes m_3 = m_1 \otimes (m_2 \otimes m_3) \tag{11}$$

Of course, if the composition operator is commutative, left and right-neutrality as well as properties to be left-/right-absorbing will coincide.

There may be many models that are absorbing or neutral. But, due to unlucky context conditions there may also be none at all. For class diagram composition, a neutral element could be the empty class diagram, which is not allowed in UML 2.1.

This formalization above would allow us to identify an algebra of composition on the syntactic level. However, when looking at the properties, we easily can see that this algebra is too restrictive to be of direct use. In fact models have a concrete syntax and the positions of white spaces or the graphical elements usually change, when models are composed or somehow otherwise modified. Furthermore, the order of presenting elements usually does not affect the semantics, but the layout of the composed result. An example in Figure 3 shows a possible key problem.

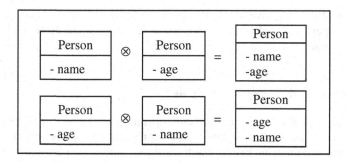

Fig. 3. Example for non-commutative model composition (on syntactic level)

This example leads us to two observations. First, the result syntactically depends on the order of the input models and thus, composition is often not commutative. Second, the result does not depend semantically on the input order, since the outputs are "semantically equal", which means that they are mapped by *sm* to the same set of systems. Therefore, we do generalize from a purely model (syntax)-based concept of composition to a semantic-based version.

3.4 Semantic-Based Composition Properties

Instead of defining associativity, etc. on the concrete syntax of models, we abstract away from irrelevant syntactic sugar and concentrate on the semantic properties of a model. Therefore, we develop the following definitions:

Definition 6. Algebraic Properties of Composition
A model $m \in M$ is called right-**neutral** vs. composition $\otimes$, iff

$$\forall\, m_1 \in M: sm(m_1 \otimes m) = sm(m_1) \tag{12}$$

Model $m \in M$ is called right-**absorbing** vs. composition $\otimes$, iff

$$\forall\, m_1 \in M: sm(m_1 \otimes m) = sm(m) \tag{13}$$

A model $m \in M$ is called right-**idempotent** vs. composition $\otimes$, iff

$$\forall\, m_1 \in M: sm((m_1 \otimes m) \otimes m) = sm(m_1 \otimes m) \tag{14}$$

Being left-neutral, -absorbing and –idempotent is defined in an analogous way.
If a model is neutral (absorbing/idempotent) from both sides, it is called neutral (absorbing/idempotent).

We call a composition operator $\otimes$ **commutative** vs. its semantics *sm* iff

$$\forall\, m_1, m_2 \in M: sm(m_1 \otimes m_2) = sm(m_2 \otimes m_1) \tag{15}$$

and **associative** vs. its semantics *sm* iff

$$\forall\, m_1, m_2, m_3 \in M: sm((m_1 \otimes m_2) \otimes m_3) = sm(m_1 \otimes (m_2 \otimes m_3)) \tag{16}$$

This formalization allows us to define an algebra with composition etc. based on semantic properties. Looking at these properties from a different angle, we can identify an equivalence relation $\cong$ on models based on the semantic mapping interpreted as homomorphism.

3.5 Properties of the Semantic Mapping

Let in this section $\otimes$ be a FPP composition operator. We know that $(\wp(S), \cap, S, \varnothing)$ defines a lattice, where intersection is both commutative and associative. Together with the semantic mapping sm we can translate the lattice properties to the language of models:

Theorem 1.
If a model composition $\otimes$ is fully property preserving, then $(M, \otimes)$ also defines a commutative, associative structure with respect to sm and $\otimes$ is idempotent for all models.

Proof: By definition of FPP we derive

Assoc.: $sm((m_1 \otimes m_2) \otimes m_3) = sm(m_1) \cap sm(m_2) \cap sm(m_3) = sm(m_1 \otimes (m_2 \otimes m_3))$,

Comm.: $sm(m_1 \otimes m_2) = sm(m_1) \cap sm(m_2) = sm(m_2 \otimes m_1)$, and

Idempot.: $sm(m_1 \otimes m_1) = sm(m_1) \cap sm(m_1) = sm(m_1)$.   □

Respecting the semantic equivalence of two models is an important property for a composition operator, because then the concrete representative is irrelevant and layout or other minor rearrangements of the model do not affect the composition result. We therefore introduce the algebra of equivalence classes on models induced by the semantic mapping:

Definition 7. Equivalence Classes of Models
The semantic mapping sm defines an equivalence relation on models as follows:

$$m_1 \cong m_2 \iff sm(m_1) = sm(m_2) \tag{17}$$

The set of semantically equivalent models is denoted by

$$[m_1] = \{ m_2 \mid m_1 \cong m_2 \} \tag{18}$$

We denote the set of equivalence classes over M by $[M]$. The composition operation can be extended to equivalence classes as follows:

Definition 8. Composition on Model Classes
Composition is extended to model classes by:

$$[m_1] \otimes [m_2] = \{ m_a \otimes m_b \mid m_a \in [m_1] \wedge m_b \in [m_2] \} \tag{19}$$

Theorem 2. [.] is a congruence for FPPs
If a model composition $\otimes$ is fully property preserving, then $([M], \otimes)$ also defines a commutative, associative structure with respect to sm, all models are idempotent, and:

$$[m_1] \otimes [m_2] = [m_1 \otimes m_2] \tag{20}$$

Proof: Follows from FPP and the definition of the equivalence classes.   □

We now have a quotient algebra ($[M]$, $\otimes$) with a number of desired properties for a syntactic composition operator:

1. Composition is fully property preserving, such that each property of the composed model can be traced back to one of the input models or both.
2. Composition is consistent with the semantics, such that it is irrelevant, which concrete representative was chosen. Thus the composition is well defined with respect to the quotient algebra.
3. Composition is commutative and associative, such that the order of composition is irrelevant.

As already discussed, unfortunately a number of composition operators will exist that do not fit this ideal scheme for a variety of reasons. E.g., it may rather often be the case that an operator is PP and CP, but not FPP. In this case, it may happen that even if the operator is commutative and associative on models, the equivalence on models is not a congruence vs. composition.

A model composition operator which depends on the order of the input or concrete representations of the model would be difficult to manage. E.g., the input order has to be saved somewhere to guarantee the equality of the results.

From theoretical computer science, we know that composition operators need to conform with semantics as much as possible. This may be achieved through a number of mechanisms. On the one hand the composition operator may be adjusted accordingly. Second, the semantic domain or the semantic mapping may be redefined, such that they go conform with composition and third, the modeling language itself may be adapted.

3.6 Summary

In the last sections we introduced some basic properties model composition operators may have such as PP, FPP, or CP. Following we give a short overview of the definitions which allow to categorize a given composition operator.

Table 1. Properties Overview of Composition

Property	Requirement	Dependencies
Property Preserving on the left (PP$_l$)	$sm(m_1 \otimes m_2) \subseteq sm(m_1)$	
Property Preserving on the right (PP$_r$)	$sm(m_1 \otimes m_2) \subseteq sm(m_2)$	
Property Preserving (PP)	$sm(m_1 \otimes m_2) \subseteq sm(m_1) \cap sm(m_1)$	PP$_l$ $\wedge$ PP$_r$ $\Leftrightarrow$ PP
Fully Property Preserving	$sm(m_1 \otimes m_2) = sm(m_1) \cap sm(m_2)$	FPP $\Rightarrow$ PP
Consistency Preserving	$\forall\, m_1, m_2 \in M:\ sm(m_1) \cap sm(m_2)$ $\neq \emptyset \Rightarrow\ sm(m_1 \otimes m_2) \neq \emptyset$	FPP $\Rightarrow$ CP

Table 1. *{Continued}*

Commutative (Com)	$\forall\ m_1, m_2 \in M:\ m_1 \otimes m_2 = m_2 \otimes m_1$	
Associative (Ass)	$\forall\ m_1,\ m_2,\ m_3 \in M:$ $(m_1 \otimes m_2) \otimes m_3 = m_1 \otimes (m_2 \otimes m_3)$	
Commutative vs. Semantics (Com$_{sm}$)	$\forall\ m_1, m_2 \in M:$ $sm(m_1 \otimes m_2) = sm(m_2 \otimes m_1)$	Com $\Rightarrow$ Com$_{sm}$
Associative vs. Semantics (Ass$_{sm}$)	$\forall\ m_1,\ m_2,\ m_3 \in M: sm((m_1 \otimes m_2) \otimes m_3) = sm(m_1 \otimes (m_2 \otimes m_3))$	Ass $\Rightarrow$ Ass$_{sm}$

Furthermore, we defined special elements with respect to composition. Table 2 gives a short overview.

Table 2. Special elements of Composition

Property of Element m	Requirement	Dependencies
Right-neutral (Rn)	$\forall\ m_1 \in M:\ m_1 \otimes m = m_1$	
Left-neutral (Ln)	$\forall\ m_1 \in M:\ m \otimes m_1 = m_1$	
Neutral (N)	$\forall\ m_1 \in M:\ m_1 \otimes m = m \otimes m_1 = m_1$	Rn $\wedge$ Ln $\Leftrightarrow$ N
Right-absorbing (Ra)	$\forall\ m_1 \in M:\ m_1 \otimes m = m$	
Left-absorbing (La)	$\forall\ m_1 \in M:\ m \otimes m_1 = m$	
Absorbing (A)	$\forall\ m_1 \in M:$ $m_1 \otimes m = m \otimes m_1 = m$	Ra $\wedge$ La $\Leftrightarrow$ A
Right-Idempotent (Ri)	$\forall\ m_1 \in M:$ $(m_1 \otimes m) \otimes m = m_1 \otimes m$	
Left-Idempotent (Li)	$\forall\ m_1 \in M:$ $m \otimes (m \otimes m_1) = m_1 \otimes m$	
Idempotent (I)	$\forall\ m_1 \in M:\ m \otimes (m \otimes m_1) = (m_1 \otimes m) \otimes m = m_1 \otimes m$	Ri $\wedge$ Li $\Leftrightarrow$ I
Right-neutral vs. Composition (Rn$_{comp}$)	$\forall\ m_1 \in M:$ $sm(m_1 \otimes m) = sm(m_1)$	Rn $\Rightarrow$ Rn$_{comp}$
Left-neutral vs. Composition (Ln$_{comp}$)	$\forall\ m_1 \in M:$ $sm(m \otimes m_1) = sm(m_1)$	Ln $\Rightarrow$ Ln$_{comp}$
Neutral vs. Composition (N$_{comp}$)	$\forall\ m_1 \in M:$ $sm(m_1 \otimes m) = sm(m \otimes m_1) = sm(m_1)$	Rn$_{comp}$ $\wedge$ Ln$_{comp}$ $\Leftrightarrow$ N$_{comp}$ N $\Rightarrow$ N$_{comp}$
Right-absorbing vs. Composition (Ra$_{comp}$)	$\forall\ m_1 \in M:$ $sm(m_1 \otimes m) = sm(m)$	Ra $\Rightarrow$ Ra$_{comp}$
Left-absorbing vs. Composition (La$_{comp}$)	$\forall\ m_1 \in M:$ $sm(m \otimes m_1) = sm(m)$	La $\Rightarrow$ La$_{comp}$

Table 2. *{Continued}*

Absorbing vs. Composition (A_{comp})	$\forall\ m_1 \in M$: $sm(m_1 \otimes m) = sm(m \otimes m_1) = sm(m)$	$Ra_{comp} \wedge La_{comp} \Leftrightarrow A_{comp}$ $A \Rightarrow A_{comp}$
Right-Idempotent vs. Composition (Ri_{comp})	$\forall\ m_1 \in M$: $sm((m_1 \otimes m) \otimes m) = sm(m_1 \otimes m)$	$Ri \Rightarrow Ri_{comp}$
Left-Idempotent vs. Composition (Li_{comp})	$\forall\ m_1 \in M$: $sm(m \otimes (m \otimes m_1)) = sm(m_1 \otimes m)$	$Li \Rightarrow Li_{comp}$
Idempotent vs. Composition (I_{comp})	$\forall\ m_1 \in M$: $sm(m \otimes (m \otimes m_1)) = sm((m_1 \otimes m) \otimes m) = sm(m_1 \otimes m)$	$Ri_{comp} \wedge Li_{comp} \Leftrightarrow I_{comp}$ $I \Rightarrow I_{comp}$

4 Related Work

Much work on specification with respect to model composition has been done in the formal methods community. Based on [13] the notion of fully abstract composition was transferred to a number of formal languages for behavioral specification. Our approach is very much in the spirit of this work, but tries to identify interesting sub-properties for model composition as well.

Model composition is also a widespread research issue in the world of UML. There are several works which concentrate on different kinds of UML-like diagrams, as class diagrams [14] or state charts [15]. Most of these works do not discuss composition or model management operators from a foundational, algebraic point of view and thus, have different objectives.

In [4] three model composition tools, namely the Atlas Model Weaver, the Epsilon Merging Language, and the Glue Generator Tool which were developed in the Modelware project [18] are introduced and discussed in detail. Furthermore, it derives some common definitions from these discussions and clarifies some basic requirements for model composition tools and frameworks. However, our work concentrates on the semantic properties of model composition, whereas [4] addresses mainly syntactic properties and their implementation in tools.

A generic semantics of the merge operator was presented in the MOMENT project [19]. It describes three steps of model merging: finding semantic equivalences, conflict resolution, and copying non-duplicated elements. In contrast to our work it concentrates on expressing semantic equalities by means of a metamodel whereas we discuss the semantic background of model composition.

A more theoretical view on different model management operators is presented in [16]. It introduces algebraic properties of model merging such as commutativity, associativity, and idempotency. The theoretical results are illustrated by two examples, merging entity relationship models and state machines, respectively. In opposition to our work the algebra of model composition is not discussed in detail. Instead the concentration lies on a general overview of model management operators and their relationships.

An algebra of merging incomplete and inconsistent graph-based views is discussed in [17]. Category theory and colimits serve as theoretical basis to express the relationships between different diagrams in opposition to our viewpoint of algebras. Furthermore, the basic intention of [17] consists in the identification of equal elements in different views whereas our work concentrates on the algebraic properties of model composition.

5   Conclusion

In this paper we gave a first contribution to shed light into the question how model composition operators interact with the semantics of models and what properties composition operators should have. For this purpose, we have abstractly described how semantics is defined. We then introduced an algebra of model composition that describes the formal relationship between the models, equivalence classes of semantically equivalent models, model composition and semantics. From this setting some results could be derived. The most important are that model composition should be a congruence induced by the semantic definition and a composition should be a commutative and associative operator with respect to the semantics.

These theoretical results lead to practical consequences for the design of model composition operators, modeling languages and semantic domains. Any composition operator should obey the properties implied by the algebra in order to allow a modular model-based development of software systems with independent compilation/ transformation of models to other representations and levels of abstraction.

This paper is concerned with the model composition operator and its implications. It can be seen as a foundation for further investigations on model management operations. However, there are a number of extensions to deal with: How to deal with a diff operator to reverse composition? How does code and test-case generation interact with composition and semantics? Are there impacts for the form of meta-modeling widely used today? What are properties of an unsymmetric composition like aspect weaving? How do UML's semantic variation points interact with composition? Will refinement preserving composition be useful and feasible? Will there be compositional refactorings? Many of these questions need to be solved for a foundational theory of model composition.

Acknowledgement. The work presented in this paper is undertaken as a part of the MODELPLEX project. MODELPLEX is a project co-funded by the European Commission under the "Information Society Technologies" Sixth Framework Programme (2002-2006). Information included in this document reflects only the authors' views. The European Community is not liable for any use that may be made of the information contained herein.

References

1. Harel, D., Rumpe, B.: Modeling Languages: Syntax, Semantics and All That Stuff. Technical Report MCS00-16, The Weizmann Institute of Science, Rehovot, Israel (2000)
2. France, R., Evans, A., Lano, K., Rumpe, B.: The UML as a Formal Modeling Notation. In: Computer Standards and Interfaces, vol. 19, pp. 325–334. Elsevier Science Publisher, North-Holland, Amsterdam (1998)

3. Parnas, D.: On the criteria to be used in decomposing systems into modules In: Communications of the ACM, pp. 1053–1058. Vol.15(12) (December 1972)

4. Bezivin, J., Bouzitouna, S., Del Fabro, M.D., Gervais, M.-P., Jouault, F., Kolovos, D.S., Kurtev, I., Paige, R.F.: A canonical scheme for model composition. In: Proceedings of the Second European Conference on Model-Driven Architecture (EC-MDA) 2006, pp. 346–361, Bilbao, Spain, (July 2006)

5. Engel, K.-D., Paige, R.F., Kolovos, D.S.: Using a Model Merging Language for Reconciling Model Versions. In Proc. Second European Conference on Model-Driven Architecture (EC-MDA) 2006, pages. In: Rensink, A., Warmer, J. (eds.) ECMDA-FA 2006. LNCS, vol. 4066, pp. 143–158. Springer, Heidelberg (2006)

6. Fabro, M., Bézivin, J., Jouault, F., Breton, E., Gueltas, G.: AMW: a generic model weaver. In: Proceedings of the 1ères Journées sur l'Ingénierie Dirigée par les Modèles (IDM05), pp. 105–114, Paris (2005)

7. Harel, D., Rumpe, B.: Meaningful Modeling: What's the Semantics of Semantics?, In: IEEE Computer, Vol. 37(10), pp. 64–72, IEEE, (October 2004)

8. Broy, M., Cengarle, M., Rumpe, B.: Towards a System Model for UML. The Structural Data Model. Munich University of Technology, Technical Report TUM-I0612. (June 2006)

9. Gurevich, Y., Kutter, P., Odersky, M., Thiele, L. (eds.): ASM 2000. LNCS, vol. 1912, pp. 22–33. Springer, Heidelberg (2000)

10. Broy, M., Facchi, C., Grasu, R., Hettler, R., Hußmann, H., Nazareth, D., Regensburger, F., Slotosch, O., Stoelen, K.: The requirements and Design Specification Language SPECTRUM, An Informal Introduction, Version 1.0, Part 1, Technical Report TUM-I9312, Technische Universität München (1993)

11. Spivey, M.: The Z Notation - A Reference Manual, 2nd edn. Prentice-Hall, Englewood Cliffs (1992)

12. Rumpe, B.: A Note on Semantics (with an Emphasis on UML). In: Second ECOOP Workshop on Precise Behavioral Semantics, pp. 177–197, Haim Kilov, Bernhard Rumpe (eds.), Technische Universität München, TUM-I9813

13. Kok, J.: A fully abstract semantics for data flow nets. In: Proceedings of the Parallel Architectures and Languages Europe, Volume II: Parallel Languages, pp. 351–368. Eindhoven, The Netherlands (June 15-19, 1987)

14. Straw, G., Georg, G., Song, E., Ghosh, S., France, R., Bieman, J.: Model Composition Directives, In: Proceedings of the 7th UML Conference, pp. 87–94, Lisbon, Portugal, (October 10-15, 2004)

15. Aldawud, O., Bader, A., Elrad, T.: Weaving with statecharts. In: Workshop on Aspect-Oriented Modeling, Enschede, Netherlands (2002)

16. Brunet, G., Chechik, M., Easterbrook, S., Nejati, S., Niu, N., Sabetzadeh, M.: A manifesto for model merging. In: Proceedings of the, international workshop on Global integrated model management, 5-12, May, 2006, Shanghai, China (2006)

17. Sabetzadeh, M., Easterbrook, S.: An Algebraic Framework for Merging Incomplete and Inconsistent Views, In: Proceedings of the 13th IEEE International Conference on Requirements Engineering (RE'05), pp. 306-318 (August 29-September 02, 2005)

18. The Modelware Project Homepage: http://www.modelware-ist.org

19. Boronat, A., Carsi, J., Ramos, I., Letelier, P.: Formal Model Merging Applied to Class Diagramm Integration. Electronic Notes on Theoretical Computer Science, pp. 5–26, Vol. 166, Amsterdam, The Netherlands (2007)

Towards the Generation of a Text-Based IDE
from a Language Metamodel

Anneke Kleppe[*]

University Twente, Netherlands
a.kleppe@utwente.nl

Abstract. In the model driven world languages are usually specified by a
(meta) model of their abstract syntax. For textual languages this is different
from the traditional approach, where the language is specified by a (E)BNF
grammar. Support for the designer of textual languages, e.g. a parser generator,
is therefore normally based on grammars. This paper shows that similar support
for language design based on metamodels is not only possible, but is even more
powerful than the support based on grammars. In this paper we describe how an
integrated development environment for a language can be generated from the
language's abstract syntax metamodel, thus providing the language designer
with the possibility to quickly, and with little effort, create not only a new
language but also the tooling necessary for using this language.

Keywords: metamodeling, domain specific languages, text-based languages,
parsing, compilers, IDE, generation.

1 Introduction

Currently, there is an increasing interest in the design of languages that are used
somewhere in the software development process. First, *domain specific modeling
languages* (DSMLs) are becoming more and more important. DSMLs are languages
for modeling software, which are focused on describing a certain aspect or viewpoint
of a software system. Second, there is a steady demand for occasional or little
languages, i.e. languages that are used for a relatively small amount of time by a small
group of people. For instance, in large, long-running projects often small (scripting)
languages are being build that enable automation of specific, reoccurring tasks in that
project. These languages are known under various names, amongst which *domain
specific languages* [1]. Special to both types of DSLs is that they have a limited
number of users, compared to general software languages like Java, C#, and UML.

Often these new languages are specified by a metamodel, which accounts for the
popularity of metamodeling toolkits like the Eclipse Modeling Framework (EMF) [2]
and Microsoft's DSL tools [3]. It is our view that metamodeling toolkits should
support the creation of a language in full. Not only should they aid the language
designer in his/her task of creating the metamodel, but they should also support the
language designer in creating the tooling for the people that are going to use the

---

[*] The author is employed in the GRASLAND project funded by the Dutch NWO (project
number 612.063.408).

D.H. Akehurst, R. Vogel, and R.F. Paige (Eds.): ECMDA-FA 2007, LNCS 4530, pp. 114–129, 2007.

language. Note that we use the term *language designer* for the person who creates the new language, and *language user* for the person who uses the newly created language and its supporting tools.

The current demands on tooling are high. For instance, if a dedicated text editor is provided, it should have syntax-highlighting and code-completion. Specially for modeling languages, tooling must include code generation software and should preferably include a debugger that is able to address the language user in terms of the domain specific model instead of the code language.

Languages targeting a limited number of users, do not warrant the effort in building such sofisticated tools, simply because the costs are too high. The only way that a language designer is able to create sofisticated tooling for such languages, is when most of it is generated by the metamodeling toolkit. In other words, the metamodeling toolkit needs to be able to generate an integrated development environment (IDE) for the language specified by the metamodel.

This paper describes the first steps towards the realisation of such a metamodeling toolkit, more specifically it describes the generation of a compiler front-end for a text-based concrete syntax of a language, based on the metamodel specification of that language. As this work is conducted within the Grasland project, our metamodeling toolkit is, for lack of a better one, named the Grasland toolkit. The Grasland toolkit is implemented in the form of a number of Eclipse plug-ins that build upon the functionality provided by the Octopus tool [4].

Section 2 of this paper outlines the process of language design as it is supported by the Grasland toolkit, and it establishes the terminology used. Sections 3 and 4 describe the two transformations that generate a grammar from a metamodel. Section 5 describes the generated static semantic analyzer. Finally, Section 6 describes future and related work.

2 Preliminaries

This section outlines the process of language design as it is supported by the Grasland toolkit, and it establishes the terminology used in this paper. Furthermore, the arguments for our approach are stated in the last subsection.

2.1 Terminology

In this paper we will use the following terms, which are formally defined to be special types of graphs.

- *Abstract Syntax Model* (ASM): a metamodel that specifies the abstract syntax of the language, which will be called *L*.
- *Abstract Syntax Graph* (ASG): an instance of the abstract syntax model.
- *Concrete Syntax Model* (CSM) or *Parse Model* (PM): a metamodel that specifies a concrete syntax of the language. (When talking about text-based syntaxes we will use *parse model*, when talking about graphical syntaxes we will use *concrete syntax model*.)

- *BNFset*: the set of (E)BNF rules that specifies a text-based concrete syntax of the language. Note that there is a correspondence between a BNFset and a parse model.
- *Parse Graph* (PG) or *Parse Tree* (PT): an instance of the parse model. (When talking about text-based syntaxes we will use *parse tree*, when talking about graphical syntaxes we will use *parse graph*.)
- *Navigations*: the set of outgoing associations and attributes of a metaclass.

Furthermore, we assume that a language can have multiple concrete syntaxes, and a concrete syntax can be either textual, graphical, or a hybrid one that combines textual parts with graphical ones, e.g. a table representation.

2.2 The Process of Language Design

Central to the process of language design as it is supported by the Grasland toolkit, is the ASM of the language. To create the tooling for the language user, the language designer needs to perform the tasks in Table 1, which are dependent on the type of concrete syntax used. Next to this, the language designer is likely to create an exchange format for abstract syntax graphs, for instance based on XML, as well as transformations from the ASM to various other metamodels, one of which will probably implement code generation.

Table 1. Tasks of a language designer for the two types of concrete syntax

Step	Text-based concrete syntax	Graphical concrete syntax
1	*Create the PM, which will include classes that represent references to other elements in the parse tree.*	*Create the CSM, which will include classes that represent graphical items like rectangles and lines.*
2	*Create the EBNF grammar, which will include keywords. Take an existing parser generator, (re)write the grammar for this generator, and generate a parser that will produce the parse tree from a text file.*	*No action needed. (Usually the CSM suffices to create a syntax-directed graphical editor, thus there is no need to create a parser.)*
3	*Create a model transformation from parse tree to abstract syntax graph (this is often called static analysis, it includes binding).*	*Create a model transformation from parse graph to abstract syntax graph.*
4	*Create a text editor dedicated to this concrete syntax, with syntax highlighting etc.*	*Create a graphical editor dedicated to this concrete syntax.*
5	*Create a tool chain such that an abstract syntax graph is created from a text file.*	*Create a tool chain such that an abstract syntax graph is created from a diagram.*

In this paper we will show how all of steps 1, 2, 3, and 5 for text-based syntaxes can be automated, i.e. none of the products are created by hand, they are all generated by the Grasland toolkit. Automation of step 4 is also possible, but not yet implemented in the Grasland toolkit.

2.3   Outline of Our Approach

Traditionally, when a new textual language is created, the main activity is to produce the BNFset. Next, a parser is created using some or other parser generator, e.g. [5, 6, 7]. The other parts of the language's compiler are implemented by hand, often by creating treewalkers that traverse the parse tree generated by the parser, as shown in Figure 1 (the shaded parts are created by the language designer). There is, in most cases, no explicit definition of the PM, nor of the ASM, although one can always extract the set of pure BNF rules, which might serve as a PM description, from the parser generator input.

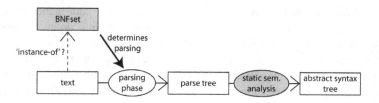

Fig. 1. The normal elements in a compiler.

In the Grasland approach, the only manual activity is to create the ASM, i.e. a metamodel and its invariants. From the ASM we generate a PM, which upholds certain requirements that will be explained in Section 3. This transformation is called *asm2pm*. From the PM we generate a BNFset, which - for practical purposes - can be generated in a format that is processable by the JavaCC parser generator [6]. This transformation is called *pm2bnf*. Next JavaCC generates a parser, which is able to produce a parse tree that is an instance of the PM in the sense that the nodes in the parse tree are instances of the Java classes that correspond to the classes in the PM. To implement the static semantic analysis, a tool is generated that transforms a parse tree into an ASG. This tool implements a model transformation from PM to ASM. Figure 2 shows the various elements in the Grasland approach; again the manually created elements are shaded.

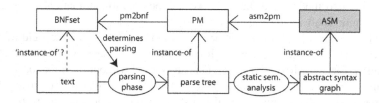

Fig. 2. The alternative process using metamodels

2.4 Rationale of the Approach

Specially for text-based languages, our approach is very different from the traditional process. Instead of focusing on BNF rules, the language designer will focus on the ASM. The PM and BNFset are automatically generated from the ASM. A number of arguments support this new design process.

The first argument is that at the start of the language creation process it need not be clear whether the new language is text based or graphical, and often the new language should support multiple syntaxes. So a specification of the concrete syntax cannot be a good starting point.

Second, although compiler construction is a formally defined area of expertise, it has one obvious omission, which is that the true ASM is not defined at all. What is usually called an abstract syntax tree in compiler construction, we call a parse tree. The abstract syntax tree is embellished with binding information and often reshuffled to produce what we call an abstract syntax graph. Note that in compiler construction the term abstract syntax tree is used for both formats. More importantly, it is the abstract syntax tree that is used for further handling, like code generation, which means that these phases lack a formal description. On this point metamodeling certainly has something to add to the area of compiler construction.

Furthermore, the power of metamodelling is larger than the power of BNF. One can express more in a metamodel. Therefore, starting with a BNF grammar and creating a metamodel from the grammar, as for instance described in [8], will result in a restricted metamodel. Most certainly, this metamodel will not be the one that the language designer wants to use as ASM.

A fourth argument is that although the syntax of the majority of programming languages can be classified as context-free, the languages themselves are often context-sensitive. That is, the static analysis phase of the compiler adds context sensitive information. For instance, variable binding may be considered context-sensitive information because a variable 'a' is not always bound to the same variable declaration, the binding depends on the context in which 'a' is found. So, to support the language designer in creating a complete toolset for a text-based concrete syntax, we need not only consider parsing but also static analysis. Currently, there are many parser generators, but as far as we know there are no generators for static semantic analysers.

From one argument comes another. Now that we have established that we have a need for a static semantic analyser, it is a good choice to generate the parse model from the abstract syntax model. In this way we have full control over the differences between the two models and therefore we will be able to automatically generate the static semantic analyser that bridges the two.

Another consideration for our choice of design process, is that the field of parsing and compiler construction is very well established. The parser generators that result from this research are tried and tested and can be used without further ado.

A final argument is a reduced 'time to market'. In the Grasland approach the language designer is able to 'play' with the abstract syntax model and for each change in this model he will be able to generate a working IDE with a single push of a button.

This means that testing the changes takes as least effort as possible. Although, as the title of this paper tells, we are still working towards a toolkit that is able to generate a complete IDE, our experiments with the generation of parts of this IDE are promising.

The next sections describe the how the steps in Table 1 are implemented in the Grasland toolkit.

3   The ASM to PM Transformation

This section describes the algorithm for the *asm2pm* transformation. This algorithm implements the creation of the parse model (or CSM), which includes classes that represent references to other elements in the parse tree. Note that this algorithm actually is defined on the meta meta level, i.e. it is not a transformation of model to model, but of metamodel to metamodel.

The algorithm, which is outlined in List 1, makes use of the composite - reference distinction in associations in the metamodel. We use a formal definition of metamodel that ensures that in any instance of the metamodel the composites form a subgraph that is really a tree. The composite relationships are subsequently used in the *pm2bnf* transformation to construct the BNF grammar. In the case that the subgraph formed by the composite associations is not a tree, but a set of unrelated trees (a forest), the algorithm will produce a set of unrelated sets of grammar rules. It is up to the language designer to decide whether this is (un)desired. Figure 4 shows an example of an ASM, Figure 3 shows the PM that is automatically generated from this ASM. The differences are marked by the colour of the classes and the font of the role names.

Note that for each of the classes for which a reference class is created (step 3), the language designer must indicate which attribute of String type is used as identifier. This knowledge is used in the static semantic analyser to implement the binding. Implementations of the Java counterparts of the classes in the ASM are automatically generated using the functionality of the Octopus tool, and the same is done for the PM.

3.1   Possibilities to Tune the *asm2pm* Transformation

The algorithm in List 1 is fully automatic and produces a parse model without any extra user effort. However, if the algorithm for the *asm2pm* transformation is executed as is, then the differences between the ASM and PM are minimal. Often the language designer wants a larger difference between the two, therefore there are options to tune the *asm2pm* transformation. Note that these differences are taken into account in the generation of the static semantic analyser as well.

The first option is to indicate that certain metaclasses in the ASM should not appear at all in the PM. Examples are the classes *PrimitiveType* and *NullType* in Figure 3. These types are only present in the ASM to provide for a number of basic elements in the language, but the language user is not meant to create new instances of these metaclasses. The language designer can indicate that these classes are hidden to the concrete syntax. Currently this is done by means of a properties file. We are investigating the possibility of indicating hidden elements using Eclipse project properties.

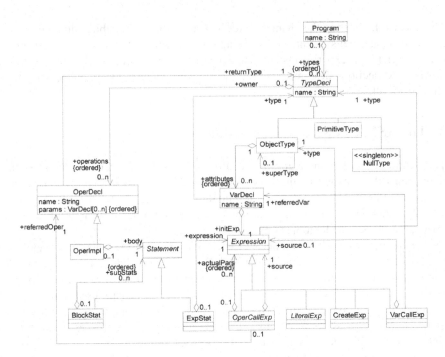

Fig. 3. Example ASM

1. Every class in the ASM becomes a class in the PM. The language designer may indicate prefix and postfix strings that are used to name the classes in the PM, in order to distinguish them from the classes in the ASM. E.g. the ASM class named *Variable-Declaration* becomes the PM class named *prefixVariableDeclarationpostfix*.
2. Every composite association is retained.
3. For every non-composite association from class A to class B a new class is introduced that represents a reference to an instance of class B. A new composite association is added from class A to this new reference class. The role name of the old association is copied to the new one, as well as the multiplicities.
4. Every attribute with non-primitive type, i.e. whose type is another class in the meta-model, is transformed into a composite association from the owner of the attribute to the class that is the attribute type. The name of the attribute becomes the role name. Any multiplicities are copied.
5. Enumerations and datatypes are retained.
6. Additionally, three attributes are added to every PM class. They hold the line number, column number, and filename of the parsed instance of the class.

List. 1. The algorithm for asm2pm

The second option is to indicate that certain attributes and outgoing associations of a metaclass need not be present in the input text file, instead their value will be determined based on the values of other elements that are present. In fact these elements

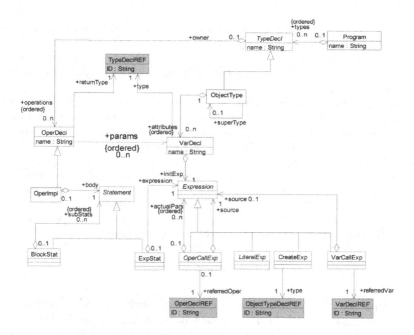

Fig. 4. Example PM

are what is known in OCL [9, 10] as *derived* elements. The language designer may indicate that a certain element need not be taken into account in the parse model, if an OCL derivation rule for this element in the ASM is provided. An example of a derived element in Figure 3 is the *type* of an *Expression*.

4 The PM to BNF Grammar Algorithm

This section describes the algorithm for the *pm2bnf* transformation, which implements the creation of the BNF rules that are used by a parser generator to produce a parser. Note that like the *asm2pm* algorithm, this algorithm too resides on the meta meta level, i.e. it is not a transformation of model to model, but of metamodel to metamodel. Alanen and Porres [11] present algorithms for the relation between PM and BNFset, which we have used and extended.

The generation of the BNFset from the PM is implemented in a single algorithm. Yet, the language designer may choose between two different output formats; either BNF, or a grammar that can directly be used as input to the JavaCC parser generator [6]. The BNF grammar that is produced is actually an extension of EBNF that uses labelling of non-terminals in the right hand side of a grammar rule. (Not to be confused with Labelled BNF [12], which uses labels on the non-terminals at the left hand side of each rule.) The labels correspond with the names of the attributes or association roles in the PM. An example in which the labels are highlighted, can be found in List 3.

---

1. Every class in the PM becomes a non-terminal in the grammar. The rules for these non-terminals are formed according to the following rules.
2. If a class has subclasses then the BNF rule becomes a choice between the rules for the subclasses. All attributes and navigations of the superclass are handled in the subclass rules.
3. For every composite association from A to B, B will appear in the right hand side of the grammar rule for A. The multiplicity is the same as in the association (for 0..1, 1, 0..*, 1..*; multiplicities of the form 3..7 are considered to be specified using invariants). Using an extension of BNF, we associate the rolename with the non-terminal in the right hand side of the rule.
4. Every attribute, all of which have a primitive type, is transformed into an occurrence of a predefined non-terminal for that primitive type in the right hand side of the rule for its owner. (We support the primitive types String, Integer, Real.)
5. Every attribute that has Boolean type, is transformed into an optional keyword. If present, the attribute has value true, if not the attribute's value is false.

List. 2. The algorithm for pm2bnf

The input for the JavaCC parser generator is such that the generated parser produces instances of the Java implementations of the classes in the PM. The algorithm that implements *pm2bnf* is given in List 2. An example can be found in List 3, which shows the BNF rules generated from the parse model in Figure 4. Note that tokens in the right hand side of the grammar rules are surrounded by angled brackets ('<' and '>').

4.1   Possibilities to Tune the *pm2bnf* Transformation

The algorithm in List 2 is fully automatic and produces a grammar without any extra user effort. However, there are a number of differences between the metamodel formalism used for the parse model and the BNF formalism and the language designer is able to influence how these differences appear in the generated grammar, thus tuning the *pm2bnf* generation.

The most apparent difference is the lack of ordering in navigations from a metaclass, versus the ordering of the elements in the right hand side of a BNF rule for a non-terminal. To indicate a certain ordering in the BNF rules the language designer can associate an index to all navigations This is done in a so-called properties file. An example can be found in List 4, where the order of the navigations from the metaclass *ObjectType* in Figure 3 is given. The first element to be included in the right hand side of the corresponding BNF rule is the attribute called *name*, the second is the optional reference to a super type, etc. Without directions from the language designer the Grasland toolkit will randomly assign an ordering.

Another difference between a metamodel and a grammar is that most grammar rules contain one or more keywords, whereas the metamodel does not. These keywords are relevant in the parser because they enable the parser to differentiate between language elements (rules). Therefore the Grasland toolkit provides the option

```
************ The grammar rules **************
```
1. BlockStat ::= <CURLY_OPEN> (**subStats**:Statement)* <CURLY_CLOSE>
2. CreateExp::= <CREATEEXP_BEGIN> **type**:ObjectTypeREF <CREATEEXP_END>
3. ExpStat ::= **expression**:Expression
4. Expression ::= (LiteralExp
   | OperCallExp
   | VarCallExp
   | CreateExp)
5. ObjectTypeREF ::= **ID**:<IDENTIFIER>
6. ObjectType ::= <OBJECTTYPE_BEGIN> **name**:<IDENTIFIER> [
   <OBJECTTYPE_SUPERTYPE_BEGIN> **superType**:ObjectTypeREF] [
   attributes:VarDecl(<SEMICOLON> **attributes**:VarDecl)* <SEMICOLON>] (
   operations:OperDecl)* <OBJECTTYPE_END>
7. OperCallExp ::= **referredOper**:OperDeclREF <BRACKET_OPEN> [**actual-
   Pars**:Expression(<COMMA> **actualPars**:Expression)*] <BRACKET_CLOSE> [
   <OPERCALLEXP_SOURCE_BEGIN> **source**:Expression]
8. OperDeclREF ::= **ID**:<IDENTIFIER>
9. OperDecl ::= (OperImpl)
10. OperImpl ::= **name**:<IDENTIFIER> <BRACKET_OPEN> [**params**:VarDecl(
    <COMMA> **params**:VarDecl)*] <BRACKET_CLOSE> <COLON> **return-
    Type**:TypeREF (**locals**:VarDecl)* **body**:BlockStat
11. Program ::= <PROGRAM_BEGIN> **name**:<IDENTIFIER> **startExp**:ExpStat (
    types:Type)* <PROGRAM_END>
12. Statement ::= (BlockStat
    | ExpStat) <SEMICOLON>
13. TypeREF ::= **ID**:<IDENTIFIER>
14. Type ::= (ObjectType)
15. VarCallExp ::= **referredVar**:VarDeclREF [<VARCALLEXP_SOURCE_BEGIN>
    source:Expression]
16. VarDeclREF ::= **ID**:<IDENTIFIER>
17. VarDecl ::= **name**:<IDENTIFIER> <COLON> **type**:TypeREF [
    <VARDECL_INITEXP_BEGIN> **initExp**:Expression]
```
************ The token definitions **************
     CREATEEXP_BEGIN ::= "new"
     CREATEEXP_END ::= "()"
     NULLLITEXP_BEGIN ::= "null"
     OBJECTTYPE_BEGIN ::= "class"
     OBJECTTYPE_END ::= "end_class"
     OBJECTTYPE_SUPERTYPE_BEGIN ::= "extends"
     OPERCALLEXP_SOURCE_BEGIN   ::= "on"
     OPERDECL_LOCALS_BEGIN        ::= "locals"
     PROGRAM_BEGIN ::= "program"
     PROGRAM_END ::= "end_program"
     VARCALLEXP_SOURCE_BEGIN    ::= "on"
     VARDECL_INITEXP_BEGIN        ::= "="
     IDENTIFIER ::= ["a"-"z", "A"-"Z", "_"] ( ["a"-"z", "A"-"Z", "0"-"9", "_" ] )*
```

List. 3. The resulting BNF rules

```
BLOCKSTAT_BEGIN=CURLY_OPEN
BLOCKSTAT_END=CURLY_CLOSE
CREATEEXP_BEGIN=new
CREATEEXP_END=()
NULLLITEXP_BEGIN=null
OBJECTTYPE_ATTRIBUTES_END=SEMICOLON
OBJECTTYPE_ATTRIBUTES_SEPARATOR=SEMICOLON
OBJECTTYPE_BEGIN=class
OBJECTTYPE_END=end_class
OBJECTTYPE_SUPERTYPE_BEGIN=extends
OBJECTTYPE_ORDER_1=name
OBJECTTYPE_ORDER_2=superType
OBJECTTYPE_ORDER_3=attributes
OBJECTTYPE_ORDER_4=operations
OPERCALLEXP_ACTUALPARS_BEGIN=BRACKET_OPEN <MANDATORY>
OPERCALLEXP_ACTUALPARS_END=BRACKET_CLOSE <MANDATORY>
OPERCALLEXP_ACTUALPARS_SEPARATOR=COMMA
```

List. 4. Part of the properties file for pm2bnf

for the language designer to indicate which keywords should be used in the grammar rule corresponding to a metaclass instance. Without keyword directions the Grasland toolkit will generate keywords based on the class and association role names.

For each metaclass there are two options to use a keyword: (1) at the start of the right hand side, (2) at the end of the right hand side. An example is the keyword 'new', indicated by CREATEEXP_BEGIN, that should appear at the start of a CreateExp instance. For each navigation there are three possibilities: (1) a keyword that should appear before the navigated element, (2) a keyword that should appear after the element, and (3) a keyword that separates the elements in a list. The last is sensible only when the multiplicity of the association is larger than one. In case that the element is optional (i.e. lower bound of multiplicity is zero), the language designer is able to indicate whether the keyword should still appear even if the element is not present. This is useful, for instance to indicate that the opening and closing brackets of a parameter list should be present even if there are no parameters. An example can be found in List 4, where the brackets are mandatory for the navigation OPERCALLEXP_ACTUALPARS. Note that a keyword in this approach can be any string, including brackets etc.

A third difference between a metamodel and a grammar is that the parsing algorithm used poses a number of requirements on the rules. For instance, the JavaCC parser generator creates LL(n) parsers, and its input should be an LL(n) grammar, where n indicates the number of lookahead tokens used. If the language designer decides to create a grammar with too few keywords, then the parser generator will produce errors and/or warnings. As the Grasland toolkit is a prototype we regard resolving these to be the responsibility of the language designer for now. By adding more keywords or by adding (by hand) lookaheads to the generated grammar the language designer will always be able to generate a grammar that is correct. Even so, the Grasland toolkit provides a minimal support in the form of the generation of lookaheads in the rule for a class with subclasses, where choice conflicts are likely because the attributes and navigations of the superclass appear in the rules for each subclass.

5   The Static Semantic Analyser

The two most important aspects of static semantic analysis are binding and type checking. This section describes how the Grasland toolkit implements these issues.

5.1   Binding

Binding is the general term for the binding of names to their definitions. These names may refer to types, for instance in a variable declaration, or to variables or operation/ functions, for instance in assignments or operation calls. Binding is often context sensitive in the sense that not all occurrences of the same name are bound to the same definition, depending on the context of the name it may be bound to a different definition, sometimes even to a definition of a different kind of element. For instance, in one context "message" may be bound to a variable, in another to a type or operation. Such a context is usually called a *namespace*.

In a Grasland generated PM all elements that need to be bound are instances of reference metaclasses (see List 1, rule 3). For each reference metaclass we know the metaclass from which it is derived. We call this metaclass the *target metaclass*.

Simple Binding. The most primitive way of binding these elements is by searching the parse tree for all instances of the target metaclass and comparing their names with the name of the element to be bound. This is the default implementation of binding.

However, it is possible for the language designer to indicate that certain metaclasses in the ASM act as namespaces. For instance in our example, the classes *Type*, *OperDecl*, and *Program* all act as namespaces. If there is a class labelled as namespace, then the *asm2pm* algorithm will produce a metamodel in which every class has the operation *findNamespace*, which will return the element's surrounding namespace. An *INamespace* interface is added to the metaclass(es) that act as namespaces for this purpose. The implementation of each of the *findNamespace* operations is specified by an OCL body expression.

The binding algorithm is in this case implemented as follows. First, find the surrounding namespace of the instance of the reference metaclass, then search this namespace for occurrences of the target metaclass and compare their names with the name of the reference element. If a match is found then the reference is bound to the found instance of the target metaclass. If no match is found, then the surrounding namespace of the searched namespace is searched in the same manner, and so on and so forth, until the outmost namespace has been searched. If no match was found, an error message is given. The search of a namespace goes down the parse tree to the leaves of the tree, unless one of the nodes is itself a namespace, then the search stops at this node.

Complex Binding. A more complex way of binding is based not only on the name of the reference element but also on the occurrence of surrounding elements. For instance, the binding of an operation call is usually determined not only by the name of the operation but also by the number and types of the parameters. In our example, the link called *referredOper* between an *OperCallExp* instance and an instance of the reference class *OperDeclREF* is an example of such a complex binding.

The language designer may indicate the use of a complex binding by stating an invariant in the ASM that must hold after the reference element is bound. For instance, for the example in Figure 3, the following entry in the properties file indicates the use of complex binding.

```
OperCallExp.referredOper=paramsCheck
```

In this case, the invariant called *paramsCheck* must be present for the class *Oper-CallExp*. It is specified by the following OCL expression. Note that the use of names for invariants is a standard OCL feature.

```
context OperCallExp
inv paramsCheck: referredOper.params.type = actualPars.type
```

Having this in place the Grasland toolkit implements complex binding more or less in the same manner as simple binding. First a list of possible matches is found based on the name only, then for each element in this list the invariant is checked. If no correct element is found then the search continues in the next namespace, etc.

An advantage of this approach is that normally these invariants need to be part of the ASM anyhow, so there is no extra effort needed from the language designer. Another advantage is that all the information that the language designer must provide is based on the ASM. The ASM is truly the focus of the language design process, even though a text-based language is being specified. This leaves room for the creation of multiple views each based on a different concrete syntax, with the possibility of combining textual and graphical views all working together on the same ASG.

Please note that this algorithm implements static semantic checking. This means that dynamic binding and dynamic scoping are by definition not covered.

5.2 Static Checking

An important observation with regard to static checking is that the rules that are checked during this phase are easily specified by OCL invariants on the ASM. These are the so called well-formedness rules. For instance, in our (simple) example the following rule provides enough information to perform type checking.

```
context VariableDecl
inv: self.type = initExp.type
```

Static checking is therefore implemented in the generated static semantic checker as the checking of invariants on the abstract syntax graph. Whenever an invariant is broken, an error message is given to the language user.

Even more complex forms of type checking involving type conformance can be handled in this manner. For instance, given the existence of an operation in the *Type* class that implements the type conformance rules, the following invariant allows for type checking with type conformance. The type conformance operation itself can also be specified using OCL.

```
context VariableDecl
inv: self.type.conformsTo(initExp.type)

context Type::conformsTo( actualType: Type) : Boolean
body: if ( actualType = self)
    then true
    else if not actualType.superType.oclIsUndefined()
        then self.conformsTo( actualType.superType)
        else false
        endif
    endif
```

The advantage of this approach is that the invariants can be used for all concrete syntaxes that may be defined for the ASM. Thus static checking becomes a common functionality instead of a functionality that needs to be implemented for each of the different concrete syntaxes.

6 Conclusion and Related Work

In this paper we have shown that it is possible to generate (parts of) an IDE, more specifically the front-end of a text-based compiler, from a metamodel. Given the tuning possibilities offered in both the *asm2pm* and *pm2bnf* transformations, the language designer can influence the resulting grammar considerably, with minimal effort from his part. Not yet mentioned is the fact that the Grasland toolkit is able to produce a deparser for the textual syntax, as well as a parser and deparser for an XML based interchange format for ASGs, and that all the generated tools described in this paper are combined to create an integrated language user environment. Because we do not foresee large difficulties in generating a language-specific editor, we conclude that it is indeed feasible to generate a text-based IDE from a metamodel, as was our initial ambition.

The idea of generating an IDE from a language specification is not new. In fact a number of metacase tools exist that perform this task, e.g. [13, 14]. What is new in our approach is that the focus of the language designer is on the metamodel, not on the BNF grammar. Keeping the focus on the ASM, instead of the grammar, is much more in line with the model driven process in which instances of the ASM are being transformed.

The process described by Wimmer and Kramler [8] starts with a grammar, from which a (raw) metamodel is built. Because this metamodel is (as they call it) "not user friendly", it is transformed into an ASM. The Eclipse plug-in set xText [15] also starts with a grammar and produces a metamodel. Hearnden et. al. describe the use of Anti-Yacc [16], which also forces the language designer to create a grammar. This grammar and a metamodel are fed to Anti-Yacc, which generates the bridging between the PM and the ASM. However, no evidence is given of how binding is handled. Finally, HUTN [17] uses an abstract base syntax that is applied to all models, which is customized to exploit specific properties of particular models. Again, our approach offers more flexibility to the language designer.

The graph grammar community has also been working on generating IDEs, see for instance [18, 19, 20]. However, their focus is on visual concrete syntaxes. Likewise, Fondement and Baar [21] describe a way to specify a visual syntax. Here too, a completely different metamodel is defined for the concrete syntax. Their approach is complementary to the one described here, as we focus on textual syntax.

The only other reference that focuses on the ASM instead of the grammar, is Jouault et al. [22]. They define a template language in which the language designer may specify the textual syntax. This syntax specification is very similar to BNF rules, thus this approach does not relieve the language designer from writing a grammar(- like) specification. Furthermore, they do not deal with complex references, nor do they handle type checking.

Concluding we can state that the Grasland toolkit produces a good, workable IDE from a metamodel. As is always the case with the generation of software, the creation of an IDE by hand could produce a better and more efficient IDE. However, it is important to compare the time and effort needed to create a reasonable well IDE using the Grasland toolkit with the time and effort needed to create a perfect IDE manually. We are confident that the comparison will favour the Grasland approach.

References

[1] Mernik, M., Heering, J., Sloane, A.M.: When and how to develop domain- specific languages. ACM Comput. Surv. 37(4), 316–344 (2005)

[2] The Eclipse Modeling Framework (2007), http://www.eclipse.org/emf

[3] Microsoft DSL tools. (2007), http://msdn.microsoft.com/vstudio/DSLTools/

[4] Octopus: OCL Tool for Precise UML Specifications (2007) http://www.klasse.nl/octopus

[5] Antlr (2007), http://www.antlr.org/

[6] JavaCC (2007), https://javacc.dev.java.net/

[7] Johnson, S.C.: Yacc – yet another compiler compiler. Technical Report CSTR 32, Bell Telephone Labs (July 1974)

[8] Wimmer, M., Kramler, G.: Bridging grammarware and modelware. In: WiSME 2005 4th Workshop in Software Model Engineering (2005)

[9] OCL 2.0 specification. Technical Report ptc/2005-06-06, OMG (2005)

[10] Warmer, J., Kleppe, A.: The Object Constraint Language: Getting Your Models Ready for MDA. Addison-Wesley Longman Publishing Co., Inc, Boston, MA, USA (2003)

[11] Alanen, M., Porres, I.: A relation between context-free grammars and meta object facility metamodels. Technical Report 606, TUCS, mar (2004)

[12] Forsberg, M., Ranta, A.: Labelled BNF: a highlevel formalism for defining well-behaved programming languages. In: Proceedings of the Estonian Academy of Sciences: Physics and Mathematics, number 52, pp. 356

[13] Reps, T., Teitelbaum, T.: The synthesizer generator. In: SDE 1: Proceedings of the first ACM SIGSOFT/SIGPLAN software engineering symposium on Practical software development environments, pp. 42–48. ACM Press, New York, NY, USA (1984)

[14] MetaEdit+ (2007), http://www.metacase.com/

[15] xText (2007), http://www.eclipse.org/gmt/oaw/doc/4.1/r80_xtextReference.pdf

[16] Hearnden, D., Raymond, K., Steel, J.: MOF-to-text. In EDOC, pp. 200–211. IEEE Computer Society, Los Alamitos (2002)

[17] Human-usable textual notation (HUTN) specification. Technical Report formal/04-08-01, OMG (2004)

[18] Bardohl, R.: GenGEd: Visual Definition of Visual Languages based on Algebraic graph Transformation. PhD thesis, TU Berlin, Berlin, Germany (1999)

[19] Minas, M.: Generating meta-model-based freehand editors. In: Proceedings of the third International workshop on graph based tools, 2006, EASST, pp. 1–11 (September 2006)

[20] de Lara, J., Vangheluwe, H.: Atom3: A tool for multi-formalism and meta-modelling. In: Kutsche, R.-D., Weber, H. (eds.) ETAPS 2002 and FASE 2002. LNCS, vol. 2306, Springer, Heidelberg (2002)

[21] Fondement, F., Baar, T.: Making metamodels aware of concrete syntax. In: Hartman, A., Kreische, D. (eds.) ECMDA-FA. LNCS, vol. 3748, pp. 190–204. Springer, Berlin Heidelberg (2005)

[22] Jouault, F., Bézivin, J., Kurtev, I.: TCS: a DSL for the specification of textual concrete syntaxes in model engineering. In: GPCE '06. Proceedings of the 5th international conference on Generative programming and component engineering, pp. 249–254. ACM Press, New York, NY, USA (2006)

Constraints Modeling for (Profiled) UML Models

François Lagarde[1], François Terrier[1], Charles André[2], and Sébastien Gérard[1]

[1] CEA, LIST, Boîte 94, Gif-sur-Yvette, F-91191, France
`firstname.lastname@cea.fr`
[2] I3S Laboratory,
BP 121
06903 Sophia Antipolis Cédex,
France
`charles.andre@unice.fr`

Abstract. The growing number of UML profiles and the resulting extensive application of stereotypes, is turning the modeling process error-prone. In order to constrain their uses, OCL lacks mechanisms for effective evaluation of stereotypes and is sometimes cumbersome. This paper describes a set of mechanisms that allow more intuitive constraint specification. They exploit the meta-model architecture to constrain a model with a focus on use of stereotypes. Two examples are given to illustrate their applicability. A dedicated assessment tool is also described.

1 Introduction

One of the purposes of Unified Modeling Language (UML) is to define a modeling language and a collection of diagrammatic notations that suit a wide-range of domains. To accommodate specific modeling concerns UML has a profiling mechanism. It adds meaning to modeling elements through stereotype applications and is a standard way of defining a domain-specific modeling language.

When a profile is defined, it is usually necessary to enrich the concepts it introduces with mechanisms that specify its use. One way of doing so, is to state constraints. For example, to depict concepts belonging to a real time system domain, we can introduce a Task concept with a stereotype «Task» and an Entry Point concept with a stereotype «EntryPoint». One of the constraints is to make sure that each task has exactly one entry point. In a broader modeling context, we must however consider not only a single profile application belonging to one domain, but also the application of more than one profile. This means expressing constraints for relationships between profiles. One illustration would be tying the above mentioned task concept with a Resource concept that is part of a profile for scheduling analysis.

An already existing solution is to enrich models with rules built into the standard Object Constraint Language (OCL). This is an effective way to describe model elements. A good illustration is the UML superstructure [1] in which most elements often several OCL expressions.

D.H. Akehurst, R. Vogel, and R.F. Paige (Eds.): ECMDA-FA 2007, LNCS 4530, pp. 130–143, 2007.
© Springer-Verlag Berlin Heidelberg 2007

However the current OCL standard lacks effective mechanisms for evaluating stereotype applications and suffers from complex writing. While an expert can write an expression, most modelers cannot readily understand or maintain them.

In this context, we introduce constructs to ease constraint relationship statements between model elements as well as among different models. The constraints can carry OCL declaration and compose rules for models having one profile application (i.e. in an intra-domain context) as well as for multiple profile applications (i.e. in a inter-domain context) and are obviously general enough for models with no applied profile. The constructs are formalized with a UML profile. It allows modelers to use a single UML environment and affords an intuitive approach to specifying constraints.

The paper is organized as follows: Section 2 gives an account on prior and related works, Section 3 presents our approach, Section 4 demonstrates its applicability by an intra-domain example and by an inter-domain example, Section 5 introduces our constraint assessment tool. We conclude with perspectives.

2   Related and Prior Work

2.1   Object Constraint Language

The Object Constraint Language (OCL) is a standard language for describing expressions in UML models. It is a twofold (query and constraint) language and benefits from the 4-layer meta-model architecture.

An OCL declaration has an element context and constrains its instance. The standard way to write expressions on elements is to create a stereotype with an extension point to the meta-element then to navigate to the element. This navigation uses a one-way navigable association relationship from Stereotype to MetaClass [1, p.686]. A given illustration introduces the stereotype «Home» to depict an EJB Home component and constrains a Home to not have owned attributes. This constraint is written as follows:

```
1   package EJBProfile
2   context Home inv:
3       self.base_Interface.ownedAttributes−>size() = 0
4   endpackage
```

If we want to navigate from a model element to a stereotype, we have to consider the OCL compliance point enabling "navigating non-navigable associations" and the role extension_Home of the association. However, its systematic use should ensure the presence of this attribute at first. Its precaution gets this theoretical solution too fragile to consider it as an practical one.

In order to specify efficient constraints, we often meet the need to express rules on elements belonging to different parts of a model. The solution is then to declare constraints in the context of the common root element. For example, to tie elements among different packages we must create a stereotype extending the Model meta-element to declare the constraints. This expression is then in charge of a multitude of rules and becomes highly complex.

To illustrate this, we consider a simplified real-time profile defining the concept of Task and Entry Point. We also identify a Resource concept that is part of a profile for scheduling analysis purpose. We need to make sure that: (a) each task belonging to a package stereotyped «RT» has exactly one operation stereotyped «entryPoint», (b) each of them should also match a class stereotyped «resource» with an equal name in a package stereotyped «SAnalysis». In order to write our expression, we introduce an ad-hoc function that collects the stereotypes applied to an element.

```
1   package RTProfile
2     def: isStereotyped(stereotype: String, e: Element):Boolean =
3     e.getAppliedStereotypes()->one(s |
4      s.name=stereotype)
5   context Task inv:
6     self.base_Class.ownedOperation->select(op |
7      isStereotyped('EntryPoint',op))->size=1
8   context RTModel inv:
9     -- collect all the classes stereotyped Task
10    let Tasks :
11       self.base_Model.nestedPackage->iterate(p, s:Set{}|
12       ((isStereotyped('RT', p)
13     and(s->union((p.packagedElement->iterate(c1, s1:Set{} |
14         isStereotyped('Task', c1)
15       and(s1->including(c1))))))))) in
16     -- collect all the classes stereotyped Resource
17     let Resources :
18       self.base_Model.nestedPackage->iterate(p, s:Set{}|
19       ((isStereotyped('SAnalysis', p)
20       and(s->union((p.packagedElement->iterate(c1, s1:Set{} |
21         isStereotyped('Resource', c1)
22       and(s1->including(c1))))))))) in
23       -- make them match
24       Tasks->forAll(c1 |
25         Resources->one(c2 | c1.name=c2.name))
26   endpackage
```

This expression quickly becomes unreadable and not maintainable. Dominik Stein et al [2] have stressed that even a simple query quickly results in a complex query expression. It is especially cumbersome when we want to query association relationships. The other drawback is that it cannot effectively indicate the reasons for a failure.

2.2 Model Comparison

To a certain extent, our problem could be considered part of a model comparison problem; a set of models is well constructed if they have a clearly identified set of elements.

In a recent paper, Alanen Marcus et al [3] defined an algorithm to compute differences and unions among models built-upon the Meta Object Facilities (MOF) which can be specifically adapted to a UML context. Yuehua Lin et al [4] emphasize that comparing models involves providing a support to visualize their differences. One possible solution is to use colors in a same way as the diff tools do.

However, current works on this subject relate more to version control problems and do not deal with the profile application.

2.3 Model Transformation

The OMG defines Query/View/Transformation [5] (QVT) specification to be used to query and to transform models built-upon the MOF. This specification includes a check-only mechanism to ensure that models can be produced by a transformation. Another possible way of solving our problem would be to find transformations that models have to respect.

In a comparable way as OCL, Devon Simmonds et al [6] showed that queries can also quickly produce complex expressions. Moreover, this specification lacks suitable implementation tools, despite promising projects, such as the one led by Frédéric Jouault et al [7] which promotes ATL as a possible implementation. For a more complete survey on this subject, the reader should refer to the Wensheng Wang report [8].

3   Our Approach

The UML superstructure defines structural information that encompasses relationships with other meta-elements and meta-properties, in addition to a set of OCL constraints. Our approach is to use this structural information to facilitate constraint formulation by means of rules for meta-elements. The models are kept intact by separating them from these rules.

The underlying goal is to identify a set of constructs to characterize meta-elements and relate them.

3.1   Conceptual Domain View

Our approach defines a set concept for the purpose of characterizing elements. This set is an AbstractSet concept with two more specialized concepts. The Input depicts an entry model element from which the rules have to be applied. The Set carries two properties to characterize members of a set. The based property states the meta-element while the stereotyped property gives a list of applied stereotypes.

Set restriction is afforded by a Restriction abstract concept which requires that members of one set match the elements of another set. As we work on sets, a existence quantification condition (alike the quantifier presented by Audris Kalnins et al [9]) is added to the constraints. This condition is satisfied if the cardinality of a set falls between a lower bound value (property atLeast) and upper bound value (property atMost). The default interval value is a lower bound equal to one and an unlimited upper bound. We also enrich this concept with an OCL capability to constrain elements of a set or among members of two sets.

We have further specialized this concept using:

- an Own concept to impose a UML content relationship with regard to the ownedMember property. This construct is our main construct for navigating through the UML hierarchy,
- a Match concept for matching elements,
- a WithThisRelationship concept that imposes a particular relationship.

Hence, a rule is composed of sets and is satisfied if one set or several sets is/are valid.

A conceptual domain view shown below (Fig. 1) sums up the key concepts and relationships. This domain view is part of a general methodology for defining a UML profile [10, p.22].

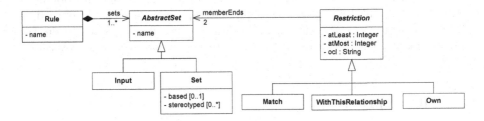

Fig. 1. Domain view

3.2   UML Domain View

The above domain view is transposed to a UML domain using a profile (Fig. 2). This is a quite straightforward operation.

An «AbstractSet» extends a Class. The name of the set is the name of the Class.

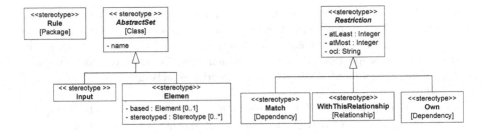

Fig. 2. Proposed profile

Our approach uses relationships to support restrictions between the sets. We extend the Dependency meta-class to support both an «Own» constraint and a «Match» constraint.

To state a constraint relationship we extend the Relationship meta-class with the stereotype «WithThisRelationship». A relationship for which the stereotype «withThisRelationship» is applied forces elements to respect this type of relationship.

4   Examples

To allow a more detailed description of our constructs, we have chosen the example of a refinement operation for an intra-domain context. To illustrate an inter-domain context, a model combining a data-driven with data-event domain is used.

4.1   A Refinement Operation

Refinement operations play a major role in the MDA process. This key concept can be defined, as suggested by Richard F. Paige et al [11], as the production of new models that necessarily enrich previously constructed models. It is the main thread leading from an abstract view to a concrete view of a given system.

Our example is a refining black-box. The first view depicts a Kahn process network and is an input point for a flow development. A Kahn process network is a group of processing units connected by communication channels via unbounded FIFO channels with a non-blocking writer and a blocking reader. Some of the processing units must be refined to an object-oriented domain model. This first view is a simplified filter specification borrowed from Rong Chen et al [12]. We consider the following filter $o(n) = k2 * i(n) + o(n-1)$ as performing data processing.

We have profiled a UML activity diagram to support the Kahn's semantics. The UML action element is stereotyped «Unit» and depicts a processing unit. The input port and output port are named connection points to manage channel communication. This level of abstraction does not represent the manner in which the input ports are connected to the output ports. We have also introduced another stereotype «isRefinable» to show which units are to be refined. The previous filter specification is represented in Figure 3.

Refinement Definition

The Adder action is stereotyped «isRefinable». The computation model requires the refined model to provide support for the two input ports (p1, p3) and the two output ports (p2, p4) and, of course, for data-processing.

To meet these requirements we apply the *expert* hypothesis that a processing unit involves a class with its own execution thread and realizes interfaces to push data into the Kahn environment and respectively uses interfaces to pull data out

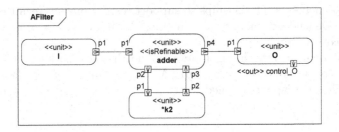

Fig. 3. Filter model

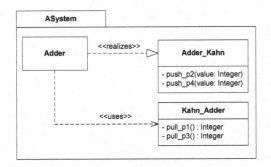

Fig. 4. Refined adder unit

of the Kahn environment. These interfaces own operations for each input and output port. They respect the naming convention push_ or pull_ followed by the port name.

Figure 4 gives a suitable refined model.

Refinement Modeling

The refinement stage is then formalized by translating a refinement execution into rules that must be satisfied by two models. We thus obtain a detailed refinement model (Fig. 5).

Its top elements are classes stereotyped «input». They maintain a mapping to the filter model and the package containing at least the expected Adder class. This information is given explicitly before evaluation. These elements have dependency relationships stereotyped «own» between K_Unit and C_Unit with default values.

The K_Unit class is stereotyped «set». It depicts actions stereotyped «Unit» and «IsRefinable». Because of the stereotype «Unit» extends the Action metaelement, we need not specify the property based. A translation could be: "consider the K_Unit set as elements simultaneously stereotyped «unit» and «isRefinable»".

This set is restricted. We require each member of the set K_Unit to exactly match a C_Unit with an equal name. We support this constraint by adding

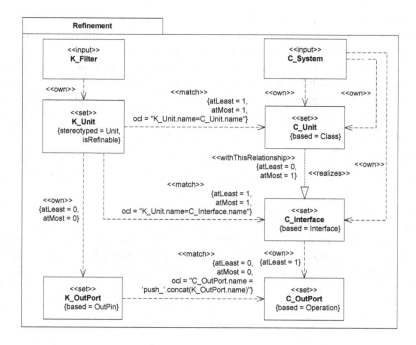

Fig. 5. Refinement model

a dependency relationship stereotyped «match» between these two sets. The property ocl carries the OCL constraint. In a similar manner, we declare another dependency relationship stereotyped «match» from K_Unit to C_Interface. This means that the processing unit has to match an Interface to support outgoing communication. Owing to space limitations we do not model the symmetric dependency relationship to manage incoming communication from K_Unit to C_Interface.

To ensure that *every* output port owned by every member of the set K_Unit implies an Operation owned by a member of the set C_Interface, we look for an output port which does not fulfil this constraint. This reformulation is similar to the data-base domain in which it is sometimes easier to find elements that do not match special criteria than to find all the matching elements. Hence the dependency relationship from K_Unit to K_OutPort has both properties atLeast and atMost equal to zero.

According to the previous guidelines, a member of the set C_Unit in charge of supporting a K_Unit has to realize or to use interfaces. Up to this stage, we have only stated the existence of such interfaces without imposing any relationship. We must thus apply the stereotype «withThisRelationship» to InterfaceRealization relationship from the C_Unit to C_Interface. We assume that a processing unit may have no outgoing communication and that the existence quantification condition is then at least equal to zero and at most equal to one.

It should be emphasized that this model does not ensure that each Action simultaneously stereotyped «isRefinable» and «unit» has a Class supporting the refinement and vice versa. The dependency relationship stereotyped «match» is directed. In our model we only ensure that each action stereotyped «isRefinable» and «unit» has a valid Class. To verify a symmetric relationship, we simply declare another model to check whether or not a C_Unit matches a K_Unit.

Assessing the Refinement

We support our approach with a tool (presented in sec. 5) that assesses rules for models. The result is provided as a graph in which nodes represent model elements.

We use our previous rules for the filter model and its refined model. We consider situations leading to a wrong evaluation to highlight constraint propagation. We add an extra output port named p5 to the processing unit Adder (Fig. 3), and we keep the refined model (Fig. 4) unchanged. The graph below (Fig. 6) is the result of the assessment.

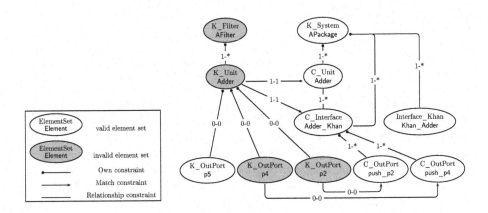

Fig. 6. Assessment graph

This graph shows that the models do not satisfy the rules. The top node AFilter is invalid. This situation is caused by the propagation of constraints from node p5 to AFilter. Output port p5 is valid because it cannot be matched to an operation. Consequently, the non existence condition from the K_Unit to the p5 is not satisfied and makes the K_Filter invalid.

4.2   A Composition Operation

We reuse our previous filter in an over-simplified controller system. This filter produces values triggering state changes in the control process over two states; Idle state and Control state. Figure 8 above shows the UML state machine model of the controller.

The overall modeling system leads to an heterogeneous interaction. On the one hand, we have a filter with a data-driven semantics, on the other hand a finite state machine model with event-driven semantics. To enable their interaction, a trigger element is introduced. This element compares a value to a range of values and sets on or off a flag. It is modeled using a new stereotype «Adapter» which extends an Action meta-class.

The next stage is to model an acceptable architecture to connect the filter, the triggering elements and the finite state machine.

Composition Definition

The component-based modeling approach offers valuable hints for composing our elements. Gregor Gössler et al [13] depict a component as a superposition of behavior models and interaction models with architectural constraints induced by connectors. To focus on the interaction models we must provide a mean for defining the connectable elements. Luca de Alfaro et al [14] introduce a formal framework in which, output and input ports are connected if they are matched by name. We have adopted this convention to depict a connectable element as being either a UML element stereotyped «in» -to encompass a required service concept- or a UML element stereotyped «out» -to encompass a provided service concept-. Two connectable elements are connected if they have an equal name and respect the in/out duality.

The unit processing O of our filter (Fig. 3) comes with an output port control_0 stereotyped «out». It is intended to produce values for triggering state changes. The finite state machine has two transitions triggered on two events; evtControl and evtIdle to activate the control or switch it off respectively. These events are triggered on values computed by the filter. Because they require information from the system, they have to be considered as input connectable elements. We therefore apply stereotype «in» to both elements.

To adapt data-driven semantics to event-driven semantics, we introduce two trigger elements TrigIdle and TrigControl (Fig. 7), both stereotyped «adapter». They act as our semantic bridge and consequently have to connect the filter to the finite state machine. According to the naming convention, both triggers have input ports named control_0 and appropriated output ports to create binding with the finite state-machine events.

Composition Modeling

Good modeling of connections involves making sure that the element stereotyped «in» match the elements stereotyped «out» with regard to the naming convention. By complying with this rule, the modeler avoids producing models with output ports for which there are no input ports.

The second rule relates to mixing semantics. Its purpose is to ascertain that an element stereotyped «adapter» exists between each filter output port stereotyped «out» and each finite state event stereotyped «in».

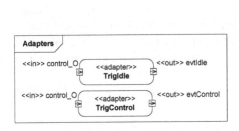

Fig. 7. Adapters

Fig. 8. Controller behavior

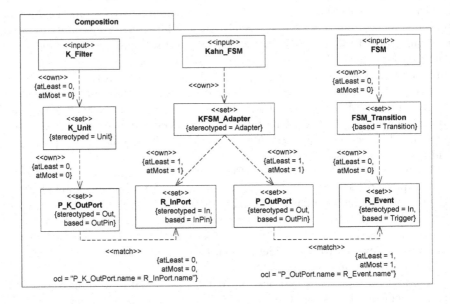

Fig. 9. Composition model

Figure 9 depicts theses rules and gives the general conditions to compose the model elements.

Such a model ensures coherence from a processing unit viewpoint. This means that we overlook any processing unit having output ports for which trigger elements are defined.

We use a naming convention to distinguish provided connectors from required connectors. A required connector is prefixed by R_ e.g. R_Input or R_Event and an output connector, or provided connector, is prefixed by P_.

The three classes K_Filter, K_Unit and P_K_OutPort have a dependency relationship stereotyped «own» with the tag value atLeast and the tag value atMost equal to zero. They initiate the question "Are there any processing units having any output port such as ...".

P_K_OutPort has a dependency relationship stereotyped «match» to R_InPort. R_InPort is the set of input ports stereotyped «in» owned by an action stereotyped «adapter». The matching condition is enhanced with anOCL constraint to impose equal name. As we search wrong processing units, the quantification existence is zero. If a P_K_OutPort element matching an R_InPort element is found, the P_K_OutPort element becomes invalid and yet fulfils the existence condition from K_Unit to P_K_OutPort.

The four classes Kahn_FSM, KFSM_Adaptater, R_InPort and P_OutPort state that a, adapter is correct if it has exactly one output port stereotyped «out» and exactly one input port stereotyped «in».

The remaining elements of the model identify event elements stereotyped «in» that are part of a transition and look for a dual output port member of the set P_Output.

In order to be thorough, constraint modeling could be supplemented by two other models. The first model will serve to make sure every UML elements owning an element stereotyped «out» has at least one dual element stereotyped «in». The second model would be reciprocal. By adding these two models, we ensure that all connectable elements are connected and that the previous model is symmetric.

Assessing the Composition

Composition assessment indicates a wrong composition if the K_Filter or the Kahn_FSM is invalid.

5   Tool Implementation

This research has led us to develop a constraint assessment tool based on Eclipse Modeling Framework Technology (EMFT) [15] library. This library provides facilities for quering a model and includes an OCL engine.

It processes in three stages. The first stage consists in reading the model in which the rules are to translate into a directed graph. A vertex is an element stereotyped «element» and edges are elements stereotyped «match». This is the support used to query and verify the models.

The following stage performs queries on models to collect the elements. It traverses the graph with a depth-first mechanism starting from each vertex having no incoming edges. For each vertex, a query is formulated contextually and performed on the models. The set of matched elements is used to build a corresponding graph. This step results in a new directed graph in which each vertex is a matched element respecting the «element» conditions.

The last stage evaluates the quantification conditions for the previous graph. Here again we use a depth-first mechanism to check conditions on each vertex. A vertex is deemed *valid* if it satisfies the condition; otherwise it is deemed *invalid*. This step is repeated while any state has changed.

On the resulting graph, each vertex represents a matched element which is either *valid* or not. To facilitate its interpretation, invalid elements are circled with red. The graph provides helpful information for locating the invalid elements.

6   Conclusions and Future Directions

In this paper, we have defined constructs for facilitating constraint specification in UML models, with a special focus on the use of stereotypes. We have also transposed our concepts to a UML profile to allow modelers to use the same environment for specifying and modeling constraints. The constraints are rules composed of sets. A set depicts elements that comply with meta-element and/or elements having a list of applied stereotypes. The sets have relationships to express constraints.

Constraint assessment is achieved by a graph and identifies the invalid element(s). This information is especially useful for the designer to correct its model.

Our approach is illustrated by a refinement operation and a composition operation that identifies the rules to be satisfied by the models.

Our tool allowed us to apply our approach to more realistic cases. It appears that constraints can be sometimes difficult to model. To overcome this difficulty, we create unitary constraints (or a more simple set of constraints). Then we elaborate a scenario to apply these unitary constraints to ensure global constraints.

The proposed constructs are general enough for application to a wide range of contexts. They can support development of a methodology for translating main modeling stages into rules.

Further work will be necessary to demonstrate the benefit of our approach for broader examples. We also require defining a theoretical foundation to support our constructs. The graph theory seems to be as one of the best candidate [16].

References

1. Object Management Group (OMG): Unified Modeling Language: Superstructure, ptc/06-04-02 (April 2006)
2. Stein, D., Hanenberg, S., Unland, R.: A Graphical Notation to Specify Model Queries for MDA Transformations on UML Models. Lecture Notes in Computer Science: Model Driven Architecture (2005)
3. Marcus, A., Ivan, P.: Difference and Union of Models. Technical Report 527, TUCS (April 2003)
4. Lin, Y., Zhang, J., Gray, J.: Model Comparison: A Key Challenge for Transformation Testing and Version Control in Model Driven Software Development. Best Practices for model Driven Software Development OOPSLA/GPCE Workshop (2004)
5. Object Management Group (OMG): MOF 2.0 Query/Views/Transformations, ptc/05-11-01 (2005)
6. Simmonds, D., France, R., Ghosh, S.: Using Directives to Implement Model Transformations. In: From MDD to Experiments and Illustrations. Hardback (2006)

7. Jouault, F., Kurtev, I.: On the Architectural Alignment of ATL and QVT. In: Proceedings of the 2006 ACM Symposium on Applied Computing (SAC 06) pp. 1188–1195. chapter Model transformation (MT 2006) (2006)
8. Wang, W.: Evaluation of UML Model Transformation Tools. Master's thesis, OOLS. University of Vienna, Business Informatics Group (2005)
9. Kalnins, A., Celms, E., Sostaks, A.: Simple and Efficient Implementation of Pattern Matching in MOLA Tool. In: Proceedings of the 7th International Baltic Conference on Databases and Information Systems (Baltic 92006) pp.159–167 (July 2006)
10. Object Management Group (OMG): UML Profile for Schedulability, Performance, and Time, ptc/05-01-02 (January 2005)
11. Paige, R.F., Kolovos, D.S., Polack, F.A.: Refinement via Consistency Checking in MDA. Electronic Notes in Theoretical Computer Science 137, 151–161 (2005)
12. Chen, R., Sgroi, M., Lavagno, L., Martin, G., Sangiovanni-Vincentelli, A., Rabaey, J.: UML and platform-based design. Technical report (2003)
13. Goessler, G., Sifakis, J.: Composition for Component-Based Modeling. Science of Computer Programming 55, 161–183 (2005)
14. de Alfaro, L., Henzinger, T.A.: Interface-based Design. In: Broy, M., Gruenbauer, J., Harel, D., Hoare, C.A.R. (eds.) Engineering Theories of Software-intensive Systems. NATO Science Series: Mathematics, Physics, and Chemistry, vol. 195, pp. 83–104. Springer, Heidelberg (2005)
15. Eclipse Modeling Framework Technology, http://www.eclipse.org/emft
16. Baresi, L., Heckel, R.: Tutorial introduction to graph transformation: A software engineering perspective. In: Corradini, A., Ehrig, H., Kreowski, H.-J., Rozenberg, G. (eds.) ICGT 2002. LNCS, vol. 2505, pp. 402–429. Springer, Heidelberg (2002)

Scenarios of Traceability in Model to Text Transformations

Gøran K. Olsen and Jon Oldevik

SINTEF Information and Communication Technology Forskningsveien 1,
0373 Oslo, Norway
{goran.k.olsen,jon.oldevik}@sintef.no

Abstract. The challenges of managing change in model-driven development are addressed by traceability mechanisms for model to text transformations. A traceability model, tailored for representing trace information between models and generated code, provides the basis for visualisation and analysis of the relationships between models and code. Usage scenarios for traceability are discussed and illustrated by our traceability implementation.

1 Introduction

Model to text transformation is one of several vital steps in model-driven development (MDD), which makes it possible to generate an extensive amount of code from models. This automation can reduce the development time and increase the quality of the code, but it also introduces some new challenges that must be addressed.

Often, the people writing transformation specifications will be different from the engineers developing the system. In this way, vital details required for understanding the systems are hidden from the engineers within the transformations. This may be a convenient way of separating the concerns of different actors in the development process. On the other hand, it may also hinder sufficient understanding of the system on the part of the engineer. One way of solving this is letting the engineer examine the design models, the transformation specifications and the generated code. This may, however, not be desirable since the engineer may be unfamiliar with the transformation language. It also reveals details that are supposed to be concealed. An alternative approach is to establish links between representations of the design artefacts and the generated code that have semantics with the necessary information for the engineers. Model to text transformations enable implicit or explicit creation of these links.

Manual updates of generated code are often required in the development process. In complex systems it can be difficult to localize the places to update, and there might also be restrictions on where changes are allowed. Traceability information can be used to ease this task.

In this paper, we describe how traceability and traceability links can be used to support the development of systems. We explain model to text traceability and how this is implemented in MOFScript [1]. Several usages of MOFScript-specific trace links are described in usage scenarios.

D.H. Akehurst, R. Vogel, and R.F. Paige (Eds.): ECMDA-FA 2007, LNCS 4530, pp. 144–156, 2007.
© Springer-Verlag Berlin Heidelberg 2007

2 Traceability

One of the main challenges in MDD is the management of relations between different artefacts produced in the development process. As systems become more complex, the number of artefacts is increasing. Furthermore, the artefacts are often generated. Therefore, trace links are needed to fully understand the many dependencies that exist between the different artefacts.

In the IEEE Standard Glossary of Software Engineering Terminology [2] traceability is defined as:

"The degree to which a relationship can be established between two or more products of the development process, especially products having a predecessor-successor or master-subordinate relationship to one another; for example, the degree to which the requirements and design of a given software component match".

2.1 Establishment of Trace Links

In the past, trace links have mostly been established manually by the different persons involved in the development process, for instance by creating trace links between word documents and use-case model elements. This task has been known as difficult, time consuming, and very often a source to errors both when it comes to the establishment of new links and keeping the existing links updated and consistent [3].

Following an MDD approach and utilizing model transformations makes it possible to generate these trace links explicitly or implicitly in the transformation specification. By implicit, we mean that some transformation tool, e.g. MOFScript, populates a trace model automatically when a transformation is executed. By explicit, we mean that additional trace code must be inserted into the transformation. This can be achieved in two ways; by writing the trace code each time or running a higher order transformation on the transformation model. The latter approach is used in the Atlas Transformation Language (ATL) [4]. The final adopted OMG standard MOF Models to Text Transformation Language also requires that the ability to explicitly create trace blocks in the code is present [5].

Storing the established trace links can be done in two ways according to Kolovos et al. [6], either by embedding them in the models or storing them externally in a separate new model. The first approach gives a human-friendly view of the trace links, but it only supports trace links between elements in the same model. The external approach has the advantage of having the trace information separated from the model and therefore avoids polluting the models.

2.2 Traceability on Different Abstraction Levels

Trace links can in theory be established between all artefacts in a system development project, for instance between requirement documents and use-case diagrams, use-case diagrams and test cases or domain and platform independent models (PIM), elements in the PIM and platform specific models (PSM), and between the PSM and generated text (e.g., code and documentation).

All these trace links are required to provide end-to-end traceability. End-to-end traceability enables a number of different analyses that can be preformed on the system, e.g. checking that a requirement is fulfilled in the implementation by following the trace links from a requirement via the PIM and the PSM to code, known as coverage analysis [7].

The trace links required to provide end-to-end traceability are intermediate and can also make the basis for useful functionality and analyses. In this paper we present several different usages of model to text traceability links.

2.3 Different Trace Link Classifications

The simplest trace link is one without any type specification other than link; it only contains references to one source and one target element which optionally can be contained in another element. According to [7-9] this may be insufficient for many projects. Hence, several different trace link classifications have been proposed.

Some examples of trace types are: The trace type *manual*, which is a trace link established manually in the trace model. The trace type *automatic* is created by a tool, and the trace type *transformation* means that the trace link is between a source and a target in a transformation. In a model to text transformation this could be from a model reference to a text segment. The trace type *dependency* is between two artefacts that are dependent of each other, and the trace type *verifies* means that one artefact verifies another (e.g. a test implementation) may verify a requirement.

2.4 Trace Link Usage

The reason to create and update traceability links is that the links can be used to support and document the development process. The information can be used in several ways, but the most obvious scenario is simple *trace inspection*. Through trace inspection it is possible to browse the trace information and get insight in how the different artefacts are connected. This is becoming more useful as an increasing number of artefacts are generated automatically from model to model and model to text transformations. The simple browsing can also be extended with additional functionality as explained in the section 0.

Walderhaug et al.[7] and Ramesh et al.[9] describe several different trace analysis scenarios:

- **Change impact analysis:** Change impact analysis is used to determine the impact a change to an artefact will have on other artefacts.
- **Coverage analysis:** Through coverage analysis, the trace user can determine the degree to which some artefacts of the system are followed up by other artefacts in the system.
- **Orphan analysis:** Orphan analysis is used to find artefacts that are orphaned with respect to some specified trace relations.

In the following section, we address traceability in model to text transformations and look at how different traceability scenarios can be provided by the traceability support in MOFScript.

3 Model to Text Traceability

For traceability to be useful, we need the ability to trace artefacts through the lifecycle of the software development process, from requirement documents to model elements and from model elements to textual artefacts such as code. The steps required to move from one level to the other are often automated by transformations. In this process, the transformation tools should be able to produce trace links.

Several model to text languages exist, and some of them have support for traceability. In the MOF Models to Text Standard [5], traceability is defined to be explicitly created by the use of a trace block inserted into the code, as illustrated below.

```
[trace(c.id()+ '_definition') ]
  class [c.name/]
  {
    // Constructor
    [c.name/]()
    {
      [protected('user_code')]
      ; user code
      [/protected]
    }
  }
[/trace]
```

This approach provides user-defined blocks that represent a trace to the code generated by the block. This is specifically useful for adding traces to parts of the code that are not easily automated. A drawback of the approach is a cluttering of the transformation code. A complementary approach, as taken in MOFScript, is to automate the generation of traces based solely on model element references.

3.1 Traceability in MOFScript

MOFScript is a model to text transformation tool and language. It can be used to generate text from EMF based models. The transformation implementation contains references to model elements that should be substituted in the generated text.

The references to model elements are the basis of MOFScript traceability. Any reference to a model element that is used to produce text output, results in a trace between that element and the target text file. The granularity is from model element to line and column in the text file [10].

```
uml.Class::main(){
    file(self.name+".java")
    'package 'packageName';\n
    import java.util.*;\n'
    self.visibility' class ' self.name'{

  self.ownedAttribute->forEach(p:uml.Property | p.association = null ){
    '    ' p.visibility' ' p.type.name' _' p.name';\n'

  }
  self.ownedAttribute->forEach(p:uml.Property | p.association !=null ){
    '// Association: 'p.name':'p.type.name'('p.lower '..'p.upper')'
    '\t' p.visibility' HashMap<'p.type.name', 'p.name '>_'
        p.name.toLower()';\n'
  }
```

The above transformation code generates the beginning of a Java class file where the references are fetched from the model. If the class property *visibility* is set to protected, "protected" will be written to the file instead of *self.visibility*. We will use the example model in Fig. 1 to illustrate the traceability support.

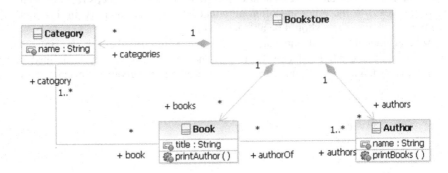

Fig. 1. Bookstore Example Model

Given the model in Fig. 1, an execution of the transformation will generate the following Java source code for the class Book.

```
package org.sintef.no;
import java.util.HashMap;

public class Book {
    private String _title ;
// Association: authors:Author(1..-1)
    protected HashMap<String, Author>_authors;
// Association: category:Category(1..-1)
    protected HashMap<String, Category>_category;
}
```

Each reference is substituted with the model element's value and a trace is created, linking the element and the code segment. The link is stored in a traceability model, an instance of MOFScript's traceability metamodel.

3.2 The Traceability Metamodel

The traceability metamodel in MOFScript was described in detail in [10]. Since then, it has been slightly modified during the implementation of the traceability support. Fig. 2 shows its concepts.

The *TraceModel* is the root of the model and contains traces, files and model element references. A *File* contains one or more blocks, which in turn contains a set of traceable segments. A *TraceableSegment* defines a position and length within a block in a file. A *Trace* references an originating model element and the segment to which it traces. The *Block* defines the positioning of the block within the file. Furthermore, a block is either protected or unprotected. A *protected block* represents an unchangeable part of a file, which is not meant to be modified by users. Conversely, an *unprotected block* represents a part of the file that is meant to be modified by the user. This could for example be the body of a method.

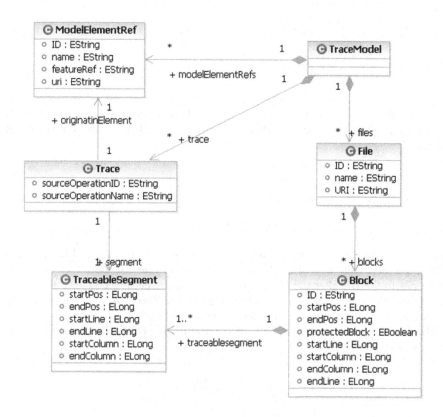

Fig. 2. Traceability Metamodel

When a transformation is executed, the MOFScript runtime populates an instance of the traceability metamodel, which is an ecore metamodel. This results in a traceability model. Fig. 3 shows an editor view of the traceability model generated from the Bookstore example model in Fig. 1.

In the traceability model in Fig. 3, *Book.java* contains, among other things, a block with id 3. In the property view we can see where the block starts and ends, and that it is a protected block. This means that editing in this area is not allowed (changes in the code will not be preserved if the file is generated again). The traceable segments represent the references that are used in the file and hold information about start and end position.

Unprotected Blocks. Setting the blocks' *protected block* property to "true" is the default behaviour of the trace generation. However, often it is required that the code is edited manually. To cope with this MOFScript supports the notion of unprotected blocks. These blocks are created with the use of the *unprotect* keyword in the transformation code, as illustrated in the transformation code for operations below.

```
self.ownedOperation->forEach(o:uml.Operation){
        '\n  'o.visibility' void ' o.name'(){'
        unprotect{
        '      //User code here for operation'
        }
        '   }\n'
}
```

The resulting code, shown below, represents the unprotected block as comments containing a *#BlockStart* and a *#BlockEnd* and an identifier for the source model element.

```
public void printAuthor(){
//#BlockStart number=4 id=_MeMJULEPEdu-Vepu7rgPLg
      //User code here for operation
//#BlockEnd number=4
}
```

Between the block comments, the user can insert or remove code, and the changes will be preserved the next time the transformation is run. All the traces that have references to the file after the block will also be generated in accordance with their new position in the file. The block comment tag (here '*//*') is controlled by environment settings and can be changed to match the target language.

The next sections elaborate on how this traceability information can be utilized and describe several scenarios.

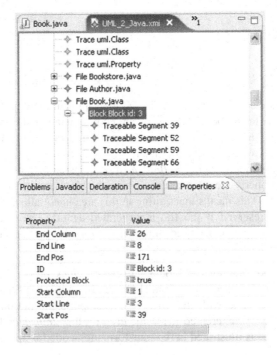

Fig. 3. Trace Model and Property View

3.3 Model to Text Specific Trace Scenarios

Trace links created in MOFScript between model elements and generated text can be utilized in several ways. This functionality can be used by different stakeholders, such as a *Transformation Architect* or *System Engineer.*

Extended Trace Inspection. The traceability model contains logical links from model elements to the code. These can be used to navigate and visualise traces in the code. For example, the user might select a specific model element and visualise the traces as highlighted code parts.

Coverage Analysis. Coverage analysis is useful for checking and ensuring that all relevant parts of the model are actually utilised by a transformation. If there are no traces from a particular model element, it is not used in the text transformation.

Impact Analysis. Impact analysis in text transformation can allow for checking the impact of a model change to existing generated code. A limitation in this regard is unprotected areas in the code that use model references, which cannot be seen from the traceability model.

Orphan Analysis. Orphans can occur in the code if model elements are deleted. There will then be traces from old model elements to the code. The transformation needs to be re-run in order to synchronise the model, the code, and the traces.

Trace Documentation. The traceability model can be used to generate different kinds of traceability documentation, for example by generated HTML documents. Such trace documentation can be provided by reusable model to text transformations [11] that have the trace model as source.

Unprotected Block Checking. When an unprotected region in the generated code has been implemented, the corresponding block in the trace model should be updated to show that it is completed. This will enable the Project Manager to check for bottle-necks, presenting a view of the remaining unprotected blocks that needs to be implemented, and if necessary move resources to a different part of the project.

Merging Traceability Models. Merging of traceability models may be used when several different transformations are executed from the same source model. The traces reference the same model elements, but sets of different target files. A merging of these will provide a more complete view of the traces from that particular source model.

Traceability Model Evolution. As models evolve, so will traceability models generated from those models. Histories of traceability models associated with a model may be used to analyse the evolution of the model with respect to code generation.

Our aim is to provide a toolset that supports the identified scenarios. Currently, we have developed a prototype that addresses some of the scenarios.

3.4 Traceability Analysis Prototype

The Traceability Model Analysis prototype is an initial version of a more complete traceability tool that also will consist of a repository for storing trace models. At this time, only MOFScript-specific trace analysis is supported. The prototype makes it possible to browse the source model in a tree editor and invoke different functionality on selected elements (Fig. 4).

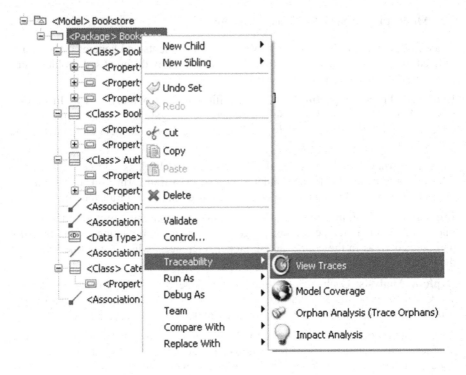

Fig. 4. Trace Menu for Model Bookstore

View Traces. This functionality gives a view of the traces for a selected model element (and its descendants). It can be used for trace inspection to locate the traces

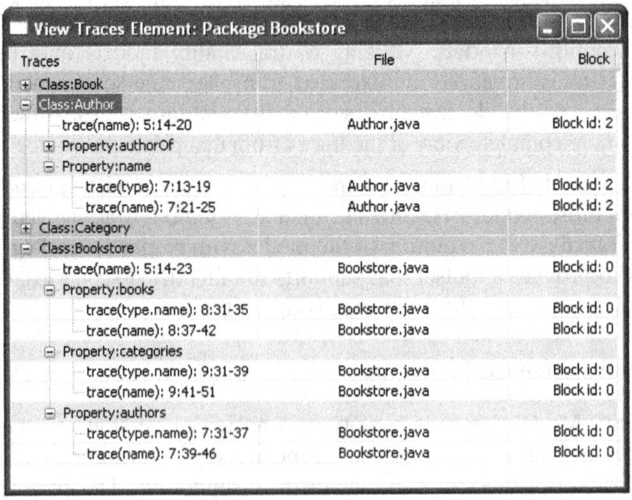

Fig. 5. Trace View

for specific model elements. Fig. 5 shows an example of this view for the Bookstore example, showing all traces generated from elements contained in the Bookstore package. As can be seen, the Bookstore class has several trace links to code segments in the file Bookstore.java.

Model Coverage. This functionality shows which parts of the model that do not have trace representations in the traceability model. It allows for checking that all intended model elements have been processed by the transformation. Fig. 6 shows the result of a Model Coverage analysis after adding two properties to the Book Class (isbn and price).

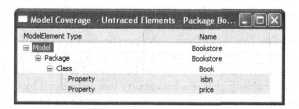

Fig. 6. Model Coverage

Orphan Analysis. This functionality allows for checking traces that are no longer valid, in that they reference model elements that no longer exist. Fig. 7 shows the result of an Orphan Analysis after the property *name* has been removed from the model element *Author*. Following the MDD approach, the normal procedure would be to rerun the transformation. However, on trace links that are created manually, this will be a useful feature.

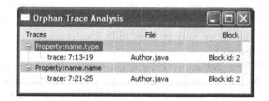

Fig. 7. Orphan Analysis after deleting a property

Impact Analysis. The functionality provided by the impact analysis checks for references in the generated code that will be affected by a modification of the model. This is basically an application of the *view traces* functionality with the source element as input to the query.

Functionality on Generated Files. The generated files also have traceability-specific actions that can be performed; this includes *view traces to file*, which will display the traces and the source elements that have this file as target and *view unprotected blocks,* which provides the user with a presentation of the unprotected blocks in the given file. The displayed unprotected blocks can be used for direct navigation into the file on the unprotected block's starting position. When the number of files and unprotected regions are many (e.g., in complex systems), this functionality will simplify the manual development task.

When text has been inserted into an unprotected block manually, the traceability model can be updated to reflect the new positions of the traceable blocks and segments in the generated file.

4 Related Work

Even though traceability is a well known problem in software engineering and the current literature contains ample publications describing the need for traceability solutions, little work has been done in the field of model to text traceability. The OMG MOF Model to Text Transformation Specification [5] specifies a trace solution with the use of trace blocks, but currently there are no implementations of the standard available. How these trace links can be utilized is not described.

Acceleo Pro Traceability [12] is a traceability tool developed by Obeo that handles traceability links between model elements and code and vice versa. This tool enables round trip support; updates in the model or the code are reflected in the connected artefacts. Analyses are also available using the traces as input, but since this is a commercial tool, restricted information describing the solution is available. It seems to be based on similar ideas as described in [10] where model elements are traced to exact positions in files.

In [13] Alexander Egyed describes a bottom up approach for trace link generation with the use of the Trace Analyser tool. The approach requires the existence of a system that is both observable and executable, a list of artefacts from the development (e.g., model elements), usage scenarios or test cases and some initial traces that links the artefacts and the scenarios. This solution creates traces from lines of executed code to requirements and thus enables traceability among all artefacts.

Reqtify [14] is a requirement traceability tool from ChiasTek. It supports traceability through the entire project from high-level requirements to models, code, test scripts, and test results.

Objecteering 6.0 from Softeam [15] provides trace functionality through a trace editor that enables the user to create traces manually between artefacts. Model elements created from wizards based on existing elements can be traced automatically.

Rational RequisitePro [16] is a requirement and use case management tool that provides the ability to display traces between parent/child relationships and showing requirements that may be affected by upstream or downstream changes.

CaliberRM from Borland [17] is also a requirement management tool that enables manual creation of trace links from top level requirements to lower level descriptions.

5 Conclusion and Future Work

This paper presents a traceability solution for model to text transformations. Usage scenarios show that the solution is viable and how the generated trace model can be utilized.

The trace generation in MOFScript is implicit, meaning that all references to model elements are traced. In the MOF Models to Text Specification [5] the creation of traces is done explicit thru the use of trace blocks (it does not state that implicit traces can not be used in addition). We believe that each approach has pros and cons and that an optimal solution should support a combination of both. Direct references from model elements to text should be generated automatically with the granularity defined by environment settings. There may also be situations where this is not sufficient to produce all trace dependencies required; therefore, explicit creation of trace links should be supported and classified accordingly. This functionality will be supported in a future version of the toolset.

In [18], Antoniol et al. have identified several challenges that must be addressed related to different aspects of traceability in MDD. Keeping trace information up to date can be an inconceivable task that often makes the links erode into an inaccurate state. The granularity of the trace links is also identified to be a challenge. The more fine-grained the trace links are, the more error prone they become. However, when traces are automatically generated, they are updated when the model changes and the code is regenerated. In this work, the challenge of keeping the trace links updated is addressed and the granularity issue is reduced.

The quantity of traces may be a challenge. In our solution, we are tracing all model element references and the number of traces might become incomprehensible and hence less useful. Furthermore, it might be a performance issue when the models and the transformation become large and complex. By adding a filtering mechanism to the traceability engine, it is possible to specify kinds of model elements that are interesting to trace and minimise performance overhead and unnecessary trace information.

Classification of traces was discussed earlier. In many traceability scenarios it may be useful or even essential to have meta information associated with traces, but it depends on the usage context. In an end-to-end traceability scenario involving different tools and artefacts, meta information will be important in order to distinguish the different traces. The scenarios we have shown here demonstrate usefulness of traces without classification.

The presented traceability solution implemented in MOFScript has its own specific traceability metamodel as shown in Fig.2. Future work includes the specification of a more generic trace metamodel (not specific to model to text) that will be implemented in a traceability tool. This tool will provide a simple interface for trace establishment both manually by users and automatically from several different MDD tools. The first step will be to integrate the trace establishment from MOFScript and then provide a user friendly interface for manual trace establishment.

Furthermore, we will investigate how to support trace model merging. Tools that do not support the provided interface of the traceability tool can supply the populated trace model, and the model can be merged into the repository's model representation. The goal will be to establish a MDD tool chain that in turn will populate the same project trace model. A typical scenario will be to model use-cases and have textual descriptions in Word documents, these artefacts will be traced to each other by manual establishment of the links. The use-cases will then be refined to different models and the proper trace links will be created manually or automatically by tools. The new models become sources to model to model transformations (e.g., an ATL transformation), which can populate the trace model in the repository. The generated target models will then act as source models to a transformation in MOFScript. The MOFScript transformation creates new trace links from the already existing model artefacts in the trace model to files, blocks and traceable segments.

With this approach, the development chain is capable of supporting end-to-end traceability where most traces are automatically created. Several end-to-end analyses similar to the model to text specific will also be supported.

Acknowledgements. This work is a result from the MODELPLEX project co-funded by the European Commission under the "Information Society Technologies" Sixth Framework Programme. (http://www.modelplex-ist.org/). Information included in this document reflects only the authors' views. The European Community is not liable for any use that may be made of the information contained herein.

References

1. Oldevik, J., et al.: Toward Standarised Model to Text Transformations. In: Hartman, A., Kreische, D. (eds.) ECMDA-FA 2005. LNCS, vol. 3748, Springer, Heidelberg (2005)
2. IEEE, IEEE Standard Glossary of Software Engineering Terminology. IEEE Std 610.12-1990. 78 (1990)
3. Egyed, A.: Resolving Uncertainties during Trace Analysis. 12th ACM SIGSOFT Symposium on Foundations of Software Engineering, pp. 3–12 (2004)
4. Jouault, F.: Loosely Coupled Traceability for ATL. ECMDA 05 Traceability Workshop (2005)
5. OMG, MOF Models to Text Transformation Language Final Adopted Specification Member doc: 06-11-01 (2006) www.omg.org
6. Kolovos, D.S., Paige, R.F., Polack, F.A.C.: On-Demand Merging of Traceability Links with Models. ECMDA 06 Traceability Workshop Bilbao (2006)
7. Walderhaug, S., et al.: Traceability Metamodel and System Solution. ECMDA 06 Traceability Workshop Bilbao (2006)
8. Aizenbud-Reshef, N., et al.: Model traceability. IBM Systems Journal 45(3), pp. 515–526 (2006)
9. Ramesh, B., Jarke, M.: Toward Reference Models for Requirements Traceability. IEEE Transactions on Software Engineering 27(1), pp. 58–93 (2001)
10. Oldevik, J., Neple, T.: Traceability in Model to Text Transformations ECMDA 06 Traceability Workshop Bilbao (2006)
11. Olsen, G.K., Aagedal, J., Oldevik, J.: Aspects of Reusable Model Transformations. ECMDA 06 Workshop on Composition of Model Transformations (2006)
12. OBEO, Acceleo Pro Traceability (2007), http://www.acceleo.org/pages/additionnal-products/en
13. Egyed, A.: A Scenario-Driven Approach to Trace Dependency Analysis. IEEE Transactions on Software Engineering 29, 17 (2003)
14. Chiastek, Reqtify (2007), http://www.chiastek.com/products/reqtify.html
15. Softeam, Objecteering 6.0 Web-Page (2007), http://www.objecteering.com/objecteering6.php
16. Software, I.R., Rational RequisitePro: reqpro/ (2007), http://www-306.ibm.com/software/awdtools/
17. Borland, CaliberRM (2007), http://www.borland.com
18. Antoniol, G., et al.: Problem Statement and Grand Challenges in Traceability. Center of Excellence for Traceability (2006)

Human Comprehensible and Machine Processable Specifications of Operational Semantics

Markus Scheidgen and Joachim Fischer

Department of Computer Science, Humboldt Universität zu Berlin
Unter den Linden 6, 10099 Berlin, Germany
{scheidge,fischer}@informatik.hu-berlin.de

Abstract. This paper presents a method to describe the operational semantics of languages based on their meta-model. We combine the established high-level modelling languages MOF, OCL, and UML activities to create language models that cover abstract syntax, runtime configurations, and the behaviour of runtime elements. The method allows graphical and executable language models. These models are easy to read by humans and are formal enough to be processed in a generic model interpreter. We use Petri-nets as a running example to explain the method. The paper further proposes design patterns for common language concepts. The presented method was applied to the existing modelling language SDL to examine its applicability.

1 Introduction

Language specifications, especially the definition of language semantics, are usually either informal or mathematical. These specifications are human readable, even though they might be imprecise or require substantial mathematical knowledge. However, it is normally hard to automatically derive computer tools from such specifications. We want to create model based language definitions that are both: comprehensible to humans and, at the same time, machine executable. Such definitions can be valuable for prototyping new languages, or creating tools for existing languages in a model driven fashion.

Meta-modelling is an already established technology to model the abstract syntax of languages in a human appealing and yet machine processable way. Other modelling techniques (based on meta-modelling) do the same for the language aspects graphical and textual notation, code-generation, or model transformations. Our contribution to the general goal of modelling languages is a method that uses existing graphical (meta-)modelling languages on a high level of abstraction to define operational semantics. We formally describe languages and can therefore execute models solely based on the according language definition by using a generic model interpreter.

Plotkin's structural operational semantics [1] is the standard way to define the operational semantics of programming languages. It uses transition systems

D.H. Akehurst, R. Vogel, and R.F. Paige (Eds.): ECMDA-FA 2007, LNCS 4530, pp. 157–171, 2007.

$\langle \Gamma, \rightarrow \rangle$, where Γ is a set of configurations γ and $\rightarrow \subseteq \Gamma \times \Gamma$ are the possible transitions between configurations. To define the operational semantics of a meta-model based language we use its meta-model M to define sets of models Γ_M. These models act as configurations. Furthermore, we use actions over models as transitions from one model of M to another model of the same M $(\gamma \in \Gamma_M \rightarrow \gamma' \in \Gamma_M)$. We use UML activities in combination with OCL to describe the actions to be executed. These activities describe sequences of model configurations: $\gamma \rightarrow^* \gamma'$. Meta-models and activities form language models which define abstract syntax and operational semantics. We developed a generic model interpreter that can process such language models. This tool interprets an input model γ_{in} by changing it as defined by the activities in the corresponding language model. The result is a model that evolves according to the specified operational semantics: $\gamma_{in} \rightarrow^* \gamma$.

In the next section we continue with related work. Section 3 explains the basic concepts of our method and shows an example language model which describes the operational semantics of Petri-nets. In section 4 we show that more complex languages need to distinguish between elements that describe abstract syntax (define the models that the user can write) and runtime elements (describe additional information that is necessary when a model is executed). Section 5 discusses reusable designs for operational semantics and presents a pattern for instantiation as an example. Section 6 briefly describes the application of our method to the modelling language SDL and thereby reasons that the framework is applicable and scales up to practical languages. The paper closes with conclusions in section 7.

2   Related Work

Work on generated or generic language tools includes frameworks for the development of domain specific languages. These frameworks use meta-models as the core of language specifications and also cover language aspects like notation, analysis, transformations, or operational semantics. Such frameworks are GME [2], XMF [3] (originated in the MMF approach [4]), AToM3 [5] and meta-programming facilities like MPS [6], kermeta [7], AMMA [8] MetaEdit+ [9]. Some of these frameworks define semantics through general purpose programming languages (MPS, MetaEdit+), others provide specialised languages to define semantics (XMF, kermeta, AToM3). Two different approaches to semantics can be identified: GME and AToM3 use model transformations into a different language or formalism (semantic domain). AMMA, Kermeta, XMF, and MPS use an action language to define operational semantics.

There are several approaches using a specific meta-language for the definition of operational semantics. In [10] Engels et al present a graphical modelling approach for UML semantics based on collaboration diagrams and graph transformations. This approach provides strong mathematical foundations, but results in very verbose semantic rules, which are hard to read and execute. In [8] Abstract State Machines (ASM) are integrated into the DSL framework AMMA

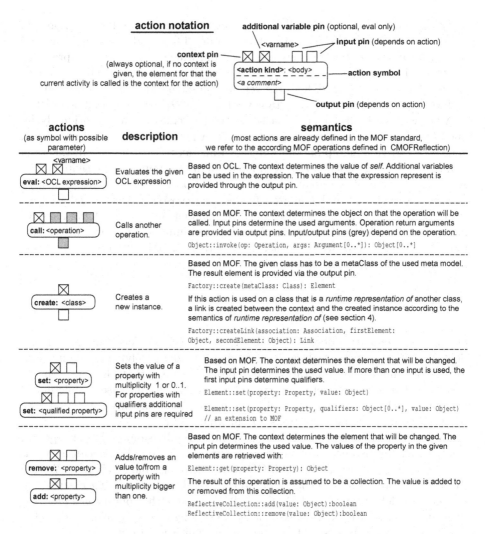

Fig. 1. A list of actions that can be used to define operational semantics

to support specification of execution semantics for DSLs, using ASMs as just another DSL. Muller et al [11] use a textual action language in combination with
OCL for high level semantics descriptions. This action language is executable
and provides the foundation for the DSL framework kermeta [7]. A similar approach is used in Mosaic [3] which uses an OCL version extended with actions
to define language semantics. We recycled the idea of using OCL for expressive model navigation in our approach. In [12] Gerson Sunyé et al explore the
possibility of UML action semantics [13] to create executable UML models and
already suggest the use of activities with action semantics for meta-modelling.
We use this idea and reduce the set of actions to those necessary to describe
operational semantics based on model changes.

We use a CMOF based modelling architecture as foundation for our approach. The reason is that the *CMOF* meta-meta-model [14] provides means for feature refinement in the context of class specialisation, which allows better expressions of abstractions in meta-models than EMOF or similar models (MOF 1.x, EMF-Ecore). The according MOF features were formalised by Alanen and Porres in[15], and we provided a programming framework for *CMOF* based modelling in [16].

Along with structural operational semantics [1], semantics are traditionally defined based on grammars for abstract syntax. A formalism, like term re-writing, is used to describe manipulation of abstract syntax trees (AST are instances of grammars). This describes interpretation of an input program represented by an AST. The formal SDL semantics definition [17] uses Abstract State Machines (ASMs) to realise a similar approach: it defines abstract syntax and runtime states with grammars and represents corresponding ASTs as evolving algebras manipulated by ASMs. Our approach replaces grammars/signatures with meta-models, ASTs/algebras with models, and re-writing/ASMs with our combination of activities, OCL, and actions.

3   Basic Concepts

Operational semantics describes transitions between models (configurations). Such transitions can be realised by changing a model (evolving configuration). To describe and execute operational semantics defined with such transitions we need: (1) changeable models; (2) types of transitions, in our case atomic model changes, which we call actions; and (3) a language to control what action is to be executed under what conditions and in what order.

Models, as instances of meta-models, aren't normally supposed to change. An UML model, for instance, does not change once it is written. But because models constantly change during editing, MOF already supports model changes. We can dynamically create new elements or update attributes of existing elements to change a model. We extended MOF's CMOF model with property *qualifiers* (as defined in UML). We use this extended CMOF language for our meta-models.

Fig. 1 defines a fixed set of atomic actions which we use in UML activities. The semantics for these actions is given by the MOF standard. The semantics for UML activities (as we use them) is founded on Petri-nets as described in [18]. Activities are connected to the meta-model via operations. The behaviour of each operation in a meta-model can be implemented with an activity. When a operation is called, the according activity is interpreted. Meta-models are object-oriented models, and calling a operation means that it is called on an instance of the corresponding class. This also means that activities are always interpreted in the context of an object. This context can be addressed with the value *self*. Operations can also have parameters, and calling an operation requires according arguments, which can be used in the activity.

Each model can be executed like a normal object-oriented program by calling an operation and interpreting the according activity. One operation has to serve as a dedicated *main* operation. There is usually a model element, known as the outermost composite, which contains all other elements. It is reasonable practice to define the *main* operation in the class that describes this element.

3.1   An Example Language – Petri-Nets

In this section we demonstrate our meta-modelling method and create a language model for Petri-nets. This model consists of descriptions for an abstract syntax and an operational semantics for Petri-nets. Fig. 2 shows this language model and an example Petri-net. We choose Petri-nets as an example language, because they have a very small abstract syntax and simple but clear semantics.

The language model specifies that a Petri-net consists of places and transitions. Places can be related to transitions, and each transition has an arbitrary number of input and output places. A place can contain any number of tokens. The figure also shows an example Petri-net, an instance of the given meta-model. This Petri-net diagram of the famous dining philosophers uses the typical Petri-net notation: places are drawn as circles, transitions as boxes. Incoming arcs show the input places of a transition, and outgoing arcs show their

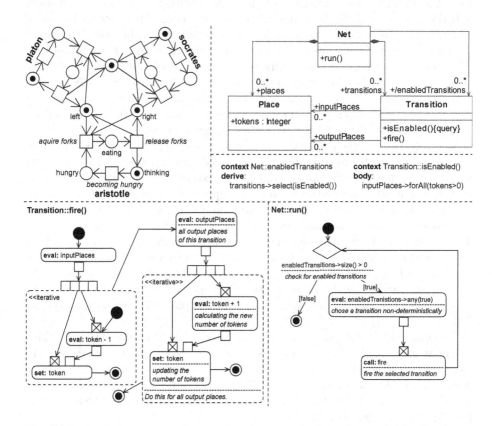

Fig. 2. Petri-nets as an example: an example net and a language model for Petri-nets containing an abstract syntax model, OCL expressions, and activities

output places. Dots inside places show the number of tokens in a place. All text in this Petri-net diagram is commentary, and no text fields are defined in the meta-model. However, we will use these names in further explanations. Please note that we mixed Petri-net structure (places and transitions) with Petri-net configurations (tokens). We will address this issue in section 4.

The semantics of Petri-nets is simple. Transitions are the only active elements in a net. They change the number of tokens in places, which are the only dynamic elements in a net. A transition changes the number of tokens in its input and output places when it is fired. But a transition may only be fired when it is enabled, and it is enabled when all its input places contain at least one token. Given these definitions, a Petri-net has the following semantics: a transition is chosen from all the enabled transitions non-deterministically. The chosen transition is fired. This means that the number of tokens in all input places is reduced by one, and the number of tokens in all its output places is increased by one. Transitions are chosen and fired until the net contains no more enabled transitions.

We describe the operational semantics with operations and derived properties. The Petri-net meta-model contains two operations, one query operation, and the derived association end `enabledTransitions`. These elements realise the informally explained semantics in a formal and executable way. The query operation and derived property can be fully determined by OCL expressions. These elements need no further refinement or implementation; the OCL expressions can be evaluated by the computer right away. `Transition::isEnabled()` returns *true* when the transition contains tokens in all input places. The derived association end `enabledTransitions` selects the collection of all enabled transitions in a net. The OCL expressions are given in fig. 2.

The behaviour of the other two operations can be specified using the activity language (see fig. 2). Imagine that the operation `Transition::fire()` is called for the transition *becoming hungry* during the execution of the example net. The first action is to evaluate the expression `inputPlaces` in the current context *becoming hungry*. This transition has only one input place: *thinking*; the result is a collection containing *thinking* only. After that, the collection is iterated. The activity in the iterative expansion region is executed for each element; in this case this is only *thinking*. This sub-activity evaluates `token−1`. This time *thinking* and not *becoming hungry* is used as context. The value $(1 - 1 = 0)$ is the result and is set to the property `token` in the context of *thinking*. After that is done, the number of tokens in each output place is increased in a similar fashion.

The operation `Net::run()` acts as *main* operation; it executes the net. This means it fires enabled transitions as long as there is at least one enabled transition left. A decision is used to continue or stop based on whether the set of `enabledTranitions` is empty or not. When it is not empty, one transition is selected non-deterministically, using OCL's `any`. After that, `Transition::fire()` is called on the selected transition.

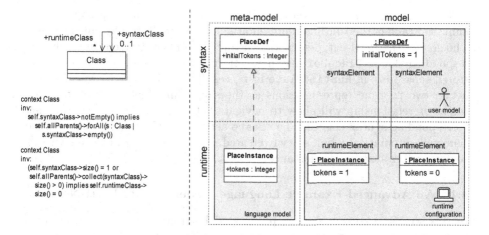

Fig. 3. A new meta-model relationship to relate syntax and runtime elements with each other

4 Distinguishing Between Syntax and Runtime Elements

In the last section we defined operational semantics by describing model changes. All runtime information needed to execute a model could be stored within the model. This approach has two flaws. One, in general we need additional data structures to describe a runtime configuration. A program, for example, is only one part of a configuration during a program run. Other parts are slots for variable values, heap memory, and program counters. The second problem is that when we change the input model it will be lost for future execution. In the moment we destroy a token in one Petri-net place and create it in another, we destroy the original marking. When we say the initial marking is part of the Petri-net, we would destroy the net by executing it. We should have stored the actual number of tokens independent from the initial number of tokens.

To describe complete configurations, a meta-model has to define both: the abstract syntax of the language and additional data-structures needed for runtime information. We distinguish between syntax classes and runtime classes. The set of all syntax classes describes what users of the language can write in their models. The set of all runtime classes describes data that can be created and used during the execution of a model. Syntax and runtime elements can be related to each other.

Fig. 3 shows (on the left side) an extension of the MOF meta-meta-model as a meta-model for a new relationship between classes. We call this relation *runtime representation of*. This directed relationship indicates that one class denotes a runtime representation of a syntax class. We use the UML realisation arrow (which has no predefined meaning in MOF) to notate this relationship. Fig. 3 also shows two corresponding OCL constraints that limit the use of this relationship: there are no circles allowed and a class cannot be runtime representation for itself.

The right side of Fig. 3 shows an example of a runtime representation: a `RuntimePlace` is the runtime representation of a `PlaceDef`. The language user, who creates the Petri-net, determines the initial number of tokens using the corresponding slot in `PlaceDef` instances. At runtime, the numbers of tokens are stored separately in `RuntimePlace` instances. That allows us to run the same net in two runtime representations at the same time. The *runtime representation of* relationship will allow to navigate between instances of runtime and corresponding syntax classes. The `create` action described in the previous section, will automatically link a newly created instance of a runtime class with the corresponding syntax class instance.

4.1   An Advanced Example Language – Hierarchical Petri-Nets

In this section we use a more sophisticated Petri-net variant to demonstrate that most semantics descriptions require to differentiate between syntax and runtime elements. In the previous section, we modelled a dinner table with three philosophers. This model already contained the same philosopher pattern three times. We model *Hierarchical Petri-nets* (also known as *modular Petri-nets*, not to be confused with Petri-nets that use sub-nets as tokens), which allow to build an abstraction for this pattern. We can model the common philosopher behaviour once, and use it for multiple philosophers. Fig. 4 shows such a hierarchical Petri-net for the dining philosophers.

Hierarchical Petri-nets contain additional concepts and notations. We can define sub-nets, notated as a smaller net inside a box. These sub-nets have dedicated interface places. In the example the behaviour of a philosopher is modelled as a sub-net. The places for his left and right fork are interface places, because each philosopher has to share this place with his right and left neighbour. In hierarchical Petri-nets each net can contain sub-net usages which are notated as a black box. Petri-net usages are related to regular places to connect interface places with real places. These connections are drawn with lines that have the respective interface place name written on them.

Since hierarchical Petri-nets contain additional concepts, we also need a different language model (fig. 5) with additional classes and different descriptions of operational semantics. We have to distinguish between the definition of a sub-net and the usage of a sub-net. `NetDef` represents Petri-net models. `NetDef` instances can contain transitions, sub-net definitions, sub-net usages, and places. Net usages are realised in the class `NetUsage`. Instances of `NetUsage` reference a `NetDef` to characterise the used sub-net. The former class `Place` is now called `PlaceDef`. Instances of this class are used to model places; we will need another place class to represent places at runtime. The connection of interface places is modelled as a qualified property of `NetUsage`. A qualified property works like a map. In this case, it associates a `NetUsage` with a `PlaceDef` based on another `PlaceDef` as key: a usage is connected to places, and each of those connections is qualified by an interface place.

Hierarchical Petri-nets use one sub-net several times. We use several instances of the same net definition to to store the number of tokens in each sub-net

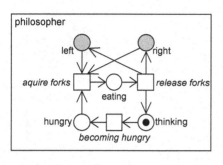
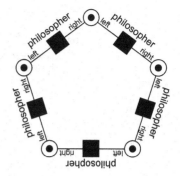

Fig. 4. A hierarchical Petri-net for the dining philosophers

instance separately. We cannot use the semantics definition from the place/ transition Petri-net example, because the places in one sub-net are now used several times in multiple usages of the same sub-net. When the number of tokens in a place of one instance changes, it would also change in the same place of all the other instances.

The definition classes `NetDef` and `PlaceDef` are syntax classes. They are used within the Petri-net model; they are classes for things the user draws in a Petri-net diagram. The dining philosopher model is a `NetDef` instance, the philosopher sub-net is a `NetDef` instance; all places in the model are `PlaceDef` instances. The other two classes `RuntimeNet` and `RuntimePlace` are runtime classes. A `RuntimeNet` can contain instances of sub-nets (other `RuntimeNet` instances) and contains `RuntimePlaces` using a qualified property with the according `PlaceDefs` as keys.

When a user provides a hierarchical Petri-net it will only contain instances of the syntax classes. Creating runtime class instances is part of the semantics. It is part of the semantics to initially instantiate the dining philosophers Petri-net, create sub-net instances for all the usages of philosopher. This instantiation task is modelled in the operation `NetDef::instantiate`. This operation will create a runtime representation of itself and all its contained places; it will furthermore create runtime representations of all used sub-nets recursively and connect its interface places to real places. Fig. 5 shows the activity diagram for this operation.

After `NetDef::instantiate` was called for the top-level Petri-net, we can use the created `RuntimeNet` by calling its **run** operation. Even though **run**'s signature hasn't changed from the previous section, it works a little different due to the changes in the meta-model. Transitions can only be fired in the context of a `RuntimeNet`. Since transition is only a syntax class with no runtime counterpart, it is also only related to `PlaceDef` (the syntax class for places). The input and output places of a transition are instances of `PlaceDef` and the number of tokens cannot be accessed or changed directly on them. The operations of transition have to access the corresponding `RuntimePlace` using a `RuntimeNet` as context. The run operation itself (not shown) also works different: it still choses one transition from all enabled transitions. But because one transition can be enabled

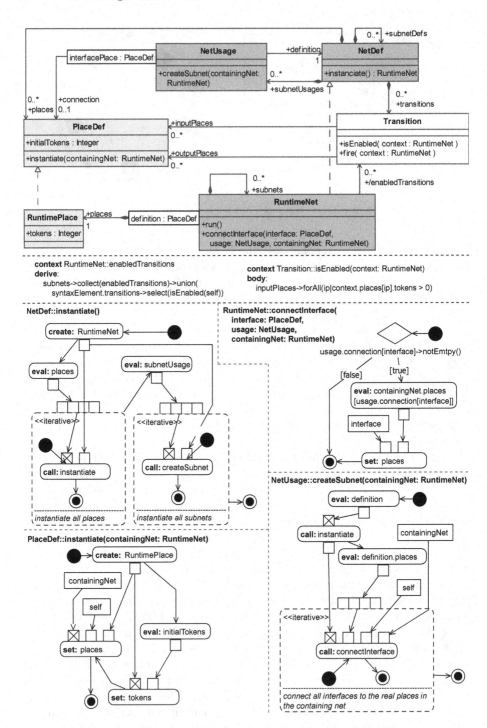

Fig. 5. A Language Model for Hierarchical Petri-nets

in different sub-nets (in the starting configuration, *becoming hungry* is enabled in all five philosophers) `run` must also chose one of these sub-nets that the chosen transition is enabled in. After transition and `RuntimeNet` are chosen, run fires the transition using the chosen `RuntimeNet` as context argument.

5   Language Design Patterns

Patterns in software engineering form a basis for reusing working designs [19,20]. We want to use patterns for language modelling. A language design pattern describes an abstract language concept. We implement these patterns as abstract

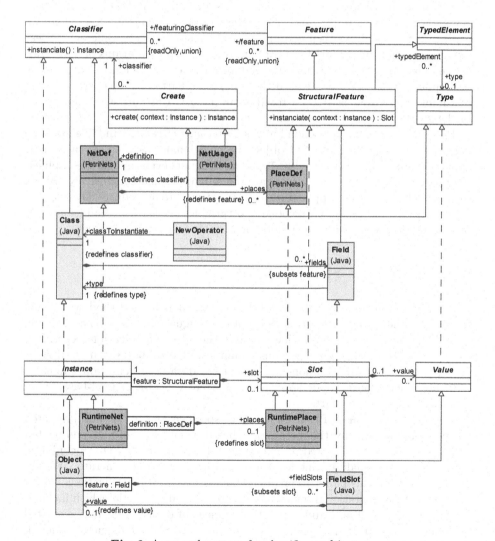

Fig. 6. A general pattern for classifier and instances

libraries (similar to the abstraction libraries in the UML meta-model). Each of these pattern implementations consists of abstract classes for syntax and runtime elements as well as their operations' behaviour. The pattern implementations can be used by usual object-oriented means: a general pattern class is specialised and its features refined to fulfil a specific purpose in a concrete context.

Fig. 6 shows such a pattern implementation (white classes) and how it is used by specialisation in two examples (grey and dark grey). This pattern describes the abstract concept instantiation. It defines `Classifiers`, which define sets of instances with common attributes defined as `Features`. These features can have a type. A `Classifer's Instance` provides a `Slot` for each `Feature`. Each `Slot` can hold `Values` of the corresponding `Type`.

This pattern is common to many languages, including MOF and UML. Without knowing it, we already used this pattern in the previous section, where we had `NetDef` (classifiers of sub-nets that can be instantiated at different places) and its runtime counterpart `RuntimeNet` (runtime representations of sub-nets). `NefDefs` have `PlaceDefs` as features and `RuntimeNets` have `RuntimePlaces` as corresponding slots. We don't need the type/value part of this pattern, because the number of tokens is always stored as an integer. But here we could extend the language if we wanted to introduce objects for tokens as in *Object Petri-nets*.

The other example application for this patterns are `Classes` and `Fields` (also known as member variables) in object-oriented languages such as Java. This application of the pattern also uses `Types` and `Values`, even though we simplified the problem in this example: classes are the only types and conclusively objects the only values. Another application for this pattern are procedure-like concepts. Procedures are classifiers, parameters and variables are features, call frames are procedure instances with proper slots for variable or parameter values.

6   SDL: A Case Study

In order to reason about the applicability our meta-modelling method, we applied it to SDL—the Specification and Description Language[21]. This is an existing graphical modelling language, widely used in the telecommunication sector. It is similar to UML but has unambiguous semantics. SDL supports structural modelling, similar to UML components, provides a data-type definition language, and allows behavioural modelling with concurrent processes, signal-based communication, and state charts.

We described the use of tools in language specifications in [22] and presented a general architecture for the meta-model-based specification of SDL and related languages in [23]. We created an experimental tool-chain for SDL, including a parser, semantics analyser, model transformations, and code-generator. We use the method from this paper to create a simulator for SDL specifications [24].

To define the operational semantics, we created a meta-model which includes runtime classes, and according operation implementations for SDL. We started to define the semantics for a representative subset of SDL. This meta-model already contains 108 classes with 257 properties and 105 operations. We composed the SDL meta-model from several design patterns. These patterns were realised in abstract libraries, which were (re-)used several times throughout the SDL language model. 30 classes are part of pattern implementations and 78 are SDL specific classes. In a first prototype we specified the operation's behaviour with Java, which is now replaced more comprehensible activities.

Three pattern implementations are used in the SDL model: the *instantiation* pattern, introduced in the previous section, a pattern for *concurrent processes and communication*, and a pattern for the *evaluation of terms*. The structural part of SDL is dominated by the instantiation pattern, because SDL-structures are defined by object-oriented classifiers, called *agents*. Agents can be recursively composed: an agent instance (instance) is a feature of another agent type (classifier). Agents can be connected through communication channels and gates. This is a combination of two patterns. The instantiation pattern is used to describe agent type and instance relations and the concurrency pattern describes interaction of different agent instances. The SDL behaviour is characterised by state machines and statements. State machine behaviour, the triggering of transitions, is realised as part of the concurrency pattern: communication as synchronisation of processes (processes in SDL are nested state machines as part of agent instances). Statements, the other part of SDL behaviour, are similar to other imperative programming languages. Expressions and data types used in those statements are realised with the evaluation pattern.

The SDL language model can be executed with our generic model interpreter. Input SDL specifications are transformed into a model representation according to the SDL language model using the tools presented in [23]. The generic interpreter runs this input SDL specification: it initially creates a runtime configuration for the specification and changes it during execution. As part of the defined operational semantics, *Message Sequence Chart* models are created from the changing runtime configuration to visualise the running SDL system.

7   Conclusions

We combine MOF meta-models with an action language based on UML activities and OCL to create language models that contain definitions for abstract syntax and operational semantics. We developed a generic model interpreter which can be configured with language models. It takes a model as input and executes the model based on the semantics defined in the language model. The used languages allow human readable graphical models of language structure and operational semantics. These language models are at the same time formal enough to be machine interpretable. With such characteristics, the method is ideal for language prototyping, creation of reference tools, and the development of domain specific languages. We created a language model for a subset of SDL. This experience showed that our method scales up to a practical language of reasonable size.

We have all tools necessary to create and interpret language models. We use a normal UML case tool (class diagrams in MagicDraw) to define the structure part of language models. We augment MagicDraw models with activities using a graphical editor, specifically developed with GEF (eclipse). As a future work, we are developing a runtime environment based on the abstract eclipse debugging plug-ins. This should allow to support the development process of language models (debugging meta-models) and also provide generic debugging facilities (debugging models).

We have to critically admit: the assessment that operational semantics modelled with our approach results in more human readable language specifications than comparable techniques (ASMs, mathematical semantics definitions, or even natural language text) is purely based on the graphical modelling argument and our prejudice experiences with it. This hyphothesis has yet to be proven by either more representable experiences or sound usability evaluations. But formal graphical models of operational semantics could play the same role that normal meta-models play for the definition of abstract syntax.

On the machine execution side, we have disadvantages and advantages. Unfortunately, but as expected, model execution, based on language models and our generic tool, compared to equivalent hand crafted tools performs less by magnitudes. It is future work to analyse and antagonize the reasons for that. An advantage, however, is that we have a meta-model based representation of the model's runtime state. Besides the fact that we can execute models right away, we can use other modelling techniques to analyse these runtime states, e.g. define constraints over them, or use model transformations on them to create different representations, e.g. record test cases.

References

1. Plotkin, G.D.: A Structural Approach to Operational Semantics. Technical Report DAIMI FN-19, University of Aarhus (1981)
2. Agrawal, A., Karsai, G., Ledeczi, A.: An End-to-End Domain-Driven Software Development Framework. In: OOPSLA '03: Companion of the 18th annual ACM SIGPLAN Conference on Object-Oriented Programming, Systems, Languages, and Applications, ACM Press, New York (2003)
3. Clark, T., Evans, A., Sammut, P., Willans, J.: Applied Metamodeling, A Foundation for Language Driven Development. Xactium (2004), http://www.xactium.com
4. Clark, T., Evans, A., Kent, S., Sammut, P.: The MMF Approach to Engineering Object-Oriented Design Languages. In: Workshop on Language Descriptions, Tools and Applications (April 2001)
5. The Modelling, Simulation and Design lab (MSDL), School of Computer Science of McGill University Montreal, Quebec, Canada: AToM3 A Tool for Multi-Formalism Meta-Modelling, http://atom3.cs.mcgill.ca/index.html
6. Dmitriev, S.: Language Oriented Programming: The Next Programming Paradigm. onBoard, electronic monthly magazin (November 2004)
7. Team, T.: Triskell Meta-Modelling Kernel. IRISA, INRIA., http://www.kermeta.org
8. Ruscio, D.D., Jounault, F., Kurtev, I., Bézivin, J., Pierantonio, A.: Extending AMMA for Supporting Dynamic Semantics Specifications of SDLs, technical report (2006)

9. Case, M.: MetaEdit+, http://www.metacase.com
10. Engels, G., Hausmann, J.H., Heckel, R., Sauer, S.: Dynamic Meta Modeling: A Graphical Approach to the Operational Semantics of Behavioral Diagrams in UML. In: Evans, A., Kent, S., Selic, B. (eds.) UML 2000. LNCS, vol. 1939, Springer, Heidelberg (2000)
11. Muller, P.A., Fleurey, F., Jézéquel, J.M.: Weaving Executability into Object-Oriented Meta-languages. In: Model Driven Engineering Languages and Systems. 8th International Conference. LNCS, Springer, Heidelberg (2005)
12. Sunyé, G., Pennaneac'h, F., Ho, W.M., Guennec, A.L., Jézéquel, J.M.: Using UML Action Semantics for Executable Modeling and Beyond. In: Advanced Information Systems Engineering. 13th International Conference. LNCS, Springer, Heidelberg (2001)
13. OMG: Action Semantics for the UML. Object Management Group, ad/2001-08-04 (2001)
14. OMG: Meta Object Facility (MOF) 2.0 Core Specification. Object Management Group, ptc/03-10-04 (October 2003)
15. Alanen, M., Porres, I.: Basic Operations over Models Containing Subset and Union Properties. In: 9th International Conference Model Driven Engineering Languages and Systems. LNCS, Springer, Heidelberg (2006)
16. Scheidgen, M.: CMOF-Model Semantics and Language Mapping for MOF 2.0 Implementations. In: MBD/MOMPES, IEEE Computer Society, Los Alamitos, CA (2006)
17. ITU-T: SDL formal definition: Dynamic semantics. In: Specification and Description Language (SDL). International Telecommunication Union, Z.100 Annex F3 (November 2000)
18. Störrle, H., Hausmann, J.H.: Towards a Formal Semantics of UML 2.0 Activities. In: Software Engineering (2005)
19. Gamma, E., Helm, R., Johnson, R., Vlissides, J.: Design Patterns: Abstraction and Reuse in Object-Oriented Designs. In: Nierstrasz, O. (ed.) ECOOP 1993. LNCS, vol. 707, Springer, Heidelberg (1993)
20. Gamma, E., Helm, R., Johnson, R., Vlissides, J.: Design Patterns: Elements of Reusable Object-Oriented Software, 1st edn. Addison-Wesley Professional, London, UK (1995)
21. ITU-T: ITU-T Recommendation Z.100: Specification and Description Language (SDL). International Telecommunication Union (August 2002)
22. Fischer, J., Holz, E., Prinz, A., Scheidgen, M.: Tool-based Language Development. In: Workshop on Integrated-reliability with Telecommunications and UML Languages (November 2004)
23. Fischer, J., Kunert, A., Piefel, M., Scheidgen, M.: ULF-Ware – An Open Framework for Integrated Tools for ITU-T Languages. In: Prinz, A., Reed, R., Reed, J. (eds.) SDL 2005. LNCS, vol. 3530, Springer, Heidelberg (2005)
24. Systeman Alysis and Modelling Group, Department of Computer Science, Humboldt-Universität zu Berlin: An Operational Semantics Model for SDL, http://www.informatik.hu-berlin.de/sam/meta-tools/sdl

Adopting Model Driven Development in a Large Financial Organization

Dov Shirtz[1], Michael Kazakov[2], and Yael Shaham-Gafni[2]

[1]Hanegev 11, Tel Aviv, Israel
[2]Metaphor Vision LTD., Givat Ram, POB 39158, Jerusalem 91391, Israel
dovshirtz@gmail.com, {mkazakov,yshahamgafni}@metaphor.co.il

Abstract. Two years ago the IT Division of a large financial organization in Israel made a strategic decision to adopt Model Driven Development as its major development methodology. This decision was based on assessing the results of several pilot projects that had run during the previous year using this methodology. The QA Department that was the main advocate of this move took upon itself to lead the adoption effort. In this paper we report on the process of adopting Model Driven Development in the IT Division of the financial organization, from inception to successful maturation. We provide details on the methodology, models and tools, and describe the challenges, benefits, and lessons learnt.

1 Introduction

In the beginning of 2005 the QA Department of a large financial organization in Israel presented its vision to the IT Division management: "Provide the IT Division with the ability to support the organization in its business goals efficiently and effectively by producing high quality software systems on time". To realize this vision the QA Department proposed three action items:

1. Change the perception of quality assurance in the IT Division.
2. Employ a new model driven development methodology throughout the software lifecycle.
3. Deploy modern software development tooling and lifecycle support tooling.

The benefits we hoped to achieve through these actions were:

1. Information sharing and improved communication between the different stakeholders involved in the development process: managers, users, analysts, testers, and developers.
2. Consistent terminology across different projects and different phases of the lifecycle.
3. Increased rate of reuse of development work-products (not necessarily code).
4. Automated generation of various work products such as documents, database schemas, tests, etc.
5. Significant improvement in the quality of software, and the software development process.
6. Accessible information and measures on project status and quality.

D.H. Akehurst, R. Vogel, and R.F. Paige (Eds.): ECMDA-FA 2007, LNCS 4530, pp. 172–183, 2007.
© Springer-Verlag Berlin Heidelberg 2007

7. Lowering development and maintenance costs
8. Faster development cycles to accelerate response to changing market needs.

In this paper we report on the process of adopting Model Driven Development in the IT Division of a large financial organization. We begin with a description of our model-driven development methodology in section 2 "Methodology and Tools". In section 3 "Adoption Process", we describe how the adoption process was performed. Section 4, "Measuring Improvement", describes our scheme for measuring improvements in productivity and quality. Section 5, "Lessons Learned", describes our insights on the challenges and lessons learnt. We conclude with future plans and challenges in section 6 "Conclusion".

2   Methodology and Tools

The classic model driven approach focuses on generating a concrete implementation in the context of a given target architecture from an abstract specification. This approach puts a lot of emphasis on design models, which are automatically transformed into the implementation.

The approach we chose in the organization emphasized using models in the early phases of the software lifecycle, especially during inception and elaboration [1]. Another area that we focused on was testing. The following principles guided us in formulating the methodology:

1. Adopting standards:
   – The model is the focus of the development process.
   – The model is written in the standard modeling language UML [2]..
   – Aiming of a component based architecture.
2. Adapting standards and tools
   – Adapting UML to the terminology, organizational standards and development disciplines by defining *Domain Specific Languages (DSLs)* [3].
   – Enforcement of standards through the modeling tools throughout the software lifecycle.
   – Integrating modeling tools with existing development tools.
3. Establishing an uniform and interlinked development stream
   – Covering all disciplines of the complete development life cycle
   – Integrating models of different kinds
   – Maximum automation and reuse possible

2.1   Models and Tools in the Software Development Lifecycle

The methodology we developed for the financial organization is derived from the Rational Unified Process [1] and based on several models along the software lifecycle each related to a specific phase. Fig. 1. presents an overview of the lifecycle phases we consider: inception, elaboration, and construction, the roles relevant for each phase, and the activities performed.. Fig. 2. depicts the models, the relations between them, and the tools. For the modeling tool IBM Rational XDE was chosen. Metaphor Builder^{TM} [4] provides the specialized models for the different phases of the lifecycle and additional adaptations for XDE.

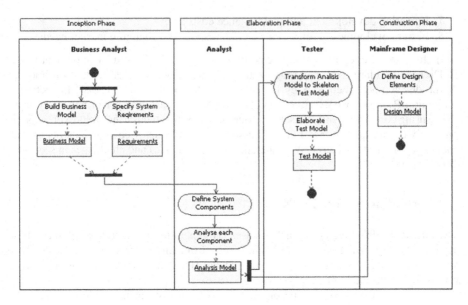

Fig. 1. Roles and Activities along the Software Development lifecycle

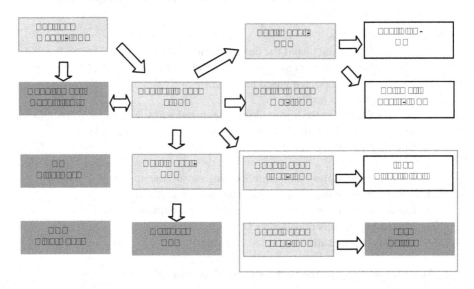

Fig. 2. Models in the Software Development lifecycle in the organization

2.1.1 Inception Phase: The Business Model and Requirements

During the inception phase a Business Analyst builds the Business Model and specifies the system requirements. The motivation for creating a Business Model is to analyze and understand the problem and to determine the initial scope for the project, and the boundaries of the system. The Business Model captures all significant information about the problem and the developing solution, and is based on Metaphor Vision's Business Modeling language:

- Terminology definitions
- Business goals
- Existing and planned business process flows
- Requirements
- Business entities (e.g. screens, persistent data, etc.)
- Business rules

Figure 2 depicts the structure of a Business Model. The model contains Business Areas each containing packages organizing the information described above.

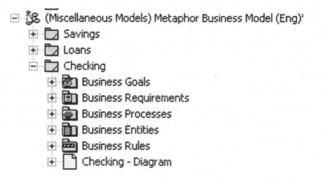

Fig. 3. Business Model structure

The Business model is automatically transformed into a skeleton for the Analysis Model, maintaining traceability between source and target elements. The Business Process Document, which is the lifecycle milestone of the inception phase, is generated automatically from the Business Model.

High-level requirements are always managed within the Business Model. The major benefit of this approach is the ease of maintaining requirements traceability. For small projects a Business Model remains the only tool capturing and managing requirements. Large projects continue managing their detailed requirements with IBM Rational RequisitePro.

2.1.2 Elaboration Phase: Architecture and the Analysis Model
During the elaboration phase Analysts define the system components and analyze each component resulting in the Analysis Model. The purpose of the Analysis Model is to analyze in detail the use cases [5] of the planned system, going into particulars of the screens, the user interaction, and the data model. The Analysis Model is based on Metaphor Vision's Analysis language and captures detailed information about the solution:

- Use cases
  Use case details are specified in a structured way by utilizing flow charts (UML Activity Diagrams) and storyboards (UML Sequence Diagrams).
- User Interface (UI)
  Different kinds of UI elements can be specified: Forms, Tabbed pages, Menus, Reports. In addition the structure of the screens is captured by field and control model elements. Relationships between screens (containment, navigation) are also kept in the analysis model.
- Data
  Data is modeled at the logical level, describing business objects and their fields.

As can be seen in Figure 3 the Analysis Model is the heart of the development process, and serves as a source for several models further down the development lifecycle. The analysis model is organized into components [6]. It is the role of an architect to define the system components. In the development organization there is no "Architect" job definition, and thus the Analysts define the system components. Once the architecture of the components is defined an automatic transformation is applied to create the initial use cases, business objects and UI forms from the Business Model. The Analysts drag the automatically generated elements to the correct component, and detailed analysis for each component proceeds. Figure 3 shows the structure of an Analysis Model. The top level packages are components, and each component is divided into layers (according to the scheme in [6]) that organize the relevant information.

Fig. 4. Analysis Model Structure

The Analysis Document, which is the lifecycle milestone of the elaboration phase, is generated automatically from the Analysis Model.

The Analysis Model serves as the basis for the various Design Models and is automatically transformed into a skeleton of the Test Model.

2.1.3 Elaboration Phase: Test Model
An additional activity that takes place during the elaboration phase is creating the Test Plan. This is where we get much of the return on investing in models in earlier phases. Testers transform the Analysis Model into a Skeleton Test Model, which is kept synchronized with the Analysis Model. The Test Model is then elaborated adding values, check points, and additional test cases. The Test Model is then automatically transformed into Mercury's Quality Center (QC) and Quick Test Professional (QTP),

in which the tests are maintained and executed. The test Model and the QC/QTP tests are kept synchronized via traceability information. The integration between the Test Model and Mercury QC/QTP is one of the features of Metaphor Builder$^{TM.}$.

2.1.4 Construction Phase: Design Model

The financial organization's IT systems are heterogeneous, and thus so are the development target languages and environments. Accordingly there are also several kinds of design models. For J2EE, .NET and data models we adopted the standard design models provided by XDE that we do not elaborate in the scope of this paper. For Mainframe applications we developed our own design language – Metaphor Vision's MF Design language, in which the MF Design Models are expressed. The language elements relate to terms used in Cobol and capture detailed information about the structure of the implementation on the target system:

- JCLs
- Programs
- Routines
- Sections
- Copy Members
- Parameters
- Data Schemes

During the construction phase Mainframe Designers define the various design elements and divide them into coding portfolios, each designated for a Coder. The designers may use elements from the analysis model in their own model, and maintain traceability to the Analysis Model by creating realization relationships between Design elements and the corresponding Analysis element. Currently there is no automatic code generation from the Design Model. Design Coding Portfolio Documents are generated automatically form the Design Model.

3 Adoption Process

The process of adopting MDD in the financial organization began as an initiative of the QA Department. Prior to this initiative most of the development in the financial organization was document based, i.e., apart from writing code the work-products of all efforts during a project lifetime were documents.

3.1 Early Preparations

Our first step was to devise a first draft of the new methodology and the accompanying Domain Specific Languages (DSLs). We made a decision early on not to abandon the documents completely; rather the documents were kept and served as the interface between the different lifecycle phases and development roles. The main difference was that the documents were generated automatically from the models.

In the same time we achieve a few pilots in different fields, each in the project/department ready to volunteer for new technology. It gave us arguments to represent for the first time our vision to IT Division management. In result we got a mandate to conduct a number of pilots along the entire division.

3.2 Implementing Pilot Projects

Our second step was to implement the methodology in several pilot projects throughout the IT Division. We allotted six months during 2005 for this step, improving the methodology and the DSLs as the pilots progressed. A total of 25 pilot projects took place covering the various systems and environments in the financial organization. One of the arguments we were confronted by frequently was that UML models cannot work with MF systems which are not Object Oriented. This obstacle was removed by creating a special DSL for mainframe design – the MF Design Language. At the end of September 2005 we had working proof that the new methodology works. We were ready to finally approach high management.

3.3 High Level Management Decision

In order to assess the pilot results we devised a survey and ran it through the personnel of the different pilot projects (60 people). The results showed 85-95% satisfaction. On one of the questions 85% of the survey participants answered that they felt that the new modeling methodology contributed and promoted them personally.

The survey results and status of pilot projects was presented before the high management of the financial organization's IT Division. As a result of this presentation high management made a bold decision to adopt the new methodology and tools throughout the IT Division of the financial organization. The QA Department received a green light to proceed with the adoption process.

3.4 Wide-Scale Adoption

The QA Department set out to plan the adoption. Organization wide adoption of a new methodology required careful planning and staging. Our adoption plan included the following items:

- Elaborating and documenting the new development methodology. Additional phases were added (such as the Business Modeling) and integration between the phases was enhanced. Each phase was documented by a detailed User Guide
- DSLs were improved according to feedback from the pilot projects.
- Courses were designed for the different professions to jumpstart the adoption.
- Special attention was given to document generation in order to produce concise and readable documents from the models.
- We understood that the change was not only a change of tools; rather it was a change in mindset, which required support. Additional consultants were hired to support the adoption process.
- Integration between tools along the lifecycle, especially between modeling and testing tools.
- Reuse of existing infrastructure and content. This included integration with organizational meta data repositories (data dictionary, message dictionary, etc.)
- Integrated management and quality measures
- Detailed staging where we set Analysis as a start point followed by Business Analysis, Test Plan and design disciplines
- Two directions of adoption – by both organization unites and large projects

Today every new project in the IT Division must employ the new Model Driven methodology.

4 Measuring Improvement

One of the major challenges we face in the process of adopting a new development methodology is proving that it is in actual fact better. This is extremely important for management making the decisions on investment in the change. There is a need to show numbers that justify the cost. For this purpose we have devised a measurement scheme based on function points [7]. We have chosen this method for measuring the "size" of a project for several reasons. First, it is independent of the amount of resources invested in a project. Second, it is independent on technology (in comparison to measuring lines of code for example). Finally, having such a normalized measure allows comparison between projects in the organization, and projects in a benchmark database.

4.1 Computing the Complexity of a Software System

The method described here is taken from Garmus & Herron's book "Function Point Analysis" [7]. The computation of the *Adjusted Function Points (AFP)* of a software system is based on the analysis model/document of the system and is done in cooperation with the system analyst. We consider five types of functional elements:

1. Internal logical files (Ilf)
2. External interface files (Eif)
3. External inputs (Ei)
4. External outputs (Eo)
5. External inquiries (Eq)

Each elements is evaluated and given a grade (Low/Average/High), which is then translated into a number. We obtain the measures for each of these elements directly from the analysis model, by running different kinds of analysis on the model (e.g. counting fields, etc.) For example, for the first element, internal logical files, we evaluate two parameters: (i) DET – Data Element Type: The number of fields in the file record. (ii) RET – Record Element Type: The number of fields that are references to other record types (similar to a foreign key in a database). We then look up the grade and its corresponding numeric value in provided tables (see Table 1 and Table 2). For example, a file with 23 record fields and 2 record types will have grade Average and numeric value 10. The computations of the grades of other elements can be found in [7].

Table 1. Grades for the element Internal Logical File

		Data Element Type		
		1 - 19	20 - 51	>=51
Record	1	Low	Low	Average
Element Type	2 - 5	Low	Average	High
	> 5	Average	High	High

Table 2. Numeric values for element grades

Component	Function Levels		
	Low	Average	High
ILF	7	10	15

The sum of the grades of the elements is the *Unadjusted Function Points (UFP)*.

$$UFP = \sum_{i=1}^{5} grade(funElem_i)$$

Next we compute the Technical Complexity Factor (TCF), which is based on 14 technical properties of the project (e.g. communication, data processing, transactions, etc.). For each property there is a question to grade the system in the range of 0-5. For Example, for the property "Data Communications" the grade is assigned according to the criteria in Fig 5. The list of properties and criteria for grading each property can be found in [7].

The *Data Communications* property describes the extent of communication used to access external data. The grade is assigned according to the following criteria:

0 – pure batch processing or stand alone.
1 – batch processing with remote data entry or remote printing
2 – batch processing with remote data entry and remote printing
3 – interactive data entry or teleprocessing to another batch process or data warehouse
4 – interactive data entry with one type of communication protocol
5 – interactive data entry with more than one type of communication protocol

Fig. 5. Example: Grade assignment for Data Communications property

The TCF is computed according to the following formula:

$$TCF = 0.65 + 0.01 \sum_{i=1}^{14} grade(property_i)$$

Finally the adjusted function points are computed according to the formula below:

$$AFP = TCF * UFP$$

This computation produces a number that measures the system complexity. Once we have this number we can use it to compare different projects.

4.2 Comparing Projects

In order to compare projects we gather for each project the following information:

- Team size
- Total resources (person months)

- Duration (calendar months)
- Number of defects during testing
- Number of defects after deployment

Dividing the number by the AFP number provide a measure for comparing projects. For example assume we have two projects A and B with the following numbers:

Project	Team size per AFP	Productivity (person months per AFP)	Delivery speed (AFP per month)	Quality (defects per AFP)
A	0.023	16	26	0.5
B	0.017	11.5	41	0.7

We can see that project B has better productivity (less person months per function point) but was slower in delivery and has more defects.

At this stage we have defined the measures and built the infrastructure to obtain measures automatically from the models. We are now in the process of gathering data on existing projects, and hope to evaluate results in the near future.

5 Lessons Learned

This section is organized as a list of questions and answers.

Q: How do you convince a large organization to adopt MDD?
A: Ultimately it has to be a high-level management decision. The real question is how to lay the groundwork for the decision to go through. It is best to start with one supporter in middle management, and with their support begin pilot projects. The choice of pilot projects is crucial. Choose projects that are run by people that like to be at the cutting edge of technology, appreciate taking risks, and have an autonomous work style. When enough promising results are gathered through pilots, go to high management.

Q: What maturity of the methodology and tools is needed to begin?
A: It is important to be successful, i.e. show benefits, on the first project. Therefore the methodology and tools need to be relatively mature, although they can be improved along the adoption process.

Q: What is the best way to stage adoption throughout the organization?
A: It is best to stage adoption according to the organization hierarchy, covering departments rather than projects. Projects are usually running in tight schedules and by the time you start to employ a new technology in one phase, the project has moved to the next phase.

Q: What is the best development phase to begin with?
A: We believe that the elaboration phase and Analysis Model are the best starting point since they are at the heart of the development process.

Q: How do you show ROI?
A: The most immediate ROI of employing analysis models is in testing.

Q: How do you measure ROI?
A: Methods we have employed are function points metrics and surveys. It is important to measure the extent to which models are being used, and to assess what is the level of detail and maturity of the models.

Q: What is the best way to teach people the new tools and work methods?
A: Courses are important to jumpstart adoption. Courses should be tailored for the different professions: Business Analyst, Analyst, Designer, Tester, etc. Documentation and User Guides are also useful. Personal consulting and support is important both for marketing the new method and easing the mindset change. The consultant should never build models themselves; their job is to teach, coach and support. Finally, creating local knowledge centers, in the different departments is essential.

Q: How do you measure success?
A: An important measure is the actual amount of people working with the new methodology and tools.

Q: What is the importance of adapting standards and tools for the organization?
A: We believe that it is crucial to adapt the methodology, and the modeling languages for each discipline along the lifecycle, and sometimes even at the project level (for large enough projects).

Q: What is the best strategy for building the methodology and tools support team.
A: Usually it is best to hire new people when a concrete need emerges. It is very difficult to convince management to provide the required human resources up front. The team should include people local to the organization, and new hires that have required knowledge.

Q: Any additional insights?
A: With respect to tools, it is most important to introduce lifecycle support tools early on: configuration management tools, etc. A good relationship with the tool company is essential; usually problems are encountered along the way that requires timely solutions.

Q: What to promise?
A: Most important is to manage expectations. Never promise what you cannot provide, always be realistic.

Q: What is the key to success?
A: Adapt standards and tools to organization and not vice versa.

6 Conclusion

Introducing changes in a large organization is a challenging task. In this paper we have described our experience with moving the IT Division of a large organization towards a model driven development methodology. We described the methodology we employed emphasizing the difference between the standard MDA view and our interpretation of MDD. We described the goals we hoped to achieve and the ways we devised to measure our progress. The adoption process is in full progress; hundreds of analysts and designers are using the model driven methodology. We believe that the reason for this success is the ability to customize UML, using DSLs and Metaphor Builder. Yet our task is far from being finished. We still face many challenges in the future: better integration between the different phases of the lifecycle and the different tools used; more automation at the construction phase of the lifecycle (design and coding); and gathering actual project data in order to compare projects that were document centric with model driven projects.

References

[1] Kruchten, P.: Rational Unified Process-An Introduction. Addison-Wesley, London, UK (1999)
[2] Object Management Group, OMG Unified Modeling Language Specification, Version 2.0
[3] Cooke, S.: Domain-Specific Modeling and Model Driven Architecture, MDA Journal (January 2004)
[4] Metaphor BuilderTM Model Driven Development Based on Domain Specific Languages, http://www.metaphor.co.il/Extras/MBExecutivePaperV1.0.pdf
[5] Jacobson, Christerson, M., Jonsson, P., Overgard, G.: Object-Oriented software engineering: A use case driven approach. Addison-Wesley, London, UK (1992)
[6] Herzum, P., Sims, O.: Business Components Factory: A Comprehensive Overview of Component-Based Development for the Enterprise. John Wiley & Sons, Inc, New York (2000)
[7] Garmus, D., Herron, D.: Function Point Analysis - Measurement Practices for Successful Software Projects. Addison-Wesley, London, UK (2000)

Reverse Engineering Models from Traces to Validate Distributed Systems – An Industrial Case Study

Andreas Ulrich[1] and Alexandre Petrenko[2]

[1]Siemens AG, Corporate Research & Technologies CT SE 1
Otto-Hahn-Ring 6, 81730 Munich, Germany
andreas.ulrich@siemens.com
[2]CRIM, 550 Sherbrooke West, Suite 100, Montreal, H3A 1B9, Canada
petrenko@crim.ca

Abstract. The paper targets the applicability of model-driven methodologies to the validation of complex systems and presents a case study of a mobile radio network. Validation relies on the availability of a collection of models formally describing various aspects of the system behavior and an execution trace obtained through monitoring the system during the execution of designated test cases. The models describe system properties and are derived from existing (informal) system specifications or other traces. The recorded trace is reverse-engineered to produce a model of the system that is used to visualize the architecture of the system during test execution and to verify the system against the specified properties using model checking technology. The obtained results and lessons learned from this case study are discussed.

Keywords: Model-driven development, reverse engineering, model verification, trace analysis, system validation, telecommunication industry, experience report.

1 Introduction

Model driven development (MDD) methodologies allow the separation of domain concerns from implementation details, which provides better quality, maintainability, and portability of the developed systems across different platforms. However, design models, which are essential to the success of the MDD approach, are not always sufficiently expressive to allow full automation of critical development activities, such as code generation. Moreover, models of complex systems, e.g., distributed applications, are seldom complete and, at best, cover only parts of the whole system. These limitations affect the applicability of MDD methodologies to system development. Nevertheless, partial models can still be used in reasoning about the developed system and its behavior. A (partial) model serves as a property that describes a singular aspect of the system. During validation, the violation or satisfaction of the property in an execution trace recorded during test execution of the system can help evaluate the functional correctness, the quality, and even the performance of the developed system.

Thus, there is a need for tools that rely on monitoring functions of distributed systems to produce log files of execution traces that can be analyzed further. This type of analysis is also known as runtime verification or passive testing of distributed systems

D.H. Akehurst, R. Vogel, and R.F. Paige (Eds.): ECMDA-FA 2007, LNCS 4530, pp. 184–193, 2007.
© Springer-Verlag Berlin Heidelberg 2007

[2]. In this context, an approach has been developed [5, 6, 7] that takes as input an execution trace of the system obtained during the execution of a test scenario. Such a recorded trace, which contains a causally ordered sequence of send/receive events or messages exchanged between system components, is reverse-engineered to produce a model in the form of a system of communicating state machines that reflects the system behavior as it occurred during the execution of that particular test scenario. The obtained model is then used to verify the specified system properties using a standard model checker. The collection of verified system properties can later be used as a partial formal model of the system.

While the underlying theoretical aspects of such approaches to system validation are understood, much work remains to be done before the appropriate technology is widely accepted in industry. In particular, we believe it is important to conduct numerous industrial case studies to a) raise awareness about it, b) stimulate development of better tools, c) identify ways of making validation technology more lightweight, and d) identify directions for further research in the field. This paper reports on such an industrial case study.

The rest of the paper is organized as follows. The next section gives a short overview of the case study. Section 3 discusses the system validation approach using trace analysis. Next, Section 4 describes an example in more detail. Before the paper is concluded, Section 5 discusses and summarizes the results and experiences gained from this case study.

2   Case Study Overview

A model checking approach to validation is particularly useful when distributed systems allow an easy capturing of their internal communications. Such monitoring is often used in telecommunication networks for debugging purposes, relying often on protocol analyzers and network tracers. In the chosen industrial case study, we focus on the applicability of a model checking based validation technology we developed earlier [5] to end-to-end testing of a 3GPP UMTS radio network [11]. Our goal is not only to demonstrate to testers that MDD can be of help to them, but also to identify research direction for improving the applicability of this technology.

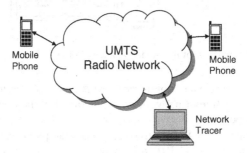

Fig. 1. Schematic overview of the UMTS radio network, which serves as SUT

When an entire 3GPP UMTS radio network is tested end-to-end, the result of a test run cannot be concluded alone from the behavior observed at the mobile phones (test probes) because of the high complexity of the network. Therefore, the communication at various internal interfaces is analyzed in addition to compute the final test verdict. In this system, communications are monitored in a non-intrusive way using designated tracing tools (network tracers) and are recorded in execution traces. Note that the whole UMTS radio network comprising several nodes (Node-Bs, RNCs etc.) serves as the system under test (SUT) as shown in Fig. 1.

3   Validation Using a Trace Analysis Approach

3.1   Outline of the Approach

The approach to validate the system based on observed traces is illustrated in Fig. 2 and can be summarized as follows:

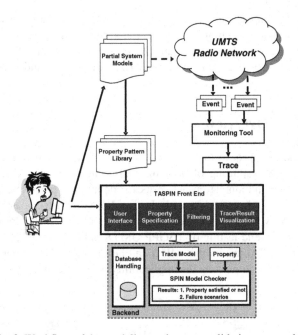

Fig. 2. Workflow of the modeling and system validation approach

- A trace during test case execution is captured that records the messages exchanged internally between different network nodes involved in the communication of two or more mobile phones.
- Traces are fed into the TASPIN front-end tool (Eclipse based) that converts the trace into a behavioral model (here: a Promela model that is input to the Spin model checker)

- Properties describing partial aspects of the system are specified in UML2 diagrams; currently sequence diagrams are used to express so-called base patterns of unique network features and activity diagrams to describe base pattern composition; a library of patterns is also built.
- Model verification: The reconstructed behavioral model (in Promela) plus the desired properties (UML2 diagrams converted to Promela Never Claim expressions) are fed into the Spin model checker backend.
- Verification results (failure traces) and the trace model itself are visualized as UML2 sequence diagrams.

The properties considered are derived from specifications of the 3GPP standards [1] and serve as a reference that must be matched in the recorded communication trace and ultimately by the SUT. They can be also considered as a repository of partial system models that are used to validate test scenarios. This repository of models will grow over time because more models are added during the course of testing and validation. The models assist not only the system validation; they are also of help when an MDD approach to develop new system features is next followed.

3.2 Implementation of the Approach

The workflow for system validation has been implemented in an Eclipse environment [3] using Spin as a model checker [8, 10] in the background. The implemented components are briefly explained (cf. Fig. 2).

- **Eclipse user interface:** Eclipse is used as the implementation environment for all the components of the tool. It comprises the following functionalities:
  - Loading and accessing traces and results in the database
  - Trace and result visualization
  - Filtering
  - Modeling in Promela
  - Property specification and selection
  - Controlling Spin
- **Database handling:** The heart of the module is the MySQL database [9] that manages all information relevant for system validation.
  - Saving/retrieving trace information into/from the database: The module takes UMTS traces recorded in XML format and stores them in the database.
  - Loading/retrieving analysis results into/from the database: Once the verification is done and the corresponding example/counter example is produced, the result file generated by the Spin model checker is read in order to retrieve the information in the original trace.
- **Filtering:** Filtering is implemented using SQL queries that select the desired messages from the database. So far there are three main categories of filters that can be combined to form user defined filters that respond to his needs and understanding of the trace:
  - Filtering by messages
  - Filtering by protocol layers
  - Filtering by parameters

- **Visualization of traces and analysis results:** This component is implemented using the Eclipse TPTP platform [4]. Its tracing and monitoring tools allow showing traces as lists of messages or as interactions between processes in a UML sequence diagram like representation. The same visualization mechanism is used to visualize both the trace and the analysis results read from output files generated by Spin.
- **Property specification:** The properties are obtained from an in-house UML editor that has been implemented as an Eclipse plug-in. The component also allows to select and instantiate a property to be considered for system validation. The detailed property specification procedure is described in Section 3.3.
- **Trace modeling:** The basic function for this module is to read the messages selected by the desired query from the database and write a model in Promela to represent them. There can be two different models produced:
  - Generate a model that does not take into account the concurrency within the SUT. In such a case, the model will consist of a single linear automaton that depicts the exchange of the recorded messages in the order of their appearance in the trace file.
  - Generate a model that features the communications between the processes and reflects the concurrent nature of the SUT. The tool generates the Promela model from a trace by defining a signal corresponding to each message and creating channels that carry the defined signals. The produced model in Spin is an asynchronous model, where processes communicate over unidirectional channels.

3.3 Property Specification

A pragmatic approach has been chosen to identify the common properties to be validated in UMTS traces. It mainly relies on the standardized 3GPP specifications of the network services that define the functionality of the UMTS network and deduces the patterns that make up the services and functions from them.

The main idea of the approach is to define so-called base patterns first and then to combine them to obtain more complex patterns. Base patterns describe a certain service taking place between the relevant network nodes. UML2 sequence diagrams (i.e., message sequence charts supporting alternative, parallel, iterative, optional and other behavior specifications) are used to specify the behavior in a base pattern. Typically the base patterns encode the behavior the system should normally exhibit (the expected behavior), but they can be also used to formulate undesired behavior, e.g., the occurrence of unexpected (error) messages.

Moreover, base patterns are parameterized by message data fields to make them applicable for other traces and re-usable for other system validation tasks. Classifying and storing base patterns in a library will foster re-use and reduce total validation efforts.

In a typical system validation task, the system engineer decides what kind of services the recorded trace of an executed test case should contain and in what order they should occur. She/he takes out the required base patterns from the library if available or creates them beforehand. In a next step, the base patterns are composed in a UML2 activity diagram to specify the expected ordering of their occurrence in the trace. Eventually the base patterns are instantiated replacing the formal parameters by actual values taken from the test run.

The following list describes the possible ways to combine base patterns:

- *Sequentially*: The last message of the first pattern occurs before the first message of the second pattern.
- *Concurrently*: The messages of the two patterns can interleave.
- *Alternatively*: If the messages of the first pattern appear in a certain trace segment, the messages of the second pattern shall not occur in the same segment.
- *Iteratively*: The messages of a pattern are repeated for a finite number of times.

Properties to be verified by Spin can be written in LTL or in *Never Claim* expressions [8]. For purposes of implementation and practicality, we have chosen Never Claim representations. First of all, LTL is more difficult to understand and to write for end users and even model-checking experts. Also it does not map well to the adopted UML diagrams.

The range of properties that can be verified in the Spin approach is defined by the expressiveness of the Never Claim expressions of the Promela language itself. In this project, we are concerned more about defining meaningful properties that help evaluate the system and offering a lightweight approach to model-checking that is acceptable by practitioners. Never Claims are sufficiently expressive for the properties considered in this project so far. Base patterns can be repeated in a trace several times and in various orders.

3.4 Using Patterns

Patterns can be devised and used for system validation following various strategies depending on, for example, the current level of confidence about system correctness. At the initial stage of testing, the system engineer may need to devise patterns from existing (informal) system specifications. If she/he already trusts several executions traces, she/he may want to make sure that certain patterns are repeated also in a newly obtained trace. Starting from a trace that is known to be correct and complete in terms of certain services and features, some base patterns can be identified and a *reference trace* (in terms of UML2 sequence and activity diagrams) is defined. The reference trace can then be used to check new traces. The traces that violate the reference trace are declared faulty unless they have been analyzed further and are known for sure to be correct, in which case the reference trace must be updated.

4 Example

The example discussed in this paper refers to a test case implementing a user scenario that tests the execution of a package-switched call between two mobile phones in order to transfer data from one mobile phone to the other one using the FTP command. Naturally, a number of network services at different network nodes and interfaces are involved in this user scenario.

In our trace-based approach to system validation we describe each required network service as a base pattern and combine them according to their temporal appearance and ordering in the user scenario as recorded in the trace. As an example of a base pattern, Fig. 3 shows the message flow of a so-called "RRC connection establishment" procedure that is issued each time a mobile phone attempts to establish a connection. Other base patterns are modeled in a similar way, but could contain more complex control structures such as parallel or alternative messages and loops.

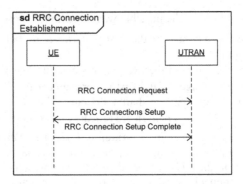

Fig. 3. Base pattern "RRC Connection Establishment"

Next, a set of base patterns is combined in a composite pattern (Fig. 4) to reflect the expected behavior of the user scenario in the trace. The UML activity diagram uses different swim lanes for each service group, here RRC and GPRS services. This kind of structuring improves the readability of the diagram in particular. The composite pattern in Fig. 4 can be also viewed as a reference trace that must reoccur each time the associated test case is performed.

A recorded trace in this example contains several hundred messages that occurred at various interfaces of the radio network during test case execution. Only about 30 messages are relevant because they are part of one or another base pattern that needs to be verified. These relevant messages could be filtered out from the trace prior to generating a Promela model. Otherwise the model is unnecessarily cluttered with unneeded messages that only slow down the model verification. At the moment, filtering is a manual process. However, we are currently discussing an approach to automatically filter out messages from the trace based on the selected patterns to be verified.

The generated Promela model of the recorded trace and the composite pattern of the expected behavior translated into a Never Claim expression are eventually fed into the Spin model checker. In the simplest case a linear Promela model is used, which does not pose much stress on the model checker. Even when using a concurrency model for the trace (see Section 3.2), the approach remains scalable if the relevant messages were filtered out before model creation.

The result of the model-checking task is a simple statement whether the verified property is contained in the model or not. In our context it means that we get assurance whether the composite pattern is matched by the recorded trace or not. In the negative case a failure scenario is produced by Spin that depicts the path from the initial state of the model, i.e., from the first message in the trace, to the state, at which diverging behavior is detected. The failure scenario is mapped back to the original trace by our tool such that the system engineer gets hints, which message violated the specified behavior of the provided composite pattern.

System engineers at Siemens used the described approach mainly during regression testing of radio network elements to validate the correct execution of user scenarios. Their validation task becomes now much simpler since before they had to analyze the produced large trace files manually in a text-based trace viewer. By means of our tool they

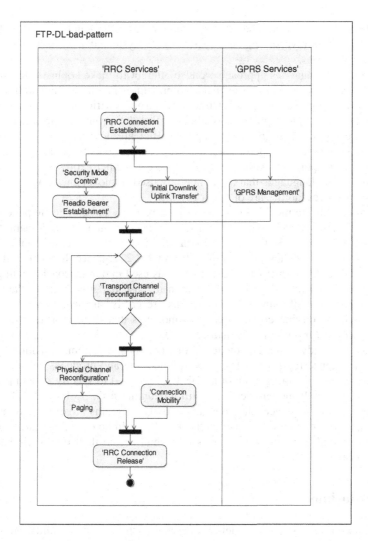

Fig. 4. Composite pattern of the expected trace behavior

are enabled to quickly decide about the correctness of network services. The graphical representation of base patterns and composite patterns is in particular helpful for them to understand the validation results and discuss them with other project members.

5 Results and Experiences Obtained

The presented approach to system validation is based on an analysis of traces recorded during the execution of test cases or by some other means. Therefore it is particularly well suited for poorly documented systems. Our approach produces a set of partial system models (base patterns and compositions) that are used to verify the correct behavior of services and other system features. They can be considered also as a starting point to reverse engineer (parts of) the system if it is desirable, e.g., for maintenance reasons.

With our trace analysis approach we also attempt to make sophisticated solutions like model-checking techniques available to practitioners who are not well trained in theoretical computer science at all. Up to now, formal verification is still an area that receives little attention in practice. We believe that this promising area can only succeed if the entry hurdle of this technology is sufficiently low. This refers in particular to the way how system properties are specified. UML seems to be again an appropriate mean for this purpose. Although it might have a smaller expressiveness compared to temporal logic languages that are commonly used in model checking, its graphical format and easy readability are of major benefit.

System models are modeled in terms of base patterns and composite patterns. This kind of abstraction works well for the discussed telecommunication domain. It might be interesting to see how this concept could be transferred to other application domains as well. Nevertheless, the mapping from UML2 sequence diagrams and activity diagrams to Promela Never Claim expressions as used in our approach is still preliminary since the semantics on the composition of base patterns in particular requires further research. While simple compositions are easily supported by our tool, our experience in specifying complex patterns indicates that there is a need to define a formal *language for pattern specification*.

In this case study it can be concluded that the chosen system validation approach based on reengineering models from traces is feasible and produces valuable results. At the same time, the integration of an UML editor used to specify system properties with an off-the-shelf model-checker is still a daunting task. So far, UML behavioral diagrams such as sequence diagrams and activity diagrams have to be transformed into an appropriate input of the model-checker. It would be desirable that future modeling tools would integrate model-checking techniques on their own such that model validation can be done more easily.

6   Conclusions

We used in our case study a model-checker approach for system validation based on traces recorded during test execution of a UMTS radio network acting as the system under test. The tool has been implemented within Eclipse and integrates with a UML editor used for the specification of properties and Spin as the model-checker. The main open problems are the completion of an extensive library of base patterns for properties in UML and a refinement of the integration with Spin. Such a refinement should result in an improved user interface to the verification task.

We believe that the presented approach to system validation is also applicable to other types of distributed systems provided that expressive traces during system runtime can be obtained. Besides applying the approach during end-to-end system testing, it could also be used in an uncontrollable environment, e.g. during field testing. Furthermore, reverse-engineering of traces seems the only feasible way to deal with systems that lack sufficient and up-to-date design documentation.

Acknowledgement

Crucial contributions of Hesham Hallal and ElHachemi Alikacem (CRIM) to tool development and support are acknowledged.

References

1. 3GPP Specifications Home; accessed, 2007-03-29 (2007) http://www.3gpp.org/specs/specs.htm
2. Colin, S., Mariani, L.: Run-Time Verification. In: Broy, M., Jonsson, B., Katoen, J.-P., Leucker, M., Pretschner, A. (eds.) Model-Based Testing of Reactive Systems. LNCS, vol. 3472, pp. 525–556. Springer, Heidelberg, ISBN 978-3-540-26278-7 (2005)
3. Eclipse – An Open Development Platform; accessed 2007-03-29, (2007) http://www.eclipse.org/
4. Eclipse Test and Performance Tools Platform (TPTP) Project; accessed 2007-03-29, (2007) http://www.eclipse.org/tptp/
5. Hallal, H.H., Boroday, S., Petrenko, A., Ulrich, A.: A formal approach to property testing in causally consistent distributed traces. Formal Aspects of Computing 18(1), 63–83 ISSN 0934-5043 (2006)
6. Hallal, H., Boroday, S., Ulrich, A., Petrenko, A.: An Automata-based Approach to Property Testing in Event Traces. In: Proc. of the IFIP TC6/WG6.1 XV International Conference on Testing of Communicating Systems (TestCom 2003), pp. 180-196. Sophia Antipolis, France (May 2003)
7. Hallal, H., Petrenko, A., Ulrich, A., Boroday, S.: Using SDL Tools to Test Properties of Distributed Systems. In: Larsen, K.G., Nielsen, M. (eds.) CONCUR 2001. LNCS, vol. 2154, Springer, Heidelberg (2001)
8. Holzmann, G.J.: The SPIN Model Checker; Addison-Wesley; ISBN. Addison-Wesley, London, UK, ISBN 978-0-321-22862-8 (2004)
9. MySQL – The world's most popular open source database; accessed 2007-03-29, (2007) http://www.mysql.com/
10. On-the-fly, LTL Model Checking with SPIN; accessed 2007-03-29, (2007) http://spinroot.com/spin/whatispin.html
11. Sauter, M.: Communication Systems for the Mobile Information Society. John Wiley, New York, ISBN 978-0-470-02676-2 (2006)

A Model Driven Software Factory Using Domain Specific Languages

Jos Warmer

Ordina, The Netherlands
jos.warmer@ordina.nl

Abstract. This paper describes the development of the SMART-Microsoft Software Factory. This factory is a fully model driven factory that makes extensive use of the Microsoft DSL Tools and is bases on the Microsoft Service Oriented Architecture. We describe the process used for developing the factory and share the experience gained in the first projects in which this factory has been used. The first project has 73% of the delivered code being generated.

1 Introduction

Within Visual Studio 2005 Microsoft has introduced the DSL Tools [5]. Using these tools anyone can define his own visual Domain Specific language (DSL). It allows one to define the concepts in the language, their visual representation, but also the corresponding code generation. The DSL Tools generate a visual editor for the language, which is seamlessly integrated into Visual Studio. Domain Specific Languages play a central role in Microsoft's Software Factories concept [1]. This eases the software development process and improves both productivity and quality through code generation.

During 2006 a complete model driven software factory has been built within the Microsoft Development Centre of Ordina. This factory is called the SMART-Microsoft Software Factory [4]. Within this factory we have used DSL technology extensively. This paper describes how we came to the DSLs that we needed and how this has led to an effective and flexible software factory. The first part describes the type of applications that the factory is targeting. The architecture of these applications plays a central role. The second part describes which DSLs we have developed to enable us to develop this type of applications as efficient as possible. We will show how the architecture has been one of the guiding principles in this process.

2 Architecture

Modern, service oriented, software systems are always based on some architecture. By defining an architecture that incorporates aspects as maintainability, security, reuse, scalability, availability etc., we are able to build better software systems. Luckily, we do not have to build a new architecture for each system. Many best practices are bundled in reference architectures. Microsoft has developed such a reference architecture for building .Net applications. Our SMART-Microsoft architecture is based on this

D.H. Akehurst, R. Vogel, and R.F. Paige (Eds.): ECMDA-FA 2007, LNCS 4530, pp. 194–203, 2007.

Microsoft architecture. The Microsoft architecture is defined at a rather high conceptual level. Therefore, for developing real applications we have made every part of the architecture explicit and defined the components and framework that we would use to build these parts of the architecture.

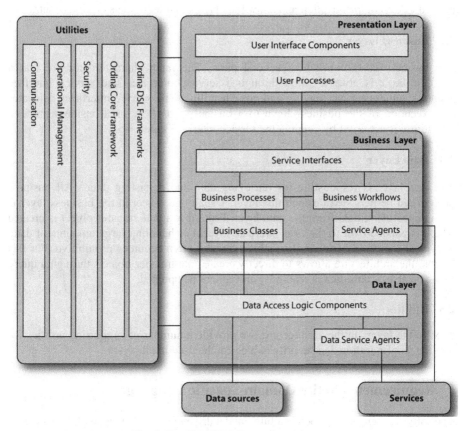

Fig. 1. The SMART-Microsoft architecture

The SMART-Microsoft architecture consists of multiple layers, with different parts within each layer. We will describe all layers in just enough detail to understand their responsibilities. This paper does not focus on architecture, therefore we will not discuss the architecture in detail.

2.1 Presentation Layer

The presentation layer consists of two parts. The UI Components part are web pages or windows forms. These are meant only to show information and do not contains any logic, except for input field validation. The UI Process part includes all navigation, state management and is responsible for calling services to either fetch information to be shown to the user, or to execute the command that the user requested. Services are always called through a generated proxy.

2.2 Data Contract Layer

In a service oriented architecture data contracts are part of the service contract. In the architecture data contracts are also the definition of the data that the presentation layer uses. Because the data contract is used inside two architectural layers we have chosen to make the data contract explicit and allow both layers to refer to the same data contracts.

2.3 Business Layer

The business layer consists of several parts, The main characteristics are that a business layer is always called through a service interface. The service interface supports authentication, logging and error handling. The service interfaces delegates the execution of the business logic to a business workflow or a business process. Scalability is achieved by keeping the service interface stateless.

2.4 Data Layer

The data layer is responsible for retrieving data and persisting data. All business objects can be persisted through this layer. Usually an object in the business layer is instantiated using data from the data layer. From this a data transfer object is created which is handed over to the user interface layer. For handling large amounts of data, as typically used in overview lists, this overhead often becomes prohibitive. For this reason, the architecture allows to directly create data transfer objects through a query to the database. This data is read-only and cannot be updated.

2.5 Utilities

Next to the layers in the architecture, we provide a number of supporting utilities for logging, configuration and security, which can be used in all layers.

3 Requirements to the Domain Specific Languages

The software factory described is a fully model driven factory. The goal of the models is to aid the developer to be more productive. We have formulated several requirements that we have used during the development of the DSLs.

3.1 Models Must Be Easier That the Equivalent Code

A model must always be at a higher abstraction level than the generated code. We do not target "coding in pictures". This means that we put concepts into a DSL, only when the concept is easier to model than it is to code. Things that take as much effort to model as to code won't become part of our DSL. A direct consequence of this approach is that we do not necessarily model 100 percent of the application. We always assume that part of the system will be modelled and part will be done in code. The code generation from the DSLs has been designed such that handwritten code is always added separately from the generated code. We have made extensive use of C# partial classes, abstract base classes, etc. to allow the developer to add his own code in separate files.

3.2 Models Must Be Productive for Less Experienced Developers

One of the goals of the software factory is to make less experienced developers with less architectural knowledge productive. This has been achieved by hiding technical details behind the models. A consequence is that a model should remain relatively simple. This has been achieved by defining multiple DSLs, each of which has a limited focus. We also allow the developer to use multiple models per DSL, such that models can remain small and understandable.

3.3 Generated Code Must Be Readable and Maintainable

The relationship between models and the generated code must be clear, especially for the more experienced developers that have the task of adding handwritten code to the generated code. For this reason the various DSLs are based on the chosen architecture. Each DSL has an explicit connection with one or more architectural parts and generates code for exactly these parts.

3.4 Regeneration Must Always Remain Possible

Code generation is only useful if you can regenerate at any moment in time. A one-off code generation where the generated code is changed by hand helps only at the very start of a project, but won't give any structural benefits. Therefore, code generation from the DSL models must always remain possible, while retaining any handwritten code. This goal influences the structure of the generated code directly. We make extensive use of frameworks and techniques as patterns, virtual operations, partial classes, abstract base classes, etc. Although this aspect does not influence the concepts in the DSLs directly, this is a mandatory requirement to be able to use the DSLs in a productive and repeatable way.

3.5 The Different DSLs Should Be Useable Separately and in Collaboration

Many MDA tools that we have encountered over the years have a tendency to be either useable completely or not useable at all. This all-or-nothing feature makes many potentially useful tools applicable in only few situations. In our environment we have many different customers with different requirements. Still we need to get as much return on investment from the DSLs that we develop as possible. By designing the DSLs as independent languages, we are able to use them separately. Still we need to ensure that the DSL can collaborate as good as possible when they are used together. This includes full validation between different DSL models, e.g. when *References* (see next sections) to model elements are being used.

4   The SMART-Microsoft DSLs

Currently we have defined four Domain Specific Languages. Each of the DSLs can be mapped to specific parts in the architecture as shown in figure 2.

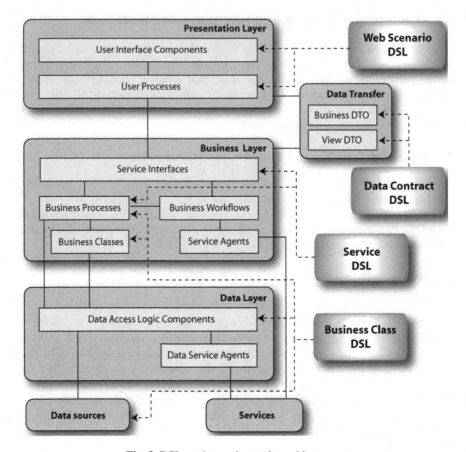

Fig. 2. DSLs and mapping to the architecture

4.1 Web Scenario DSL

The Web Scenario DSL is used to model the presentation layer. As most of our customers require web applications we have chosen to create a DSL for web interfaces. We have investigated the use of one DSL for both Web and Windows user interfaces. However, the structure of these interfaces is quite different. Instead of trying to generalize this, we have chosen to stay close to our target architecture. If we have enough customers that require windows interfaces, we plan to develop a separate Windows Forms DSL, which can then be used as an alternative to the Web Scenario DSL.

The key concept in the Web Scenario DSL is the *user action*, a combination of showing a web page to the user and performing an action by the user. Figure 3 shows an example of a Web Scenario Model. In this model *Search Orders* is a user action of type *List*. It contains a *Reference to OrderDTO*, a model element that has been defined in another Data Contract model (see figure 4). The *Edit Order* is an Edit Action with a reference to *OrderDTO*. From this model web pages (ASPX) are generated that allow editing of an *OrderDTO*. Note that the *Reference* elements are defined in properties, which are not shown in the example model.

For the condition "Is Order Open" in the model the skeleton code is generated, such that it will be called at the right place. We decided that modelling conditions is as much work as writing them in C#, the developer should write the actual condition in C#. This is an example of how we combine generated and hand-written code in a well-defined way.

The element *Add Product* is a reference to another Web Scenario, defined in a separate Web Scenario model.

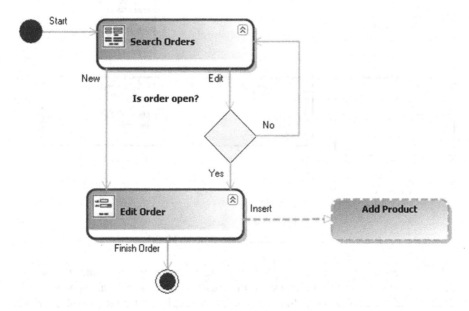

Fig. 3. Example Web Scenario Model

4.2 Data Contract DSL

A Data Contract model is used to define Data Transfer Objects (DTO). They allow us to define all data objects that are used to communicate between the layers in the architecture using services. Figure 4 shows several DTO objects. *OrderDto*, *ProductDto*, *CustomerDto* and *OrderLineDto* are business DTO's, which means they represent a business object. A view DTO, like *CustomerOrdersDto* is used for modelling lists. *ProductDescriptionDTO* is a filter DTO and represents a limited view on the attributes of a business DTO. The example also shows a composite DTO named *OrderOrderlineDTO*, which is a composition of a *OrderDTO* and its *OrderlineDTO's*.

4.3 Service DSL

SMART-Microsoft has a service oriented architecture. Therefore, we needed a DSL to model the services. The parameters of the services always are DTOs, which are defined in a Data Contract model. This is done by special *Reference to DTO* model elements in the Service model.

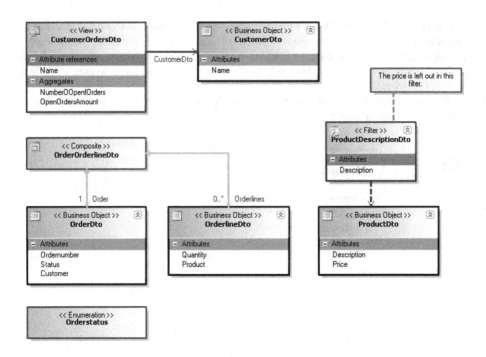

Fig. 4. Example Data Contract Model

When generating code we follow the architecture; we generate the service interfaces, and also the skeletons of the business processes that implement the services. For standard services like the CRUD (Create, Read, Update, Delete) services for business objects the implementation of the business process is generated as well. The implementation of other services is done in C#, using partial classes to separate the handwritten code from the generated code.

Figure 5 shows the CRUD services with types <<Insert>>, <<Select>>, <<Update>>, and <<Delete>>. The input and output parameters are references to DTOs defined in a Data Contract model. *ImportProducts* is a custom service, for which the developer needs to write the implementation by hand.

4.4 Business Entity DSL

The Business Entity DSL allows the developer to model business classes, including their attributes and relationships. From the Business Entity DSL the code for the Business Class layer is generated. We also generate the complete code for the data layer from the business entity model.

Figure 6 defines five business entities. Apart from the attributes and relationships *Customer* also has a business rule *MaximumOpenOrders*. As with conditions on the Web Scenario, the implementation of the business rule is written in C#. The generation process ensures that the business rule is called at the right places at the right time.

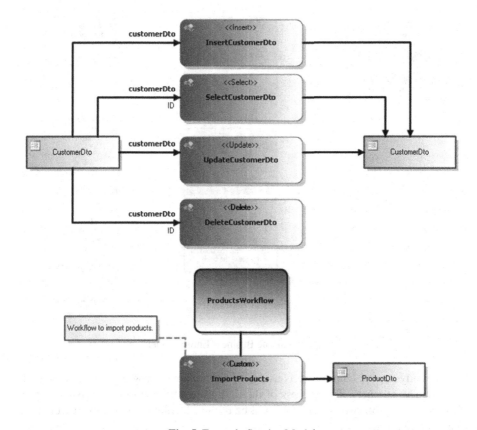

Fig. 5. Example Service Model

The Business Entity DSL doesn't contain operations or methods. The added value of putting these in the models is too limited, all we can do is generate the method template. Writing the method template directly in C# is just as much work. One of our goals was that models should save work, and this doesn't apply for methods. Therefore we have chosen to write methods for business classes in C# through partial classes.

5 Project Experience

The first release of the model driven software factory went into production in September 2006. The first project (a fixed price, fixed date customer project) was finished in December 2006 on time and within budget. After finishing the project, measurements showed that 73% of the code was generated. The developers in the project had no experience with the underlying architecture, but the model driven approach ensured that they could develop the application within the time planned, fully compliant to the architecture. More than 50 different domain specific models were used.

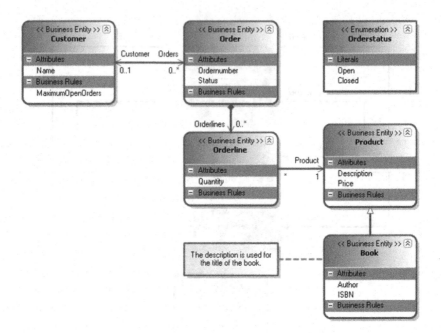

Fig. 6. Example Business Entity Model

Currently several other projects using the factory are in progress, but it is too early to show any numbers. The success of the first project has led to the decision that the SMART-Microsoft software factory will be used as the default development environment for all projects.

In the near future we expect to extend the software factory with additional DSLs, thereby making it applicable to a wider variety of application.

6   Conclusion and Lessons Learned

Below we summarize the main conclusions that we can draw from both developing and using the software factory.

- Before developing SMART-Microsoft we had extensive experience with more traditional MDA approaches using UML with a separate modelling tool as the modelling language. Using small DSLs has been a positive experience compared with the traditional approaches.
- Taking the target architecture in account while defining DSLs has proved to be a good choice. It ensures that the models are suitable for the architecture. Also, it ensures that the models can easily be mapped to specific parts of the architecture. This allows incremental code generation per DSL model.
- Taking the target architecture as the basis for the DSLs leads to a natural boundary of the domains for the different DSLs.

- Within the Microsoft DSL Tools a DSL model is stored in one file. Managing models through these small model files has proven to be a positive experience. A model file is handled the same way as a code file. All tools for version control and multi-user access can be used as is.
- Having multiple models allows us to mix and match which DSLs we use in a given project. The applicability is much wider than with typical "Main Model" approaches.
- Validation between DSL models is neccesary. As the Microsoft DSL Tools didn't support this, we built our own component to allow information exchange between models for validation and other purposes.
- The combination of modelling and programming works very well. Full integration of the DSLs in the VisualStudio IDE makes it much more accessible for developers to use. In this environment the approach of mixing models and code seems to be a natural one to developers. It is neccesary to coach developers where they can extend the generated code. For this purpose we have established a Wiki, where all developers add their project experience.

One of the differences with typical MDA approaches is that we work with multiple small DSLs and multiple small models per DSL. We call this approach *Partial Models*. A preliminary paper on this has been published at the OOPSLA workshop on Domain Specific Languages [3]. A more extensive in-depth paper has been submitted to ECDMA 2007 [2].

Our experience has been gained with the Microsoft DSL Tools. However, the conclusions are applicable to any other environment where tools exist to easily create your own DSLs. One example of such an environment is the Graphical Modelling Framework (GMF) [6] in Eclipse. The same approach can be used to develop a model driven software factory in such an environment.

References

[1] Greenfield, J., Short, K., Cook, S., Kent, S. (eds.): Software Factories, Assembling Applications with Patterns, Models, Frameworks, and Tools. John Wiley & Sons, New York (2004)
[2] Warmer, J., Kleppe, A.G.: Partial Models: Getting rid of mthe "Main" model. Submitted to ECMDA-FA (2007)
[3] Warmer, J., Kleppe, A.G.: 2. Building a Flexible Software Factory Using Partial Domain Specific Models. In: Proceedings of the 6th OOPSLA Workshop on Domain-Specific Modeling (DSM'06), Computer Science and Information System Reports, Technical Reports, TR-37, University of Jyväskylä, Finland, ISBN 951-39-2631-1 (2006)
[4] SMART-Microsoft Website, http://www.ordinasoftwarefactory.nl/Default.asp/id,285/index.htm
[5] Microsoft dsl tools (2006), http://msdn.microsoft.com/vstudio/DSLTools/,
[6] The Eclipse Graphical Modeling Framework (2006), http://www.eclipse.org/gmf

Towards a Model Driven Approach
to Automatic BPEL Generation*

Xiaofeng Yu, Yan Zhang, Tian Zhang, Linzhang Wang,
Jianhua Zhao, Guoliang Zheng, and Xuandong Li

State Key Laboratory for Novel Software Technology
Department of Computer Science and Technology
Nanjing University, Nanjing, P.R. China 210093
yuxiaofeng@seg.nju.edu.cn, lxd@nju.edu.cn

Abstract. Both complex separate Web services and composite Web services
need orchestration specification. However, on one hand, the process of manually creating orchestration specification is time-consuming and error-prone; and
on the other hand, application developers are in a dilemma to choose between vi-
rous orchestration languages and engines. In this paper, to reduce the complexity
of creating Web services orchestration specification, and to make orchestration
models isolate from orchestration languages and engines, we propose a model
driven approach to generate orchestration specification. Web services orchestration is modeled using the CCA (Component Collaboration Architecture) of the
UML profile for Enterprise Distributed Object Computing (EDOC). Then transform CCA specified orchestration models to BPEL via transformation rules. The
same orchestration model can be transformed to different orchestration specifications though we take BPEL as the transformation target. Moreover, the transformation process is automatic.

Keywords: model transformation, EDOC, BPEL generation.

1 Introduction

Web Services are emerging as the most promising technologies to implement loosely
coupled distributed applications, and to perform application integration within and
across organization boundaries. Each Web service exposes interface via a WSDL file
which defines fairly atomic and low-level operations. If a Web service has a complex interface consisting of several operations which are invoked in a sequence according to a
specification, a WSDL file is not able to define the behavioural details of this specification. On the other hand, to increase reuse and to deal with complex business processes,
there is great need to orchestrate discrete Web services into a higher value composite
Web service. But before implementing composite Web services, there are some issues
to be addressed such as orchestration specification. Therefore, either a complex separate Web service or a composite Web service needs an orchestration specification to

---

* Supported by the National Natural Science Foundation of China (No.60673125,
No.60425204), and the National Grand Fundamental Research 973 Program of China
(No.2002CB312001).

D.H. Akehurst, R. Vogel, and R.F. Paige (Eds.): ECMDA-FA 2007, LNCS 4530, pp. 204–218, 2007.

describe dynamic behaviors. However, the process of manually creating orchestration specification for Web services is time-consuming and error-prone. Though there are CASE tools such as IBM Websphere [1], Oracle BPEL Process Manager [2] which offer a user-friendly visual interface for designing and creating orchestration specification, these tools are specific to orchestration languages. Unfortunately, more than one orchestration languages exist currently, such as BPEL [3], WSCI [4] and BPML [5], but none of them has been declared as the winner up to now. Moreover, each orchestration engine can execute only one language. Therefore, developers using such tools have to face the risk of exhausting migration between different orchestration languages and execution engines.

The Model Driven Architecture (MDA) [6] initiated by OMG is an innovative software development method which focuses on separating system functions from the platforms that the system will be implemented on. MDA makes models the first entities in systems. The models which specify the functions of a system without taking into consideration of the technology platforms of the system are called Platform Independent Models (PIMs). Whereas the models which specify technical details of the platform that the system will be implemented on are called Platform Dependent Models (PSMs). A PIM can be transformed to different PSMs via different transformation rules, thus isolating business logic from implementation platforms.

In this paper, to reduce the complexity of manually creating orchestration specifications, and more important is to separate orchestration from languages and execution engines, we present a MDA based approach. This approach models Web service orchestration as PIMs using EDOC CCA, then transforms CCA described PIMs to BPEL specified PSMs through transformation rules. The BPEL generation process of this approach is automatic, thus decreasing the complexity of manual work. Moreover, in this approach, the same orchestration model can be transformed to different orchestration language defined specifications by applying different rules, thus liberating developers from migration nightmare. Though we make BPEL as the target orchestration language in this article, the approach is applicable to other orchestration languages.

The remainder of this work is structured as follows. Section 2 and section 3 give an overview of EDOC CCA and BPEL respectively. Section 4 presents detailed transformation rules from EDOC CCA to BPEL process. The transformation rules are then illustrated through a case study in section 5. Section 6 discusses the related work. The last section concludes and outlines the future work.

2 Overview of EDOC CCA

The UML Profile for EDOC (Enterprise Distributed Object Computing) [7] conforms to MDA and provides facilities to model distributed component based enterprise computing. The EDOC Profile consists of several profiles each of which is constituted by a set of Profile Elements. The Component Collaboration Architecture (CCA) is the core Profile Element of the EDOC Profile. CCA models the structure and behavior of the components that comprise a system in a platform independent way. In our approach, the structural aspects of PIMs are specified with CCA Structural Specification, whereas

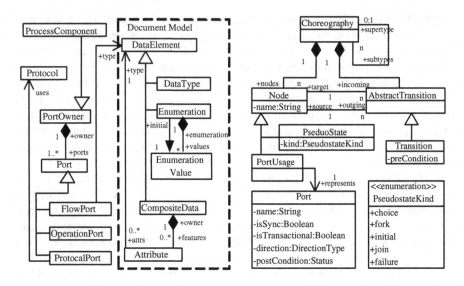

Fig. 1. CCA Structural Spec. Meta-model   **Fig. 2.** CCA Choreography Meta-model

the dynamic behavior of the PIMs are specified with CCA Choreographies. The simplified meta-models of CCA Structural Specification and CCA Choreography are illustrated in Fig. 1 and Fig. 2 respectively.

As shown in Fig. 1, the primary elements of the CCA Structural Specification are:

- ProcessComponent - It describes the contract for a component.
- Port - It realizes a conversation for a ProcessComponent or Protocol.
- FlowPort - It is a Port which produces or consumes a single data type on behalf of the owning component or protocol.
- OperationPort - It represents the typical call/return pattern of an operation.
- ProtocolPort - It is a Port which uses a Protocol to realize complex two-way interactions between components.
- Protocol - It specifies the conversation between two ProcessComponents.

The cental elements of the CCA Choreography meta-model are shown in Fig. 2:

- Choreography - It is an abstract class inherited by Protocol and ProcessComponent which expresses the behavior of ProcessComponents. A Choreography specifies how messages will flow between PortUsages.
- Node - It is an abstract element that specifies something that can be the source and/or target of a transition and thus ordered within the choreographed process.
- PortUsage - It expresses the usage of a Port as part of a Choreography.
- PseudoState - It specifies starting, ending or intermediate states in the Choreography. A PseudoState depends on it's kind attribute which can be one of the following enumeration values: choice, fork, initial, join, success and failure.
- Transition - It specifies the ordering that the related nodes will activate.

3   Overview of BPEL

BPEL is an XML-based language for orchestrating Web services. Fig. 3 depicts the simplified meta-model for BPEL based on [3].

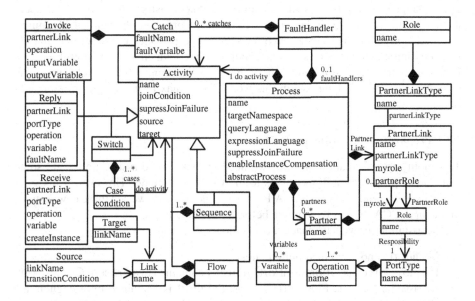

Fig. 3. A Simplified Meta-model for BPEL

We briefly sketch the BPEL concepts that are relevant for the proposed mapping from CCA as follows:

- Process - It is the root in the BPEL specification.
- PartnerLink - It represents a bilateral message exchange between two parties via a reference to a PartnerLinkType.
- PartnerLinkType - It defines the roles and PortTypes of two partner services.
- Variable - It holds workflow data and messages exchanged between parties.
- FaultHandler - It provides a way to define custom fault-handling activities.
- Invoke -It denotes a synchronous request/response or an asynchronous one-way operation to invoke a Web service.
- Receive - It denotes receiving a request from other web services.
- Reply - It denotes sending a response to a request previously accepted via a synchronous Receive activity.
- Sequence - It specifies that Activities are executed sequentially.
- Flow - It specifies that Activities are executed in parallel, possibly with some synchronous Links.
- Switch - It specifies that alternative branches are chosen to be executed based on the value of some Variables.

4   From CCA to BPEL Using OMG's QVT

Several transformation languages and specifications have been proposed to specify transformation rules, such as OMG's Final Adopted QVT Specification [8], YATL [9], ATL [10]. Since the OMG Final Adopted QVT Specification defines standard transformation languages, we use this specification to define transformation rules. This specification defines three QVT languages: Relations, Core, and Operational Mappings. However, only the Operational Mappings language provides constructs commonly found in imperative languages (loops, conditions, etc.) which are very useful to specify complex transformation rules. Therefore we define transformation rules using the Operational Mappings language in this work. The syntax of this language references to [8].

4.1   Preparation for Transformation

To simplify transformation process, we need to make some assumptions, add some constraints, properties and operations to the CCA meta-model. However, it does not mean that we intend to alter the CCA Profile. On the contrary, we add these new features to the input CCA models by a plugin before transformation.

The assumptions we have made are as follows:

- MultiPort is not used in system modeling.
- If a FlowPort or an OperationPort is directly contained in a ProcessComponent, we assume that this FlowPort or OperationPort is contained by a cognominal ProtocolPort which is directly contained in the ProcessComponent.

The constraint validProtocol is added to the CCA meta-model which specifies that a Protocol can be inherited by only one pair of ProtocolPorts. Thus we can navigate between ProtocolPorts which use the same Protocol. This constraint is defined using the Object Constraint Language (OCL) (the OCL code is left out).

The following properties are added to the CCA meta-model to facilitate the transformation process (the OCL expression of these properties is omitted):

- outermostProtocolPort: It represents the ProtocolPort which contains the current Port and is directly owned by a ProcessComponent.
- partnerPort: It represents the Port which interacts with the current Port.
- ownPort: It represents the Ports with respect to the 'responder' role of the Protocol that the current ProtocolPort uses.
- lastNodeType: It represents the types of the last nodes of all branches of the current ChoiceState. It is a set which consists of SucessState, FailureState, MerageState, and JoinState
- isSync: It is a Boolean value which indicates whether the current Transition is used as a synchronous control between two concurrent Nodes. If the current Transition works as a synchronous control, this property must be set with 'true'. Otherwise the value of this property must be 'false'. The default value of this property is 'false'.

The operations we add to the CCA meta-model is listed below(OCL code of these operations is very big, so we omit the details):

- getNextNode: It returns the next Node to the current Node.
- getPreviousNode: It returns the previous Node to the current Node.
- getMatchJoinState: It returns the matching JoinState of the current ForkState.
- getMatchForkState: It returns the matching ForkState of the current JoinState.
- getSyncTrans : It returns the synchronous control Transitions which will be mapped to BPEL <links> in a corresponding BPEL <flow>.
- getRootTrans: It checks whether a Transition is directly nested in a ForkState.
- getLinks: It returns the <links> which are mapped from the synchronous control Transitions directly nested in the current ForkState.

Besides, we define a PseudoState named MergeState. A MergeState has one outgoing Transition and several optional incoming Transitions only one of which can be enabled at a time. A MergeState is used to merge the outgoing Transitions of a corresponding ChoiceState.

4.2   From CCA to BPEL

Based on semantic equivalence and the new features we defined for the CCA meta-model, we propose the rules mapping from CCA Choreography to BPEL (see Table 1):

Table 1. The rules mapping from CCA Choreography to BPEL

Rule	Input(CCA)	Constraint	Output(BPEL)
fp2var	FlowPort		<variable>
fp2ch	FlowPort	in OperationPort postcondition !='success' direction ='responds' owner.direction ='initiates'	<catch>
fp2inv	FlowPort	not in OperationPort direction ='initiates'	<invoke> with <inputVariable>
fp2rec	FlowPort	not in OperationPort direction = 'responds' or in OperationPort direction ='responds' owner.direction ='responds'	<receive>
fp2rep	FlowPort	in OperationPort direction ='initiates' owner.direction ='responds'	<reply>
op2inv	OperationPort	direction ='initiates'	<invoke> with <inputVariable> and <outputVariable>
ProPort2x	ProtocolPort		<PartnerLinkType> and <PartnerLink>
fs2fl	ForkState		<flow>
pc2def	ProcssComponent		WSDL <definition>
cca2bpel	Choreography		<process>

Table 1 shows that not all the BPEL concepts can be transformed from CCA models. For those BPEL elements, such as <assign>, <pick>, <correlations>, there are no corresponding elements in CCA that have equivalent semantic to them. The complete description of all these rules in Table 1 is very big, therefore we only give the code for part of these rules: **fp2rep**, **op2inv**, **fs2fl** and **cca2bpel**.

The rule **fp2rep** (see Fig. 4) maps a FlowPort to a BPEL <reply> activity. If an 'initiates' FlowPort is owned by a 'responds' OperationPort, it is used to return messages to synchronous calls from other ProcessComponents. Therefore such a FlowPort can be mapped to a BPEL <reply> activity.

```
transformation fp2rep(in cca:CCA, out bpel:BPEL)
main(){cca.objectsOfType(FlowPort)→map fp_to_rep();}
mapping FlowPort::fp_to_rep():Reply{
  when{this.owner.oclIsTypeOf(OperationPort) and this.owner.direction='responds'
       and this.direction='initiates'}
  partnerLink := this.outermostProtocolPort.resolveone(#BPEL::PartnerLink);
  portType := this.partnerPort.outermostProtocolPort.resolveone(#WSDL::PortType);
  operation := this.owner.resolveone(#WSDL::PortTypeOperation);
  Variable := this.resolveone(#BPEL::Variable);}
```

Fig. 4. The transformation rule fp2rep

The rule **op2inv** (see Fig. 5) maps a CCA 'initiates' OperationPort to a BPEL <invoke> operation. Since an OperationPort represents a synchronous call/return operation, the generated <invoke> has both the <inputVariable> and <outputVariable>.

```
transformation op2inv(in cca:CCA, out bpel:BPEL)
main(){cca.objectsOfType(OperationPort)→map op_to_inv();}
mapping OperationPort::op_to_inv():Invoke{
  when{this.direction = 'initiates'}
     var iPort := this.ports→select(fp|fp.direction = 'initiates');
     var oPort := this.ports→select(fp|fp.direction = 'responds' and
       fp.postcondition = 'success');
     partnerLink := this.outermostProtocolPort.resolveone(#BPEL::PartnerLink);
     portType := this.partnerPort.outermostProtocolPort.resolveone(#WSDL::PortType);
     operation := this.partnerPort.resolveone(#WSDL::PortTypeOperation);
     inputVariable := iPort.resolveone(#BPEL::Variable);
     outputVariable := oPort.resolveone(#BPEL::Variable);}
```

Fig. 5. The transformation rule op2inv

The rule **fs2fl** (see Fig. 6) maps a CCA ForkState to a BPEL <flow> activity. Each outgoing branch of the ForkState is mapped to a BPEL <sequence> which will be added into the corresponding BEPEL <flow>. The transitions which are used to express synchronization dependencies are mapped to <links>.

The rule **cca2bpel** (see Fig. 7) calls all the other rules sequentially to map a Choreography of a ProcessComponent to a BPEL <process>. This rule traverses a Choreography from its initial node to its end nodes, and applies other transformation rules to each node according to the type of the node. Since a <process> needs to refer to its WSDL specified interface, the rule **cca2bpel** reuses the rules mapping from CCA ProcessComponent to WSDL that we have proposed in [22] (see Table 2).

```
transformation fs2fl(in cca:CCA, out bpel:BPEL)
main(){cca.objectsOfType(ForkState)→map fs_to_fl();}
mapping ForkState::fs_to_fl():Flow{
  links := this.getLinks();
  activity := this.outgoing.iterate(og; acc:Set(BPEL::Sequence)|
    var seq : BPEL::Sequence;
    var nd : CCA::Node := og.target;
    while (nd <>this.getMatchJoinState){
      seq.activity→append(nd. resolveone(#BPEL::Activity));
      nd := nd.getNextNode();}
    acc→including(seq);)
}
```

Fig. 6. The rule fs2fl

```
transformation cca2bpel(in cca:CCA, out wsdl:WSDL, out bpel:BPEL)
extends transformation dt2pdt(DM,WXS);            extends transformation en2st(DM,WXS);
extends transformation cd2ct(DM,WXS);             extends transformation fp2x(CCA,WSDL);
extends transformation opp2ptop(CCA,WSDL);        extends transformation fp2var(CCA,WSDL);
extends transformation fp2ch(CCA,WSDL);           extends transformation fp2inv(CCA,WSDL);
extends transformation fp2rec(CCA,WSDL);          extends transformation fp2rep(CCA,WSDL);
extends transformation op2inv(CCA,WSDL);          extends transformation proPort2x(CCA,WSDL);
extends transformation syncTran2lk(CCA,WSDL);     extends transformation cs2sw(CCA,WSDL);
extends transformation fs2fl(CCA,WSDL);           extends transformation pc2def(CCA,WSDL);
extends transformation choreography2bpel (CCA,BPEL);
main(){
  cca.objectsOfType(DataType)→map dt_to_pdt();
  cca.objectsOfType(EnumerationType)→map en_to_st();
  cca.objectsOfType(FlowPort)→map fp_to_x();
  cca.objectsOfType(OperationPort)→map opp_to_ptop();
  cca.objectsOfType(FlowPort)→map fp_to_var();
  cca.objectsOfType(FlowPort)→map fp_to_ch();
  cca.objectsOfType(FlowPort)→map fp_to_inv();
  cca.objectsOfType(FlowPort)→map fp_to_rec();
  cca.objectsOfType(FlowPort)→map fp_to_rep();
  cca.objectsOfType(OperationPort)→map op_to_inv();
  cca.objectsOfType(ProtocolPort)→map protocolPort_to_x();
  cca.objectsOfType(Transition)→map syncTran_to_lk();
  cca.objectsOfType(ChoiceState)→map cs_to_sw();
  cca.objectsOfType(ForkState)→map fs_to_fl();
  cca.objectsOfType(ProcessComponent)→map pc_to_definition);
  cca.objectsOfType(Choreography)→map choreography_to_bpel();
}
```

Fig. 7. The rule cca2bpel

Table 2. The rules mapping from CCA to WSDL

Rule	Input(CCA)	Constraint	Output(BPEL)
dt2pdt	DataType		<PrimitiveDataType>
en2st	Enumeration		<SimpleType>
cd2ct	CompositeData		<ComplexType>
fp2x	FlowPort		<Message> and <PortTypeOperation>
opp2pto	OperationPort		<PortTypeOperation>

5   The Illustrative Example

To exemplify how our approach works, we choose an illustrative example of an E-Store. The E-Store provides customers with on line purchasing service. A customer sends an order to the E-Store, then the E-Store calculates the price, arranges the shipment and the shipping schedule. Finally, the E-Store sends an invoice to the customer.

Fig. 8 illustrates the CCA specified E-Store PIM and its collaborative partners. The ProcessComponent E-Store includes four ProtocolPorts which are selling, shippingCallBack, invoiceCallback and scheduling. The ProtocolPort selling has an 'responds' OperationPort sendOrder, the ProtocolPort shippingCallback has an 'initiates' OperationPort requestShipping and a non-operationPort-owned FlowPort sendSchedule, the ProtocolPort scheduling and invoiceCallback only contain nonoperationPort-owned FlowPorts. Each of these ProtocolPorts interact with its partner port using a corresponding Protocol (see Fig. 9).

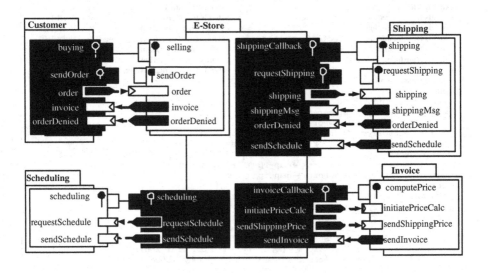

Fig. 8. The PIM of the E-Store and its partners

The Choreography of E-Store ProcessComponent is depicted in Fig. 10. The Choreography shows that, firstly, a customer makes a purchase order to the E-Store component. Then the E-Store component uses the Invoicing component to calculate the price, uses the Shipping component to arrange the shipment, and uses the Scheduling component to handle scheduling. The E-Store component performs these three tasks concurrently. There are two control dependencies: the shipping price is required to complete the final price calculation and the shipping date is required to complete the scheduling. Finally, the E-Store component sends an invoice to the customer.

After the necessary information for transformation is available, we can apply the transformation rule **cca2bpel** to the E-Store ProcessComponent and its Choreography, thus automatically generating the WSDL file and the BPEL file in listing 1.1 and

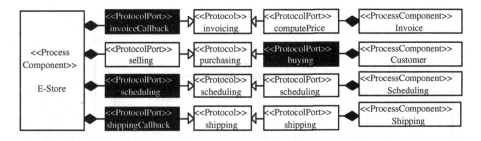

Fig. 9. The contract of the E-Store

listing 1.2 respectively in the appendix. In order to automatize the transformation process, we are engaged in developing an execution engine. A plugin is also in the process of development which adds the new features to the input CCA models. These features include the properties and operations that we have defined for the CCA meta-model. The transformation process with the execution engine and the labelling plugin is shown in Fig. 11. Firstly, a CCA model expressed in XMI (XML Metadata Interchange) is input into the labelling plugin. Secondly, the plugin adds new features to the CCA model and transmit the altered CCA model into the execution engine. Finally, the engine executes transformation rules to generate a BPEL process and a WSDL file for the altered CCA model.

6 Related Work

The interface models for Web services are specified using WSDL, whereas the orchestration models are specified using one of the various nonstandard orchestration languages, such as BPEL and BPML. Our previous work covers model driven WSDL generation from CCA Structural Specification [22]. This article focuses on model driven BPEL generation from CCA Structural Specification and CCA Choreography.

Besides our work, [11] presents a model driven approach to semi-automatically generate BPEL from healthcare domain workflows. However, our approach is independent of application domains. [12] shows how BPEL process definitions for parties involved in a choreography can be derived from a global WS-CDL [13] choreography model. However, WS-CDL is not a modelling language, hence, mapping from WS-CDL to BPEL is not usable during the analysis and design phases of the development cycle. In contrast, this article generates BPEL from EDOC CCA models. Since the EDOC profile is a standard modelling language, our approach is applicable to both the analysis and design phases.

BPMN [14] provides a business process modeling notation that is readily usable by business analysts, technical developers and business people. [15] provides a technique which can generate BPEL from BPMN automatically. Since UML is the most widely used modelling language and we use a standard UML profile (the EDOC profile) to specify the source models in transformation, our approach is more widely applicable than that of [15]. In the OMG BPMN specification [16], a mapping between BPMN and

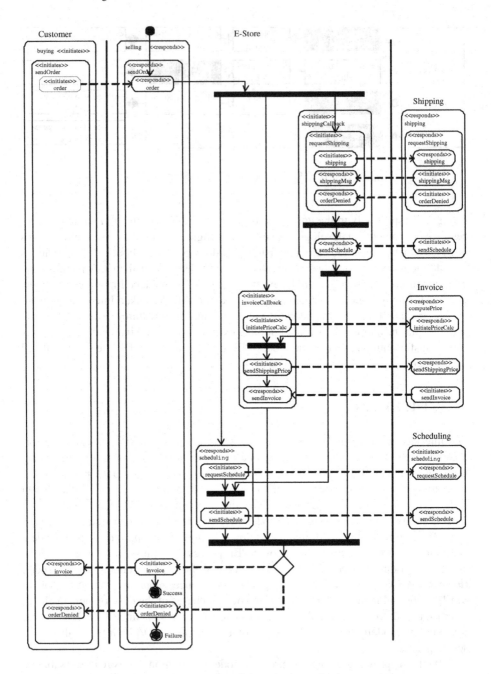

Fig. 10. The Choreography of the E-Store purchasing process

BPEL is also provided. On one hand, BPMN does not to provide an executable business process and no system can directly execute BPMN models, but BPEL processes can be

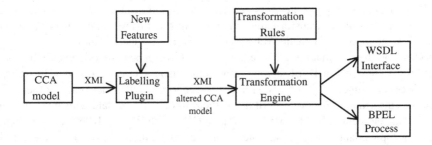

Fig. 11. The transformation process with an execution engine and a labelling plugin

directly execute by many engines. On the other hand, we intend to generate executable orchestration models from design models. Therefore, we choose to specify a mapping between CCA and BPEL instead of between CCA and BPMN.

Further related work is BPEL generation from UML in MDA context. [17] proposes a method to generate BPEL from UML 1.4 Activity models. However, this method depends on their own profile which is not a standard UML profile. In addition, [17] does not provide formal transformation rules. On the contrary, our approach sits on the top of the ECOC profile which is a standard UML profile, furthermore, we give detailed formal transformation rules. [18] presents a mapping from UML Activity diagrams to BPEL without any author added constructs , but the authors do not provide complete transformation rules. [19] shows how PIMs specified by UML 2.0 Sequence diagrams can be transformed to BPEL, and gives informal definition of the transformation rules. [20] provides the transformation from UML 2.0 Activity diagrams to BPEL, and shows few transformation rules. The difference between our approach and [18,19,20] is twofold. First, this work is part of our whole project as introduced in [22] which aims to support model driven development for component based enterprise distribute computing systems, therefore, we use the EDOC profile instead of the pure UML 1.4 or UML 2.0 to specify PIMs. Second, we present much more complete formal transformation rules .

Finally, as far as we know, the closest work to ours is [21], one of the focuses of which is to transform EDOC behavior models to BPEL. However, [21] does not give any concrete transformation rules. On the contrary, we propose detailed transformation rules which are critical to BPEL generation from EDOC behavior models.

7   Conclusions and Future Work

The core contribution of this work is to propose model driven transformation rules which can automatically generate BPEL specified Web service orchestration specification from EDOC CCA models. Though currently we do not provide formal proof for semantic consistency in transformation, we have implemented a prototype of these rules as a proof of concept. This approach can reduce the complexity and speed up the process of creating Web service orchestration specification by generating BPEL automatically. Further, this work offers a substantial approach to leverage the reuse of design artifacts advocated in the MDA, because we can apply this approach to other target platforms

(BPML, WSCI, etc), or to later version of the same platform based on the same source models by revising the transformation rules. Therefore, this works provides a platform independent approach to create Web service orchestration specifications.

This work reveals that not all the elements of CCA can be transformed to BPEL, and not all the elements of BPEL can be transformed from CCA meta-model. In CCA, a MultiPort combines a set of ports which are behaviorally related and each of them will "buffer" information sent to it until all of them have received data. However, there is no such an element in BPEL corresponding to CCA MulitPort. In BPEL, the <assign> activity copies data from one variable to another. Nevertheless, there is no element in CCA corresponding to BPEL <assign>. If we want to generate a BPEL Process which includes all the elements of BPEL specification, either we need to add BPEL related elements to the CCA meta-model, or we need to add some elements to the generated BPEL Process manually. Since on one hand, adding BPEL related elements to CCA meta-model will make the EDOC profile more BPEL specific, and on the hand, most of the BPEL elements can be generated automatically using our approach, we choose to alter the Process manually if needed.

Two-way transformation is not supported in our current approach, because when one CCA element is mapped to more than one BPEL elements, the reverse mapping is impossible. But we are planning to enable two-way transformation for one-to-one mappings.

Integrating nonfunctional artifacts into the transformation process and deriving definitions on other orchestration languages are both our current consideration.

References

1. http://www-306.ibm.com/software/websphere/
2. http://www.oracle.com/technology/products/ias/bpel/index.html
3. Andrews, T., et al.: Business Process Execution Language for Web Services, Version 1.1., BEA, IBM, Microsoft, SAP, Siebel (2003)
4. Arkin, A., Askary, S., Fordin, S., Kawaguchi, K., et al.: Web Service Choreography Interface (WSCI) 1.0. W3C Note 8 August World Wide Web Consortium (2002)
5. Arkin, A.: Business Process Modeling Language (BPML). Specification, BPMI.org (2002)
6. OMG. Model Driven Architecture (MDA)- document number ormsc/2001-07-01 (2001)
7. Object Management Group. UML Profile for Enterprise Distributed Object Computing Specification(EDOC). OMG Document Number: ptc/2001-12-04 (2001)
8. Object Management Group. Meta Object Facility (MOF) 2.0 Query/View/Transformation Specification, Final Adopted Specification, ptc/05-11-01 (November 2005)
9. Patrascoiu, O.: YATL: Yet Another Transformation Language.First European Workshop MDA-IA (2004)
10. ATLAS Group. ATLAS Transformation Language. Reference site: (February 2005),
    http://www.sciences.univ-nantes.fr/lina/atl/ or
    http://www.sciences.univ-nantes.fr/lina/atl/
11. Anzbök, R., Dustdar, S.: Semi-automatic Generation of Web Services and BPEL Processes - A Model-Driven Approach. In: van der Aalst, W.M.P., Benatallah, B., Casati, F., Curbera, F. (eds.) BPM 2005. LNCS, vol. 3649, pp. 64–79. Springer, Heidelberg (2005)
12. Mendling, J., Hafner, M.: From WS-CDL Choreography to BPEL Process Orchestration. Technical Report JM-2006-07-24. Vienna University of Economics and Business Administration (2006)

13. Barros, A., Dumas, M., Oaks, P.: A Critical Overview of the Web Service Choreography Description Language (WS-CDL). BPTrends Newsletter 3 (2005)
14. White, S.A.: Business Process Modeling Notation (BPMN) Version 1.0. Business Process Management Initiative, BPMI.org, May (2004)
15. Ouyang, C., van der Aalst, W., Dumas, M., ter Hofstede, A.: Translating BPMN to BPEL. BPM Center Report BPM-06-02, BPMcenter.org (2006)
16. Object Management Group. Business Process Modeling Notation Specification. Final Adopted Specification dtc/06-02-01
17. Skogan, D., Grønmo, R., Solheim, I.: Web Service Composition in UML. In: Proceedings of the 8th IEEE International Enterprise Distributed Object Computing Conference (EDOC'04), pp. 47-57 (2004)
18. Bézivin, J., Hammoudi, S., Hammoudi, S., Lopes, D., Jouault, F.: Applying MDA approach to B2B applications: A road map. In: Proceedings of the Workshop on Model Driven Development (WMDD 2004), The 18th European Conference on Object-Oriented Programming (ECOOP 2004) workshops (2004)
19. Bauer, B., Müller, J.P.: MDA Applied: From Sequence Diagrams to Web Service Choreography. In: Koch, N., Fraternali, P., Wirsing, M. (eds.) ICWE 2004. LNCS, vol. 3140, pp. 132–136. Springer, Heidelberg (2004)
20. Bordbar, B., Staikopoulos, A.: On behavioural model transformation in Web Services. In: Wang, S., Tanaka, K., Zhou, S., Ling, T.-W., Guan, J., Yang, D.-q., Grandi, F., Mangina, E.E., Song, I.-Y., Mayr, H.C. (eds.) Conceptual Modeling for Advanced Application Domains. LNCS, vol. 3289, pp. 667–678. Springer, Heidelberg (2004)
21. Kath, O., Blazarenas, A., Born, M., Funabashi, M., Hirai, C.: Towards Executable Models: Transforming EDOC Behavior Models to CORBA and BPEL. In: Proceedings of the 8th IEEE International Enterprise Distributed Object Computing Conference (EDOC'04), pp. 267-274 (2004)
22. Yu, X.F., Hu, J., Zhang, Y., Zhang, T., Wang, L.Z., Zhao, J.H., Li. X.D.: A Model Driven Development Framework for Enterprise Web Services. In: Proceedings of the 10th IEEE International Enterprise Distributed Object Computing Conference (EDOC'06), pp. 75-84 (2006)

Appendix

Listing 1.1. snippet of the generated WSDL file of the E-Store ProcessComponent

```
1  <definition name="purchasing" targetNamespace=" "
2      ...
3    <types>
4      <xs:complexType name = "ShippingInfo">
5        <xs:elemente name = "problem" type="xs:string"/>
6        <xs:elemente name = "keyword" type="xs:string"/>
7      </xs:complexType>
8    ...
9    </types>
10   <message name="order">
11     <part name="order" type="CustomerOrder"/>
12   </message>
13   ...
14   <portType name="sellingPT">
15     <operation name="sendOrder">
16       <input message="order"/> <output message="invoice"/> <fault name="orderDenied" message="orderDenied"/>
```

```
17    </operation>
18   </portType>
19    ...
20   <plnk:partnerLinkType name="invoicingLT">
21     <plnk:role name="invoice">
22       <plnk:portType name="computePricePT"/>
23     </plnk:role>
24     <plnk:role name="invoiceCallback">
25       <plnk:portType name="invoiceCallbackPT"/>
26     </plnk:role>
27   </plnk:partnerLinkType>
28    ...
29   </definition>
```

Listing 1.2. snippet of the BPEL process of the E-Store **ProcessComponent**

```
1   <process name="selling" targetNamespace=" "
2      ...
3    <partnerLinks>
4      <partnerLink name="invoicingLK" partnerLinkType="invoicingLT" myRole="invoiceCallback" partnerRole="invoice"/>
5      ...
6    </partnerLinks>
7
8    <variables>
9      <variable name="order" messageType="order"/>
10     <variable name="invoice" messageType="invoice"/>
11     ...
12   </variables>
13
14   <faultHandlers> ...</faultHandlers>
15
16   <sequence>
17     <receive partnerLink="selling" portType="sellingPT" operation="sendOrder" variable="PO"/>
18     <flow>
19       <links>
20         <link name="requestShipping_to_sendShippingPrice"/>
21         <link name="sendSchedule_to_sendSchedule"/>
22       </links>
23       <sequence>
24         <invoke partnerLink="shipping" portType="shippingPT" operation="requestShipping" inputVariable="shipping"
25             outputVariable="shippingMsg">
26           <source linkName="requestShipping_to_sendShippingPrice"/>
27         </invoke>
28         <receive partnerLink="shipping" portType="shippingCallbackPT" operation="sendSchedule"
29             variable="sendSchedule">
30           <source linkName="sendSchedule_to_sendSchedule"/>
31         </receive>
32       </sequence>
33       ...
34     </flow>
35     <switch>
36       <case condition = "order is denied"> </case>
37       <otherwise> </otherwise>
38     </switch>
39     <reply partnerLink="selling" portType="sellingPT" operation="sendOrder" variable="sendOrder"/>
40   </sequence>
41   </process>
```

Author Index

Lecture Notes in Computer Science

For information about Vols. 1–4415

please contact your bookseller or Springer

Vol. 4478: J. Martí, J.M. Benedí, A.M. Mendonça, J. Serrat (Eds.), Pattern Recognition and Image Analysis, Part II. XXVII, 657 pages. 2007.

Vol. 4477: J. Martí, J.M. Benedí, A.M. Mendonça, J. Serrat (Eds.), Pattern Recognition and Image Analysis, Part I. XXVII, 625 pages. 2007.

Vol. 4476: V. Gorodetsky, C. Zhang, V.A. Skormin, L. Cao (Eds.), Autonomous Intelligent Systems: Multi-Agents and Data Mining. XIII, 323 pages. 2007. (Sublibrary LNAI).

Vol. 4475: P. Crescenzi, G. Prencipe, G. Pucci (Eds.), Fun with Algorithms. X, 273 pages. 2007.

Vol. 4472: M. Haindl, J. Kittler, F. Roli (Eds.), Multiple Classifier Systems. XI, 524 pages. 2007.

Vol. 4471: P. Cesar, K. Chorianopoulos, J.F. Jensen (Eds.), Interactive TV: a Shared Experience. XIII, 236 pages. 2007.

Vol. 4470: Q. Wang, D. Pfahl, D.M. Raffo (Eds.), Software Process Dynamics and Agility. XI, 346 pages. 2007.

Vol. 4468: M.M. Bonsangue, E.B. Johnsen (Eds.), Formal Methods for Open Object-Based Distributed Systems. X, 317 pages. 2007.

Vol. 4465: T. Chahed, B. Tuffin (Eds.), Network Control and Optimization. XIII, 305 pages. 2007.

Vol. 4464: E. Dawson, D.S. Wong (Eds.), Information Security Practice and Experience. XIII, 361 pages. 2007.

Vol. 4463: I. Măndoiu, A. Zelikovsky (Eds.), Bioinformatics Research and Applications. XV, 653 pages. 2007. (Sublibrary LNBI).

Vol. 4462: D. Sauveron, K. Markantonakis, A. Bilas, J.-J. Quisquater (Eds.), Information Security Theory and Practices. XII, 255 pages. 2007.

Vol. 4459: C. Cérin, K.-C. Li (Eds.), Advances in Grid and Pervasive Computing. XVI, 759 pages. 2007.

Vol. 4453: T. Speed, H. Huang (Eds.), Research in Computational Molecular Biology. XVI, 550 pages. 2007. (Sublibrary LNBI).

Vol. 4452: M. Fasli, O. Shehory (Eds.), Agent-Mediated Electronic Commerce. VIII, 249 pages. 2007. (Sublibrary LNAI).

Vol. 4451: T.S. Huang, A. Nijholt, M. Pantic, A. Pentland (Eds.), Artifical Intelligence for Human Computing. XVI, 359 pages. 2007. (Sublibrary LNAI).

Vol. 4450: T. Okamoto, X. Wang (Eds.), Public Key Cryptography – PKC 2007. XIII, 491 pages. 2007.

Vol. 4448: M. Giacobini et al. (Eds.), Applications of Evolutionary Computing. XXIII, 755 pages. 2007.

Vol. 4447: E. Marchiori, J.H. Moore, J.C. Rajapakse (Eds.), Evolutionary Computation,Machine Learning and Data Mining in Bioinformatics. XI, 302 pages. 2007.

Vol. 4446: C. Cotta, J. van Hemert (Eds.), Evolutionary Computation in Combinatorial Optimization. XII, 241 pages. 2007.

Vol. 4445: M. Ebner, M. O'Neill, A. Ekárt, L. Vanneschi, A.I. Esparcia-Alcázar (Eds.), Genetic Programming. XI, 382 pages. 2007.

Vol. 4444: T. Reps, M. Sagiv, J. Bauer (Eds.), Program Analysis and Compilation, Theory and Practice. X, 361 pages. 2007.

Vol. 4443: R. Kotagiri, P.R. Krishna, M. Mohania, E. Nantajeewarawat (Eds.), Advances in Databases: Concepts, Systems and Applications. XXI, 1126 pages. 2007.

Vol. 4440: B. Liblit, Cooperative Bug Isolation. XV, 101 pages. 2007.

Vol. 4439: W. Abramowicz (Ed.), Business Information Systems. XV, 654 pages. 2007.

Vol. 4438: L. Maicher, A. Sigel, L.M. Garshol (Eds.), Leveraging the Semantics of Topic Maps. X, 257 pages. 2007. (Sublibrary LNAI).

Vol. 4433: E. Şahin, W.M. Spears, A.F.T. Winfield (Eds.), Swarm Robotics. XII, 221 pages. 2007.

Vol. 4432: B. Beliczynski, A. Dzielinski, M. Iwanowski, B. Ribeiro (Eds.), Adaptive and Natural Computing Algorithms, Part II. XXVI, 761 pages. 2007.

Vol. 4431: B. Beliczynski, A. Dzielinski, M. Iwanowski, B. Ribeiro (Eds.), Adaptive and Natural Computing Algorithms, Part I. XXV, 851 pages. 2007.

Vol. 4430: C.C. Yang, D. Zeng, M. Chau, K. Chang, Q. Yang, X. Cheng, J. Wang, F.-Y. Wang, H. Chen (Eds.), Intelligence and Security Informatics. XII, 330 pages. 2007.

Vol. 4429: R. Lu, J.H. Siekmann, C. Ullrich (Eds.), Cognitive Systems. X, 161 pages. 2007. (Sublibrary LNAI).

Vol. 4427: S. Uhlig, K. Papagiannaki, O. Bonaventure (Eds.), Passive and Active Network Measurement. XI, 274 pages. 2007.

Vol. 4426: Z.-H. Zhou, H. Li, Q. Yang (Eds.), Advances in Knowledge Discovery and Data Mining. XXV, 1161 pages. 2007. (Sublibrary LNAI).

Vol. 4425: G. Amati, C. Carpineto, G. Romano (Eds.), Advances in Information Retrieval. XIX, 759 pages. 2007.

Vol. 4424: O. Grumberg, M. Huth (Eds.), Tools and Algorithms for the Construction and Analysis of Systems. XX, 738 pages. 2007.

Vol. 4423: H. Seidl (Ed.), Foundations of Software Science and Computational Structures. XVI, 379 pages. 2007.

Vol. 4422: M.B. Dwyer, A. Lopes (Eds.), Fundamental Approaches to Software Engineering. XV, 440 pages. 2007.

Vol. 4421: R. De Nicola (Ed.), Programming Languages and Systems. XVII, 538 pages. 2007.

Vol. 4420: S. Krishnamurthi, M. Odersky (Eds.), Compiler Construction. XIV, 233 pages. 2007.

Vol. 4419: P.C. Diniz, E. Marques, K. Bertels, M.M. Fernandes, J.M.P. Cardoso (Eds.), Reconfigurable Computing: Architectures, Tools and Applications. XIV, 391 pages. 2007.

Vol. 4418: A. Gagalowicz, W. Philips (Eds.), Computer Vision/Computer Graphics Collaboration Techniques. XV, 620 pages. 2007.

Vol. 4416: A. Bemporad, A. Bicchi, G. Buttazzo (Eds.), Hybrid Systems: Computation and Control. XVII, 797 pages. 2007.